The Author

ALVIN L. SCHORR is Deputy Assistant Secretary, U.S. Department of Health, Education, and Welfare. He was formerly Deputy Chief of Research and Planning at the Office of Economic Opportunity. Editor-in-chief of *Social Work,* and the author of many articles that have appeared in *The New York Times Magazine, Harper's, The Public Interest,* and other leading periodicals, Mr. Schorr is also the author of *Poor Kids: A Report on Children in Poverty* (Basic Books, 1966).

Explorations in Social Policy

EXPLORATIONS IN
SOCIAL POLICY

Alvin L. Schorr

FOREWORD BY JOHN W. GARDNER

BASIC BOOKS, INC., PUBLISHERS
New York • *London*

For Kenneth, my son,
who knows the excitement of building with
his hands and with his mind. I can wish
him no better gift. This book is for him;
he will understand the challenge that led
to it, whatever work he himself does.
The imperfect world that the book reflects
is also his; it will answer to him
when he requires it.

Foreword

JOHN W. GARDNER

Chairman, The Urban Coalition
Formerly Secretary of the U. S.
Department of Health, Education, and Welfare

————◀◆▶————

The topics covered in this book are among the most difficult issues of social policy facing the nation today. Most Americans—even many informed Americans—hardly know the relevant questions. And of the small number who do, too many have highly dogmatic answers.

Most of the issues are puzzling and complex. They deserve to be the subject of lively continuing national discussion. But the plain truth is that few men have the combination of policy experience and intellectual cutting edge to contribute to the subject. Too much of current writing is either the emasculated prose and thought of government commission reports or the literate fantasies of men who have never come near the arena in which social policy is hammered out.

Alvin Schorr is as much at home in the world of action as he is in the world of reflection. He respects the complexity of the issues. He approaches the questions with that combination of compassion and cool intellect that alone will bring us to workable solutions. Both his heart and his mind are in good working order.

He wrote these essays while working at the Department of Health, Education, and Welfare and the Office of Economic Opportunity. They provide convincing evidence that there is room in government for the wide exploration of ideas and the forceful expression of views. Both government as an institution and the government employee as an individual stand to profit from that fact.

Contents

Introduction   1

1. Social Policy: A Personal Review   3

Part I.   The Socially Orphaned   17

2. Problems in the ADC Program   21
3. ADC: What Direction?   44
4. The Socially Orphaned: The Next Step in Social Security?   57

*Part II.   Filial Responsibility and
Family Policy*   69

5. The Fifth Commandment   71
6. Current Practice   77
7. Social Security and Filial Responsibility   101
8. Beyond Pluck and Luck   132
9. Family Policy in the United States   143

Part III.   The Air We Breathe   165

10. The Nonculture of Poverty   167
11. The Population Recipe   176
12. Housing Codes and Financial Incentive   195
13. Planned Development: Vision or Fancy?   205

*Part IV.   Community Services: Penalties of
Pragmatism*   211

14. Urban Services   213
15. Social Services in France   220
16. The Future Structure of Community Services   247

Part V.   One Nation . . . Indivisible   259

17. Policy Issues in Fighting Poverty   261
18. National Community and Housing Policy   272
19. Alternatives in Income Maintenance   288

Index   301

Introduction

1

Social Policy: A Personal Review

The essays that are collected here are the product of a seven-year search for a connection between government policy in social matters and specified objectives. During most of that period I was absorbed in understanding how policy might promote two particular objectives—a reduction in poverty and more rewarding family relationships. In any ordinary sense, it was an accident that offered the opportunity for this search inside a government agency. When the Social Security Administration undertook to examine its impact on family relations, I was a practicing social worker and conveniently at hand.

The search led to conclusions that proved controversial and always, it seemed, drew powerful opposition from some quarter of the agency. In the end, two commissioners of Social Security authorized publication of the major pieces of work. Such determination leaves even commissioners exposed and is not universal. I was trying to show that a free exchange of ideas—within the government as well as without, whether a particular idea wins or loses the day—would make for richer research and sounder government programs. The trial struck me in some small measure as convincing but will quite possibly go unnoticed among many pressures for circumspection.

The method of the essays is basically empathetic and intuitive;

I should say this at once. It is not an accident that the title of this book reduces to E.S.P. Word is abroad that amassing data is research while intuition is poetry, perhaps, or clinical practice. The notion reflects an analogy to a science-that-never-was or technical flight from the risk of making errors, and it will find no support here. Intuition must be subjected to trial by data and by theory. However, it is only the glimmering of an idea or of a solution that makes the endless data bearable.

Although the essays are rearranged here to bring together those with a common subject, the order in which they were written will be apparent. The reader may follow the evolution of a method. Evaluation of Aid to Families with Dependent Children (AFDC) was conducted by reading hundreds of program studies to ask what the studies were saying. Poor design or a researcher bent on making his own point often overrode a study's message, but grasping the total import of the studies was simply an exercise in attention. On the other hand, this method makes evaluation very much a prisoner of each program's framework. Data are derived from studies which, in the formulation of their questions, tend to accept basic program assumptions and stereotypes. Nor do such studies provide much basis for asking whether quite another type of program would have done better.

After AFDC, I preferred to phrase broader questions: What are the relations of adult children and their parents? What might government do to wipe out poverty? Approached more broadly, the questions contained the relevant programs rather than the other way around. Unfortunately, the research formulations that can be brought to bear on such questions are few. To administrators who seek answers to use in doing business, social scientists seem like solipsists on a retreat. Many studies bear on issues that trouble the private worlds of sociology and psychology, but relevance to the outside world does not seem to have a high order of priority. It proved necessary to gather the research evidence concerning each issue in order to discover what current practice is or even what a reasonable objective is. As it developed, this was an exciting task. Jigsaw-puzzle bits of data turned out, when pieced together, to look rather different than the picture we imagined we would see. Assembling them forced attention to issue-related research that would have otherwise been overwhelmed by irrelevant data, and was itself a service to policy development.

Once the work on AFDC was published, important groups of public welfare officials thought it either "controversial" and therefore to be avoided, or mistaken and therefore to be opposed. I took such reactions to be natural, that is, compounded of defensiveness and a tactical judgment that criticism of the program would be used against its clients. On the other hand, the work on filial responsibility drew only public approval (except for the complaint of a syndicated columnist that it was intended to destroy the American family), but of legislative and policy movement there was for a time none. In "Beyond Pluck and Luck" (Chapter 8), while speaking out a bit more warmly and directly on the issue, I tried to account for the persistence of relative responsibility laws despite their patent undesirability. To put this another way, it seemed that persistently irrational policies must serve some function. Applying a Freudian technique to uses of social policy, I imagined that irrational behavior might be made to go away by exposing its sources. Legislatures did not appear to be moved by this attractive strategy.[1]

In retrospect it appears that the first problems were approached as if their solutions were open and rational. If we knew the circumstances of socially orphaned children, we might know what to do. If we knew what old people need and want from their children, we might know how to support the children in giving it. Increasingly, however, I found myself mixing such analysis with questions of value and ulterior motive. If American public policy is not in general a pursuit of family integrity, why not? And why do we pretend that it is?

I was influenced by a conversation with E. Franklin Frazier. He seemed to carry a profound sense of disappointment about the personal reactions of people who should have honored him. Yet he would not recede from naming unpleasant truths when he saw them: Acrid honesty was a barrier to the appreciation he would have liked and at the same time the core of his duty and honor. In accounting for public policy rather than trying to say what it should be, I found myself tending in an analogous manner to deal with unpleasant truths by naming them. This was to stand up to them even if I could not change them. The intellectual role of commentator has its compensations, when one is forced back upon it; yet I could never rest with it. I was dealing with social policy in order to change it. The belief that change occurs creates a responsibility to say what a rational policy would be.

I had begun to work upon solutions and was stumbling upon problems. One problem had to do with the lack of fit between social science research and problems of social policy. Was it said that AFDC tended to break up families? In 1959, researchers had not explored the matter and did not seem to know. By 1965, it was widely asserted that AFDC did have this effect but little more research had been done. Indeed, the relevant portion of the law had been amended, offering an unequaled opportunity for research, but no one troubled. Is it said that poor housing causes poverty? Research has been largely confined to statistical correlations, which fail to demonstrate a causal relationship, and which fail to demonstrate that housing is not causal. When poor people moved into decent housing and it promptly deteriorated, the public concluded that poverty caused poor housing rather than the other way around. On the whole, research has abandoned the question at this unsatisfactory point.

The two examples are different in a variety of ways. The absence of information about AFDC may be accidental; it may reflect a chasm between sociology and social work; or AFDC may be unrelated to theoretical issues of any moment. The absence of information about the effects of poor housing may reflect the preoccupation of social science with *social* relationships, or it may reflect the complexity of housing and its connections with people's behavior. The two examples share one quality, however: Research did not act as critic and prod to social policies though they were clearly vulnerable. Research did not ask what the objectives of social policy were and silhouette achievements against objectives. The lack of fit between social research and social policy may, in large measure, result from the popularity among social scientists of the so-called value-free orientation.

The problem of the value-free orientation is not new. In 1938, standing between a great depression and a great war, Robert S. Lynd asked what role the social sciences were playing, and quoted Auden: "Lecturing on navigation while the ship is going down." As the nation was suffering from a human rather than a technological failure, interest was centering on the social sciences. Yet the social sciences—economics, psychology, sociology—seemed preoccupied with descriptive statements and analyses of "problems accepted largely at their face value." Lynd observed: "More data avail us little if they are data on false or misstated problems." [2] Neither was Lynd a fatalist by temperament. He prescribed several general remedies and listed twelve "outrageous" hypotheses that would assure research centered upon social needs. The hypotheses may seem less outrageous now, but they have yet to be tested.

The problem that Lynd capsulated as "Knowledge for What?" has not been resolved. However, we may see it in a broader context today. It has been painstakingly argued, by Ellul among others, that we have become possessed by the technological and technical instruments that we possess. We have not simply lost our way; we are captured by the laws of development of a technological society. Therefore, we are "committed to the quest for continually improved means to carelessly examined ends." [3] We are disciples of know-how rather than know-why.

In this circumstance, there is a painful circularity in the relationship between social science and national policy. The significant questions today are not *how* but *whither* and *why*. How to end poverty is a less difficult question than what is the end of poverty. How to secure civil rights is less difficult than what are the objectives of civil rights. Two presidents have declared that our first need is a sense of purpose or consensus. All the while, the social sciences devote themselves to the means to achieve whatever it might turn out that their purposes might be, doggedly evading the very questions of purpose that would give meaning to their data. The law of a technological society according to Ellul—that the means *are* the ends—engulfs us and cannot be confronted here by dropping a slogan or two in passing. So far as I perceived the problem, however, it meant several things to my work.

First, it was necessary to move back and forth continuously between social objectives and programs or techniques. Unstated objectives could not be assumed. Unstated, I could not be sure myself that I was sticking to the main point. Second, I was no doubt unjustly suspicious of the technical accouterments that the social sciences were taking on—data processing, mass surveys, econometrics. They give such an appearance of activity, whether or not they say anything. Their sophistication and the sheer volume of their data easily hide from sight the assumptions at their core. Finally and most important, all the tedious work of analyzing one social policy or another was an act of faith, an affirmation that man is sooner or later in control.

A second problem that I stumbled upon is what Hylan Lewis has called "the politicality of knowledge." Knowledge and the political climate are far from readily distinguishable. On one hand, the times appear to call for a certain kind of knowledge and to bring it forth. For example, prior to World War II, when comparatively few women worked, research demonstrated that working mothers tended to have delinquent children. After the war, it became plain that much larger numbers of women were working, and researchers reexamined the issue. Then it conveniently appeared that children were not led into delinquency because their mothers worked. Only those who received irregular care, for whatever reasons, showed a tendency to be delinquent. Similarly, research on the fertility of poor families for many years emphasized the attitudes that are peculiar to their situation and lack of scientific knowledge. From about 1963 on, the emphasis has shifted to how much the poor resemble people who are not poor in their desires regarding family size and in their competence to plan families. Both styles of fertility research contain truths. Apparently it is difficult or impolitic to present both sets of truths at once.

On the other hand, the staging of research is itself a political fact. It is common knowledge that research may be staged mainly to create familiarity with and acceptance of a new idea. Research, it has been pointed out, may be a euphemism for deliberately trying to produce a change.[4] Even apart from deliberate manipulation, a program demonstrating the effects of work experience for public assistance clients was followed by a national program— *before* the results of the research were in. Research was called for on the effect of permitting public assistance recipients to retain a portion of their earnings; the provision was written into law *be-*

fore research was well under way. One sometimes wonders whether the outcome of research is significant—or is research the shadow cast before itself by social change?

A greater danger than selected data or biased conclusions lay in the choice of research issues. Styles of research inevitably lead to oversimplification and I found myself always tempted to right the balance by leaning the other way. This surely explains the irony of spending so much time on primitive matters such as housing and nutrition, despite my training in and fascination with the subtleties of interpersonal relationships. Styles in the conduct of research must reflect more than a tendency to oversimplification. I have naturally wondered whether we hear so much about the culture of poverty because it excuses our failure to do the expensive physical things—feed poor children and build low-cost housing. At a deeper level, I have wondered if we are so estranged from sensuousness and the physical world that we must deny their influence upon poor people and, by extension, upon ourselves. Thus, the gaps in research hold more mystery than the work that is in process. What is being done reflects the direction of social movement; what fails to be done, what we *don't* do, is what we are satisfied not to know. I have tried to keep asking what we do not want to know, and why.

These elements of the politicality of knowledge—that research may provide the proof that the moment requires, that it may more exactly be a precursor to than a cause of action, and that it may fail to deal at all with the most uncomfortable questions—are fairly straightforward possibilities. The recent history of public assistance, in particular its relationship with non-cash social services, illustrates these problems in combination. Moreover, it indicates how difficult taking time for research or retaining room for scepticism may be when the urgent political need seems otherwise.

In 1956, Congress amended the statements of purpose in the major public assistance programs to specify that appropriate social services should be furnished to recipients. In rather a low key, Congress was reflecting awakening anxiety about costs of public assistance and rising juvenile delinquency. By the time a new Democratic administration came to office in 1961, Aid to Families with Dependent Children was in more serious difficulty. It was regularly attacked in the press for promoting immorality and laxity. The Senate Appropriations Committee had said it was "greatly concerned about the sharp increase in illicit relations, which in turn had greatly augmented the caseload in the 'aid to dependent children' program. . . ." The committee was shortly to ask for a national review of the program, in "a concerted effort to eliminate any abuses of the program."

The newly appointed Secretary of Health, Education, and Welfare therefore declared that "the time has come to meet new situations in new ways. . . ." [5] He asked leaders in the field of public and private welfare to distill their accumulated knowledge; with their help, he evolved a new program. "Its byword," said the Secretary, "is prevention; where that is too late, rehabilitation—a fresh start." [6] Key provisions of his program were to train personnel in the helping professions and to encourage states to provide helping services in the administration of their programs. As the 1956 declarations of purpose had been notably ineffective, in 1962 Congress provided cash subsidies to states that would follow its lead.

Despite formal encouragement from the leadership of social work and public welfare and the virtual absence of professional objection, the rehabilitative provisions were open to grave doubts from the beginning. It had been estimated that public welfare already required three times the number of trained social workers that were graduating each year.[7] And the Secretary had himself said that nine out of ten recipients of public assistance could not do other than receive help—because they were old, or blind, or otherwise disabled, because they were children, or because they were mothers who had to care for children. In short, though helping services would mean self-support for a few and would undoubtedly improve the living conditions of others, services would probably not fundamentally alter the scope of public assistance.

On the other hand, the administration's willingness to do anything at all about AFDC—a willingness that was novel and refreshing, if only the simplest realism—may have protected the program from the rising fury of Congress and the slick magazines. By 1962 Congress not only provided additional money for social workers; it broadened AFDC, notably to include children in need because their fathers were unemployed. Malingering and immorality now yielded newspaper space to accounts of human misery and self-help. Several million poor children continued to receive aid. If some mothers were inordinately harassed to show that self-support was feasible, others received help who would not have been eligible earlier, and still others received an attention or a bit of advice that was new.

How might one have summed up the matter in the year or two that followed? Probably, the functional analysis of the problem was faulty but the political analysis seemed faultless. It might have been demonstrated that helping services were a BB gun pointed at a mammoth problem of human need. In that event, Congress might not have broadened the program; it might, in frustration, have found ways to restrict it. Many of the same social workers who had advised Secretary Ribicoff in 1961, within three or four years were calling for the abandonment of AFDC and its helping services also.[8] If they had made that recommendation to the Secretary, would he have sought to implement it? One cannot know. If they had made that recommendation, would social workers have seemed to be against providing helping services at all? Possibly, for social policy seems to proceed by simplicities. We have not yet had a campaign in domestic social policy like the one we had in foreign policy, when President Kennedy set out deliberately to teach American people the necessity for a complex policy in a complex world.

Yet that summing up would have proved premature. In 1967, the House Ways and Means Committee observed with a certain crispness that "those [1962] amendments have not had the results which those in the administration who sponsored the amendments predicted." [9] The committee drafted a bill which its chairman described as tough but not mean. More realistic provision was made for social services that might reasonably help mothers to work—extensive day care, for example. At the same time, a large measure of choice about working was removed from mothers. In an unprecedented act, a ceiling was placed on the number of children that the federal government would aid. For the third time in little more than a decade, Congress acted upon a judgment that knowledge or research might have tested and would certainly have undermined—that social services applied to the AFDC program could substantially alter its costs or caseloads.[10] If that judgment had earlier bought a respite for needy women and children, in 1967 it was used against them.

This is the dilemma: Half-right may serve the political need more soundly than all-right; so it would have seemed in 1962 or 1963. That the promise of social services was used against recipients in 1967 obviously calls into question even its earlier political soundness. Still, it is not entirely clear that virtue and scepticism would have been the best course throughout. The government's determination to pursue the social services solution from failure to failure must raise the question whether, in a deep sense, facts or knowledge would have any influence at all. Or is it rather a profound American faith in self-improvement that drives us to this solution, even when it is plainly inappropriate? If that is the case, who will conduct the research that contravenes this faith and what audience will attend to its findings?

To all these doubts and questions that I have labeled the politicality of knowledge, there are no certain answers and probably not even general answers. However, it became clear to me that, even at its most descriptive and technical, social science is not outside social policy. I had to reconcile my consciousness of being partisan with a certain fastidiousness about the conduct of intellectual inquiry. In this attempt at rationalization—at harmonization, as Europeans say—unpopular conclusions were an ally. One must perforce be scrupulous if each separate omission or defect, whether significant or not, is likely to be held to contaminate the substance of an argument. Taking pains to state values was also an ally; if my detachment was compromised, at least my biases were presented as part of the data. None of these observations harmonizes my taste for an objectivity outside the system with a passion for making the system answer to my own conception of human ends. The two drives are not compatible; still, I was never able to give myself to one or the other exclusively.

A third problem overlapped all the rest: It seemed increasingly difficult to develop new information, in the ordinary manner, and then bring about changes. The problem has two major aspects, called professionalization and bureaucracy—I use the terms invidiously. Professionalization, while it multiplied skill and depth, seemed to mean an increasing estrangement from closely allied skills and from the clients who were meant to be the object of it all. This is hardly an original statement: The doctor, the lawyer, or the social worker who sees in his office a person rather than a constellation of professional stereotypes (a diagnosis, the professional says) is becoming increasingly rare. (The poverty program may have altered this for the moment; we shall see.)

As I am a social worker, I had ready access to my own profession and the route to changing it was at least theoretically open to me. I criticized the trend to ordering other people's lives;[11] I called for less judging and more partisanship with poor people, attitudes not alien to the history of social work. It should be said that social work did not strike me as more culpable than other professions. Social workers did not cover themselves with glory in the generation after World War II, but where were the newspapermen and sociologists who heap scorn upon them now? Covering other stories and publishing or perishing. I criticized social work because I knew it and spoke to my own profession. But the burden of my argument is that all professions are prisons, impeding communication with our peers and empathy with our clients. The valuable men in this situation are marginal men—Jews, psychiatrists, expatriates, poets, comedians, Negroes, and neurotics.[12] Marginal men are frequently not solid citizens of course; many of them pay a price for multiple or ambiguous vision.

The problem of bureaucracy is analogous to the problem of professionalization but more pervasive, because it is the organizing principle of our society. Looking out from one bureaucracy at many others, it often seemed hopeless to try to achieve the simplest and most self-evident changes. The aspect of bureaucracy that troubled me most was the surrealistic separation of activities from their purposes, the tendency for functions to become more important than people. This quality of bureaucracy seems little open to change, although obviously bureaucracies have had changes imposed upon them. I have thought that there must be a way of building sedition into bureaucracy and, from time to time, grandly conceived my role in this fashion. Yet I never possessed sufficiently broad knowledge of bureaucracy or, perhaps, sufficient imagination to formulate this solution systematically.

The record of the Nuremberg trials and, particularly, the trial of Adolph Eichmann in Israel led me to what may seem a far-from-technical solution. Eichmann's central defense was, of course, that he was a correct functionary. It is as if we have been offered a warning while we are still able to discern it. In the face of the number of people we have come to be and the powerful forces we must command, bureaucracy is fated to proliferate. Function will seek to mold us to its needs which we take to be our own. Nothing will help us except each man's countervailing conviction that he is personally responsible for his client and neighbor.

With that assertion, I am content to offer the essays that follow.

NOTES

1. However, in 1965, the federal government forbade states from holding adult children liable for their parents' expenses in relation to medical assistance. Shortly afterward, the New York State legislature, preoccupied with the new medical care programs, wiped out relative responsibility in all of public assistance as well as in medical care. A wish for administrative simplicity seems to have played a role in this decision. Thus, though the efforts over a period of time of various citizens' groups may have prepared the way, the actual change was brought about obliquely by federal legislation and practical administrative considerations.

2. Robert S. Lynd, *Knowledge for What?* (Princeton, N.J.: Princeton University Press, 1939), pp. 2, 122.

3. Jacques Ellul, *The Technological Society* (New York: Alfred A. Knopf, Inc., 1964), p. vi.

4. The Dean of Teachers College, Columbia University, New York, complained that universities "docilely" do research on the educational innovations that foundation executives have determined to sell to the American public. Stephen M. Corey, "Research or Propaganda?", *Phi Delta Kappan*, XXXIX, No. 1 (October 1957).

5. Abraham Ribicoff, "The New Administration Looks at Social Welfare," *The Social Welfare Forum, 1961* (New York: Columbia University Press, 1961), p. 23.

6. Abraham Ribicoff, "The New Look in Public Welfare," *The Social*

Welfare Forum, 1962 (New York, Columbia University Press, 1962), p. 25.

7. Alvin L. Schorr, "Need for Trained Social Work Staff: A Ten-Year Goal," *Social Security Bulletin*, XXIV, No. 8 (August 1961).

8. For example, the National Association of Social Workers adopted the following statement in November 1964: "The means test—a comprehensive examination of means and resources, applicant by applicant, as a basis for financial assistance to millions of people— nullifies the objective of guaranteeing to every individual in our society the right to an adequate and certain income, and does violence to basic human values."

9. *Report of the Committee on Ways and Means on H.R. 12080, Social Security Amendments of 1967*, August 7, 1967 (Washington, D.C.: United States Government Printing Office, 1967), p. 96.

10. For example, an analysis of the increase in AFDC over a five year period indicated that three out of ten additional recipients came on because Congress itself liberalized the program. Four out of ten came on because of general increase in the number of socially orphaned children in the population. (John M. Lynch, "Trend in Number of AFDC Recipients, 1961–65," *Welfare in Review*, V, No. 5, May 1967.) Shortly after this analysis appeared, a welfare official estimated for newspapers that as many more children in similar circumstances were not receiving assistance as were carried on the program. (Joseph H. Meyers, Deputy Administrator, Social and Rehabilitation Service, January 27, 1968.) In sum, population trends and the unavoidably liberal response of legislators to rising wealth increase the AFDC load. Even if this were not so, a large reservoir of needy children wait to take the places on AFDC of those who might move off. Services are presumably useful for those who are helped, but it is idle to suppose that they will override these underlying trends.

11. Alvin L. Schorr, "The Trend to Rx," *Social Work*, VII, No. 1 (January 1962).

12. A number of authors have pointed to the role of marginal people— people who are both of and not of their societies—in different places at different times. In 1919, Thorstein Veblen wrote of the European Jew that he pays "the cost of losing his secure place in the scheme of conventions into which he has been born, and . . . of finding no similarly secure place in the scheme of gentile conventions into which he is thrown. . . . He is in a peculiar degree exposed to the

unmediated facts of the current situation; and . . . takes his orientation from the run of facts as he finds them, rather than from the traditional interpretation of analogous facts in the past" ["The Intellectual Pre-eminence of Jews in Modern Europe," *The Political Science Quarterly*, XXXIV, No. 1 (March 1919), 39–41]. Erik Erikson makes a similar observation about Jews in *Childhood and Society* (New York: W. W. Norton & Company, Inc., 1950).

Regarding marginality in comedians, see Victor Goertzel and Mildred George Goertzel, *Cradles of Eminence* (Boston: Little, Brown and Company, 1962). Regarding marginality in psychiatrists, see Karl Menninger, *A Psychiatrist's World* (New York: The Viking Press, 1959), pp. 415–424, 477–496; and Jurgen Ruesch and Gregory Bateson, *Communication: The Social Matrix of Society* (New York: W. W. Norton & Company, Inc., 1951), p. 20. Regarding marginality in Negroes, see any work of James Baldwin or Ralph Ellison.

PART I

The Socially Orphaned

AUTHOR'S NOTE

The public assistance program for children is now called Aid to Families with Dependent Children (AFDC) but was called Aid to Dependent Children (ADC) for many years. Chapter 2, "Problems in the ADC Program," was an attempt to give a balanced statement of what sparse evidence seemed to say the problems were. I tried to find a position that was neither a tender defense of the status quo nor a brash sweeping away of everything that welfare might mean. The next chapter, "ADC: What Direction?" was prepared about a year after the first appeared and is in part a restatement. With the careful research statement made in the first article, I permitted myself a certain vigor of expression in the second to convey more clearly the points I wished to make.

Three out of the four problems described in Chapter 2 have since received legislative attention. States are now permitted in certain circumstances to give aid to children living with both parents. States must overlook specified amounts of earned income in determining need. States that wish to have a medical assistance program must include within it those on AFDC, an attempt to prevent scapegoating of the children's program. Even the fourth problem, the effect of AFDC on family stability, has been addressed in part by the social services added to the program. In the absence of a broad, objective appraisal of the program, however, skepticism is in order. With services addressed primarily to making mothers and children self-supporting, the effect may be to increase movement off assistance and then back on again.[1]

Chapter 3, "ADC: What Direction?," was written to say that the program's problems would not be solved within the program itself. Amendments that give states the option of improving their programs, such as the one permitting assistance to children with both parents present, have been implemented by a minority of states. The states with the poorest AFDC programs have patently gone as far as they are able or wish to go. (The 1966 Advisory Council on Public Assistance, undoubtedly influenced by such evidence, recommended federal standards of assistance and a much heavier infusion of federal funds.[2] These would certainly lead to a stronger federal role in determining policies.) "What Direction?" concluded by suggesting that the solution lay outside the AFDC program.

Obviously, my interest had turned to the need for a new step in social security. Chapter 4, "The Socially Orphaned," followed five years later, more forthrightly stating the need for a new program without making a case for a particular one. Rising interest in a new income maintenance program had been limited at that time to the idea of a negative income tax. Various such proposals with trivial differences or with major differences that were masked (for example, whether or not they were intended to replace all other social security programs) were being urged upon the American public. It seemed to me that the evident need for a new program, the evident capacity to provide it, and the fact that public opinion would have to be prepared for it offered a rare opportunity for an informed national choice. Yet no one able to catch the public eye seemed willing to make clear to the American people that they could choose markedly different forms of a new program.

Chapter 4 was written to explore three programs with fundamental differences. If the alternatives could be made familiar, perhaps public interest would turn to their underlying differences. For example, entitlement to a negative income tax rests on income falling below a certain level; fundamentally, it is sophisticated and highly simplified public assistance. Fatherless child insurance follows the social security principle; it particularly resembles survivors' insurance. The family allowance rests on the principle of payment to all members of an age group, regardless of other circumstance. Its concept is different both from programs resting on a test of income and from social insurance programs in which people pay for protection against a common risk. Any one of these programs would, if it made substantial payments, represent a considerable improvement over existing provision for children. In the end, differences were really developed in public when people started arguing for one program against another. To keep no secrets, my personal preference is for children's allowances. Chapter 19 indicates the reasons.

NOTES

1. See Edmund Sherman, "Public Assistance Services before and after the 1962 Amendments: An Analysis of Change in Two Public Assistance Settings," unpublished doctoral dissertation (Bryn Mawr College, Bryn Mawr, Pa.: 1966). This small study shows how narrowly services may be focused on self-support, to the exclusion of other important considerations.
2. Advisory Council on Public Assistance, *Having the Power, We Have the Duty* (Washington, D.C.: United States Government Printing Office, Dept. of Health, Education, and Welfare, 1966).

2

Problems in the
ADC Program

It is not strange that a program should develop problems during a quarter of a century, particularly when the problems arise in large part from changing social circumstances. Two kinds of social change go the heart of the Aid to Dependent Children program:

1. The risk of losing one's parents by death is now all but replaced in public concern by the risk of losing or never having a parent because of divorce, separation, or illegitimacy.
2. More women nowadays prefer gainful employment to the other alternatives that are open to them.

The propositions that follow are not an evaluation of the ADC program. An evaluation would give overriding weight to the provision of food and shelter and mothering to millions of children. It would give credit to the attempts of social workers to be helpful against what seem at times to be overwhelming odds. It is precisely these odds that the following propositions attempt to state. If they are accurate, it is time to design a more constructive way to meet the needs of children.

A considerable number of studies, statistical summaries, and program descriptions have been examined in the course of arriv-

Reprinted from *Social Work*, V, No. 2 (April 1960), 3–15, by permission of The National Association of Social Workers.

ing at this statement. They do not compel the conclusions that are drawn—studies that have been designed with sufficient care to compel any conclusion are exceptions—but most of the evidence is consistent with the following propositions. The propositions do not state all the problems in ADC—the attempt is to describe major problems which are interrelated in such a way that they reinforce one another in damaging effects upon families. These are (1) the scapegoat problem in ADC, (2) the work dilemma, (3) whether ADC is directed to strengthening the whole family or to establishing a maternal family, and (4) the unsettling effects of the program.

THE SCAPEGOAT PHENOMENON

Under tension, wrote Kurt Lewin, groups will select one member to receive their concentrated hostility. The operation of this pattern, which he called the scapegoat phenomenon, frees the rest of the group to deal with each other in a more relaxed manner. Without implying that the forces operating in a small group are the same as those operating in society, the ADC program is analogous in being the focus of recurrent public attack, in concentrating in one program a group of people of whom there is widespread disapproval, and in receiving less-favored treatment than other public assistance programs.

The group that receives ADC is on the whole disadvantaged and characterized by many of the symptoms of social breakdown. Its members are relatively less well educated than average, have inferior job training and experience, and a high proportion are Negro. Broken families are characteristic. This general picture is reflected, with additional details, in almost any local study. For example, in New York State, four out of five ADC children come from broken homes, four out of ten have been deserted by their fathers, a third were born out of wedlock. ADC children live in families "with a long low-income experience." [1] In California a great number had "disturbing family and social problems which were admittedly outside the usual scope of vocational rehabilitation." [2] In Georgia "there are usually a multiplicity of disabilities and complaints . . . emotional disturbances . . . behavioral disorders." [3] One study in Pennsylvania counted problems and arrived at an average of seven different problem areas for each ADC family.[4] These are the unattractive facts; they are well and widely known.

Attacks launched on the program in the press and in legislative hearings cite statistics of divorce, desertion, and illegitimacy —with case illustrations. They usually suggest the vital connection that ADC causes or makes feasible disordered behavior which the absence of assistance would prevent. For example, a resolution of the Louisiana legislature says ". . . most of said [ADC] subsistence money is being spent by the parents selfishly . . . since this subsistence policy has been in existence there has been an appalling increase in the number of illegitimate children born. . . ."[5] There is usually the assumption that some needy families ought to be receiving assistance, particularly the families of widows, but that many or most are abusing the program.[6] The high percentage of Negroes may more or less frankly be an issue.

Investigation tends to show that two kinds of forces are operating.[7] First, changes in the general population are reflected in the ADC case load; that is, there are proportionately more children and more families in the population. As insurance people would say, the population "at risk" in terms of ADC is *proportionately* larger. Divorce, separation, and illegitimacy have increased generally. Remarriage rates are so high as to present many fathers with the choice of supporting one family or another. The likelihood that the father will marry someone else has a similar effect on support of illegitimate children. The income of broken families is not rising at the same rate as the income of whole families. Thus, generally, we have more broken families and their income is relatively lower than it used to be.

Second, special factors operate that make disordered families loom larger in the ADC program. Survivor insurance removes the most sympathetic figure, the widowed mother, from the ADC program. With increased mobility, certain urban areas feel unduly the effects of economic problems in rural and depressed areas. Negroes, overrepresented in the low income group, may place more emphasis on the tie between mother and children and less on marriage—the grandparents of some would not have been permitted to marry by the laws of their state. Unequal migration makes for a large surplus of young Negro women over men in some urban areas, and the reverse in other areas. In the end they cannot place illegitmate children for adoption if they wish to.

These are the basic forces to be borne in mind. We shall see in four stated propositions how certain aspects of the ADC program aggravate recipients' problems. None of them will suggest, however, that the ADC program is chiefly responsible or that the absence of assistance would do anything but create worse problems. What has happened, as a social accident, is that ADC—designed in one social era and moving into another—now operates selectively to serve people of whom social problem and community disapproval are characteristic.

If ADC operates selectively, there must be needy children who are not served. In the District of Columbia it is estimated that less than a third of families having children and living on submarginal income receive ADC.[8] In New York public relief recipients represent less than one-fourth of all persons with total income below public assistance standards.[9] (This estimate does not separate out ADC, but we shall see that ADC turns out to be favored in no set of figures.) Nationally, about 2.2 million children receive ADC. In addition, there were about 600,000 children in families receiving General Assistance in March 1958. As the roughest sort of measure of children in need, on the other hand, 8 million live in families with incomes of less than $2,000 a year. What of the other more than five million needy children? Many are in families where a father is present and not disabled (the Social Security Act excludes these from ADC). Others are excluded by other policies or budgeting levels, and no doubt some choose not to apply. The five million children whose needs are not being met have some bearing on the assertion that ADC serves a selected disapproved group. For, if all needy children were served by ADC, the percentage of disordered behavior in their background picture would be somewhat reduced, but it would still be high enough to cause considerable concern, and this would bring out clearly the fact that disordered behavior is a problem of American society and not of an intransigent group. Purely punitive action, such as some newspapers and legislators have suggested, would be more difficult to contemplate.

This situation might not be serious for the families who are served by ADC if public disapproval did not reflect itself in the administration of the program. The caseworker and administrator are also part of the public; no public agency is entirely independent or can for very long be entirely independent of public attitudes. There is evidence that public attitudes—on the desirability of work, for example—get translated into imperatives from the caseworker to the client, sometimes faster and further than administrators desire.[10] *Future Citizens All* documents two points suggesting the impact of disapproval: first, a substantial number of recipients have payments terminated while they are still in need—25 per cent. Second, the highest percentages still in need are among those who are most disapproved: Negroes compared with whites, long-term recipients compared with short-term, and illegitimate children in unstable homes compared with children in more acceptable situations.[11]

Bills that are presented by legislators and sometimes enacted may seem punitive in intent. In trying to evaluate intentions, however, and the content of changing regulations, one is on very difficult ground indeed. An examination of relative budget levels of ADC and the other programs is easier, for it is at least quantitative. The average monthly grant per recipient in ADC in September, 1959 was $28.58, less than half the average payment of any other federally aided category of public assistance.[12] Average payments may not fully reflect recipients' income because they may have other income—from earnings, for example, or from support. However, the budget standards which states set are also lower in ADC than in the other programs.[13] One may also examine the maximum grants which states prescribe in each category, for they carry a quality of conscious legislative or administrative intent. Maximum grants, among the twenty-five states which have them in all categories, turn out to be as high *for one person* in the other three federally aided categories as they are for *an adult and one child* in ADC.[14]

It has been implied that the relative disadvantage of the ADC program has grown as social change affected the clients it serves and it became identified in public consciousness as serving social undesirables. Table 2–1 indicates the rate at which payments in

Table 2-1

PERCENTAGE INCREASE IN AVERAGE PAYMENTS PER RECIPIENT
IN 1947–1949 DOLLARS [a]

	Aid to dependent children	Old age assistance	Aid to the blind	Aid to the permanently and totally disabled	General assistance (per case)
1936–1949	43	41	77	—	109
1950–1957	12	21	42	32	28

[a] Based on *Trends,* Department of Health, Education, and Welfare (1959), p. 60.

various programs have increased in purchasing power. (A second set of figures is given from 1950, when Aid to the Permanently and Totally Disabled began and the child's caretaker might, for the first time, be included in the ADC payment.) ADC shows the smallest overall increase by 1957. Moreover, by the 1950 to 1957 period, Old Age Assistance has moved up from about the same rate of increase to almost twice the rate of increase as ADC. Aid to the Blind has also considerably widened its advantage.

It only remains to note that lower levels of payment are not just a relative matter, but mean that levels of payment are below what is commonly regarded as adequate. In fact, measured against United States Department of Agriculture food costs, only one state appears to meet the needs of recipients fully.[15] The inherent conflict within a program intended to be rehabilitative but suffering from public disfavor is poignantly noted by the rehabilitation studies that are being made in increasing number. In one way and another these frequently say, "The economic deprivation prior to and subsequent to receipt of ADC means [the ADC parents] have lived in deprivation for a number of years. In addition to the complete depletion of material resources they have quite often an accompanying depression of motivations, self-confidence, mutual respect between spouses, personal dignity . . . [which] have made the rehabilitation of the parents . . . much more difficult. . . ." [16]

First proposition: *In the present social context, the ADC program operates selectively to serve families who are not only disadvantaged economically but who meet with social disfavor. Many needy families with children are excluded from the program;*

those who are included receive less favored treatment than other public assistance recipients.

THE WORK DILEMMA

When the assumption that women would stay at home with their children if they were not in grave financial need accorded with the feelings of most women, the program had little problem in this area. Now women elect to work even though they have children, and particularly those mothers elect to work whose husbands' income is low or who are without husbands. The problem now arises not only in connection with the general question of whether women should work. There are the conceivably more important questions of what is being done to the mother's area of choice about work and to the quality of her feeling about work.

In its early years, the ADC program fitted into the economy in such a way as to offer a genuine choice to a mother. This is not to say that the program assured that she could get a job if jobs were scarce or if what she offered to an employer was very little. On the contrary, it is evident that the program was written when it seemed desirable to attract women out of the labor market, leaving more jobs for men. The effect, however, was that if a mother desired to work and could find employment, she did. If she preferred to stay at home, her right to do so was affirmed in accepting her for ADC. The *Handbook of Public Assistance* says that ADC should "make it possible for a mother to choose between staying at home to care for her children and taking a job away from home." The role of the public assistance agency is "to help the mother arrive at a decision that will best meet her own needs and those of her children." It should make it possible for an ADC mother "to exercise some degree of choice as to what course of action she should follow with respect to seeking or continuing employment and to make a decision in consideration of her special circumstances, especially the extent to which the age or condition of her children may make her continuous presence at home desirable or necessary." The emphasis is all on choice and particularly on free choice to stay at home.[17]

The situation is different when there are jobs for women and when work for women is acceptable, if not (for public assistance clients) approved. The free choice that these mothers once had is now being eroded from opposing directions. On one hand, seventeen states formally specify that mothers must work if they can make adequate provision for the care of their children. Even where the attempt is made to administer these policies most thoughtfully, in the end there must be criteria to determine whether or not a mother is expected to work—not by her own but by welfare department standards.[18] Seven states may deduct from the ADC grant what they calculate would have been the earnings of a mother who refused available employment. In many counties and states where there is no formal policy, the caseworker and administration are apt to assert their own expectation that mothers work. Where there are no formal policies there will not, naturally, be criteria, but the extent of the pressure on the mother measures the diminution of her freedom to choose.

On the other hand, the basic legislative design of the program —that is, the way the budgeting process relates a mother's income to her grant—makes work meaningless as a means of increasing her income. With exceptions we shall mention, the money she earns is deducted from her grant; consequently she is no better off financially.[19] To be sure, a woman who can work full-time at a moderately good salary can often earn a great deal more than her ADC payment. The typical ADC mother, however, does not have advanced skills or job training; with children, full-time work is apt to be unsuitable. Consequently her earnings remain near ADC budget level; as income is deducted, with or without work, her income remains approximately the same. The point is often made that earning part of one's own income, even if it does not add to income, is conducive to pride. Aside from this, women may want to work for other personal or family reasons. It will be generally conceded, however, that especially in an ADC family's circumstances the major incentive is financial. For the ADC mother the financial incentive is effectively excised.

There are two kinds of exceptions to more or less automatic reduction of payments when a mother earns income. One only appears to be an exception. States will budget for a working mother an increased amount to allow for travel or other expenses created by the fact that she is working. Although this may increase the grand total for which her family is budgeted, these are new expenses that must be met and there is no more money available to the family. The other exception is in those states that establish a maximum payment in ADC; though budgeted need may be more, the family receives only the specified maximum. In this situation, the family may earn the difference without reducing the grant. (One bears in mind that the opportunity is created by paying grants below what the state has established as need; this has other effects which we are not attempting to appraise.) Here, then, is a limited opportunity for the ADC mother to increase her usable income. Comparison of the rate at which mothers work in the states which provide this limited incentive and in those which do not should give some indication of the effect of the budget process.

In late 1958 the median state had 10.4 per cent of its ADC mothers working.[20] Of 34 states *with* a maximum or similar limitation on payments, 23 states had a higher percentage and 11 had fewer mothers working. Conversely, of 16 states *without* a maximum, only 2 had a higher percentage and 14 had fewer mothers working than in the median state. Obviously these figures are affected by administration and state conditions (the availability of work, for example), but there is an apparent tendency for mothers to work where it will produce some financial result for them. States that provide this small measure of incentive show an increased percentage of working mothers over those that do not; by contrast, the number of working mothers in states with a formal work requirement, as compared with those that do not have it, shows a smaller increase.

To recapitulate, then, we have moved away from a situation where ADC provided a choice to mothers in terms of their appraisal of the family's situation. In the present situation, the option to stay home may be ruled out by fiat and the choice to work made meaningless by the budget process. At the same time that modern efforts are focused to maintain and increase self-dependence, in this major area real choice is removed. The mother with low earning capacity finds that acceptance of her application no longer affirms a right to stay at home or to have a choice. In many states and counties she is likely to be expected to work, whether she wishes to or not. On the other hand, earning money brings her no financial advantage. The absence of financial advantage is not new in the ADC program, of course, but this was unimportant when there were no jobs or no desire to work; it is crucial when a mother may prefer to work. To put it another way, it was appropriate that a program for women who prefer not to work should design out the incentive to work. But when women prefer to work and the program may press them to work, it is not appropriate that it should bring them no profit.

Much of the discussion of this problem to date has been polarized around two points of view: first, that mothers ought to be encouraged to stay at home because, in addition to humanitarian considerations, this is the only way to safeguard the development of children; second, that in the present social situation the mother's happiness and, indeed, the child's, depend on her being self-sufficient when she can. Moreover, it is not reasonable to spend public funds for families who can, without special damage, support themselves. In the assertion of one point of view or the other, and the organization of welfare department policy around whichever one is dominant, there has been a tendency to lose sight of the fact that the mother may be more competent to decide her family's needs than administrators.

Having taken on the responsibility to make this decision, public policy moves firmly to north and south at once—that is, simultaneously to require and discourage work. If policy reflects, as it undoubtedly does, growing agreement that women may or even should work, then provision of an incentive should reduce the need for legislative and policy requirements. Still, room should be left for a mother to choose not to work. Obviously, there is a broader question here of the effect of the means test, as it has been applied to date, upon incentive to work when earning ability is low. In ADC this question had no importance until women wanted to work and the public wanted them to work. Now it has importance.

How does this ambivalent policy seem to the ADC mother upon whom it focuses? She finds herself at the center of conflicting pressures and, to the extent that she feels she has a choice, she faces a dilemma. This is the conflict inherent in her situation:

She is more or less officially pressed to work and she has her own urgency to pay her bills or buy more, but work increases her load and does not add to her income. How can she resolve this dilemma? She can hold fast to her function as a mother and see herself as doing an important job at home, despite want and social pressure. Some women are able to do this. She can drop out of the program or not even apply. That cases are being closed has been amply reported; these will be touched on again in discussing stability. She can become apathetic. She can acknowledge what has become a fact for her, that the welfare department and not she determines whether she shall work, and respond visibly but without vigor to whatever are the department's current requirements. And she can move back and forth between the possibilities —work irregularly, occasionally, erratically. (Irregular work may have the advantage of not being or seeming to be reportable.) All the alternatives but the first move not to but away from self-dependence, and they have all been remarked in ADC programs.[21] They are progressive, making for poor work experience and a cycling of resentment and resignation. Finally, they establish work as something closer to indenture than to self-advancement, and prepare a problem for the mother after her children are grown.

Second proposition: *The operation of the ADC program removes from the ADC mother effective choice about whether she will or will not work to supplement her income. To the extent that she feels any right to decide at all, she feels pressure to work when she is at home and little or no financial advantage when she is working.*

MATERNAL FAMILY OR WHOLE FAMILY?

It is an axiom in physics that to every action there is a counteraction. The ADC program is fundamentally a force for keeping mothers in the home; in counterpart it thrusts away the husband and father. This is serious now because in the large majority of cases the father is alive. The operative factor is, of course, the legislative requirement of death, absence, or incapacity of a parent. The assertion is a familiar one: that, since he must, the father will absent himself or the family will conceal his presence in order to be eligible for a grant. It is a plausible argument and, though one could wish for more direct studies of the issue, what evidence there is supports it.

As an isolated piece of behavior, it is hard to conceive that a man who would otherwise stay at home will desert his family so they may receive ADC. The situation is usually more complex—families in trouble have more than one kind of trouble. Deprivation may lead to family conflict, or vice versa. This is especially likely if, as in the subculture of Negroes and perhaps in the attitude of any low-income group in prosperous times, the family's respect for a man hinges on his capacity to support them.[22] Then, particularly if the family has received ADC once or knows of it, the steps from deprivation through marital conflict to agreement, tacit or angry, that everyone will be better off if the father leaves—these steps are not hard to visualize. On the other hand, the father may leave home out of no conflict at all but in search of a job. If he is unsuccessful, the effects of his failure on him and his family can only be compounded by the fact that his return stops ADC. The New Mexico Department of Public Welfare, analyzing the effect of the recession on its ADC case load, notes that 26.6 per cent of the applications in its recession case load were precipitated by loss of the wage earner, compared with 19.7 per cent ordinarily. "Previous studies have indicated," it says, "that as economic tensions increase so do desertions. . . ."[23]

All public assistance agencies face the problem of deciding what parental absence means. Many take a pragmatic position that when there is a stable, though nonlegal, union the condition of parental absence is not being met. To take any weaker position would seem to encourage living together rather than marriage. To take a stronger position (which some departments do) penalizes children for the infractions of their parents. In any event, the local department needs to know when there is a man in the picture and exactly what the relationship is. When departments look into this, they generally discover a number of cases that meet their test of stable union or whatever test they have established. The number they find varies. Beyond this, they frequently report that some parents—one or two,[24] 9 per cent,[25] or as many as 39 per cent, "were apparently apart for our benefit."[26] Moreover, the stable-union policy, while it gives no advantage to living together over marriage, shifts the premium to casual sexual contacts. In New Orleans, for example, we find that "we have had several clients . . . tell us that they were going out with men [and] practicing prostitution and we later learned that this was untrue. Generally this is told us to protect a rather stable relationship." [27]

This begins to provide a picture of the maze of conflicting attitudes, unresolved by the basic law, through which a department must thread its way to reach an interpretation of absent parent that applies to marital and sexual absence. Concern for the child is often at odds with anger at the behavior of the parent. Furthermore, the definition of absence gives advantage to certain kinds of sexual behavior. Though one's tendency might be to encourage behavior which is most like marriage, the logic of a definition of absence moves in the opposite direction. That is, the mother of an illegitimate child by a brief adventure meets the definition more readily than a couple who are married in all respects but the legal ceremony. The department evaluating these considerations is now deep in moral attitudes, and a further consideration comes into play. It is in a position (and often is pressed) to enforce, by the withholding of money, moral standards which the community will not enforce in its courts. These problems are described here not to sympathize with the public welfare administrator—though one may pause to sympathize—but to make clear that the ". . . plight of mothers and their children often ceases to be the issue." [28] Determinations are not being made in terms of the need of the whole family. Considerations are moral, even humanitarian, but the standard which is not applied to policy is, "What unites the whole family?" On the contrary, the emphasis is on getting rid of the man and insulating the mother, and presumably the children, from contacts with other men.

The program's emphasis on parental absence is fundamentally created by the Social Security law, but state policy and practice may aggravate the problem. There is indication that the longer a family receives ADC, the weaker the father's connection with it. [29] In a study of absent fathers, it was found that one half the men who returned to their families had been absent less than a year. Interest in the whole family, then, would dictate efforts to reduce the period of absence, but on the contrary a number of departments set a minimum period—three months, for example—in order to be eligible for ADC.[30] ADC checks are rarely written to the father even though he is at home, not because this suggests itself as more constructive or certain, but because the father is not considered. The family is dealt with "as if he were already dead." [31] Caseworkers are found pressing mothers into separation —joining the "girls' club"—so they may be eligible for ADC.[32] A Utah study of the outlook for self-support of its ADC recipients proved inaccurate because possibilities for employment were considered but marriage, which in the end affected almost as many, was not considered.[33]

It is possible that the residence requirement operates in a special manner in ADC to promote separation. The numbers affected may be small; this is impossible to ascertain. Though American families tend to move as a unit, men in depressed areas who have exhausted their resources are likely to go ahead by themselves to seek work. This seems a prudent way to proceed. But the father's return to his wife and children makes them ineligible for public assistance. Bringing them to him, if they are in another state, produces the same result. One may argue that it is unwise to move the family before the father is beyond the likelihood of needing public assistance. A New York State study suggests that the period needy families take to establish themselves may be a little more than a year.[34] It has already been indicated that the length of separation has a bearing on the likelihood of reconciliation. A program centered on the whole family might not seek to change the initial separation which prudence may require, but it would not introduce an external barrier to reunion to lengthen this period.

We have already noted that Negroes constitute a high percentage of ADC case loads. The cultural tradition of the Negro, developed during slavery and in the plantation system afterward, is one in which the mother is the focal person in the family. The father's interest was "adventitious" and his influence often curbed by some outside authority.[35] Relative lack of opportunity for Negro men in education, training, and employment operates to perpetuate this family pattern. In rural areas, some balance is established because planters seek families with a male member.

No such factor comes into play in urban areas, where there are three times as many Negro families with female heads (30 per cent of all Negro families) as in rural areas. It is a curious coincidence, but an effective one, that the ADC program—product that it is of an advanced stage of industrialization—keys in with this folk heritage of Negroes to support the matriarch and weaken the role of the father among the families who apply for help. To state this in reverse, a program designed to deal with families orphaned by death moves unwittingly into dealing with families orphaned by their culture—and reinforces that culture.

There is a temptation to shift the responsibility for many of these problems to the caseworker, to his lack of skill or failure to focus on the whole family, but this is a temptation which should be resisted. Two things are inherent in the absent parent provision: (1) there is payment when the father is absent, and there is not when he is present; and (2) the definition of absent parent, applied not to death but to sexual behavior, involves welfare department and caseworker in value judgments and the dispensation of justice. The inevitable result is a focus on a maternal family; the caseworker who can avoid this result day after day is skillful and well trained indeed.

While the concern being expressed here is for the effect of the ADC program on the man's place in his family, the mother and children are affected beyond their relations with him. For the focus on a fatherless family inevitably eliminates from ADC a number of families who will not accept or cannot meet the policies that are established. Without returning to the general question of the program's coverage, the point here is that application of the absent parent provision means that children who would otherwise be found in need do not receive assistance. One study indicates that 9 per cent of children in families dropped from assistance for these reasons went into institutional or foster placement within a year.[36] In the Junior Village study 40 per cent of the children in the institution on "census day" had been denied assistance within the past year, more than half of them for reasons connected with the absent parent provision.[37] In some cases where the children remain at home, there is increased income from work or from support; in others the children continue to be in need.

Third proposition: *Though the emphasis of the ADC program is on the whole family when the family is defined as children and a mother, the effect is to divide the family in the sense of man and wife and father and children.*

TOWARD STABILITY?

Dependability and regularity are important features of healthy nurture for children, but it is characteristic of ADC that the family situations are in constant movement. Though much of this movement is undoubtedly because these are troubled families to begin with, it is important to inquire whether the ADC program reduces or aggravates uncertainty. There is clinical evidence that children will work out some adjustment to desertion or cruelty, provided they can know what to expect, but that vacillation and recurrent change leave them even more seriously damaged. Recent investigations of the connection between juvenile delinquency and working mothers point to the nature of the work as the key: whether it is sporadic, whether regular plans are made for the children, and so on.[38]

The observation that constant change is characteristic of ADC cases is based chiefly on an impression of case reports. Only a few attempts have been made to count change within families; they are not comparable with each other, and there is no "normal" group to use as a standard. *Future Citizens All* measured shifts in family structure from first ADC payment to termination.[39] (For example, of 2,649 families that started as homemaker and children only, 295 added a spouse by the time of termination.) Between initiation and termination (median time twenty-five months), 27 per cent showed a *net* change in family structure. A Marin County study notes that ten of their nineteen "marked improvement" families showed change in membership—"*some* [emphasis supplied] were probably for the better." [40] In their "deteriorating" group of fifteen cases there were three desertions, eight illegitimate pregnancies, five moves out of the county, and one mother who sent the children to relatives out of the county. The absent parent study notes that in more than two-fifths of the situations in which fathers returned to their families, the recent estrangement was not the first.[41]

Change in family structure is the most critical type of internal change, but other types are also significant. It has already been suggested that irregular work is characteristic of ADC mothers. The 1959 Bureau of Public Assistance study must raise some question about the regularity and dependability of the plans that can be made for the care of children in these circumstances. In families with children under twelve years of age, 14 per cent had made no arrangement for their care, and 11 per cent had left them in the care of other children, seventeen or younger.[42] The financial problem is basic to ADC; even aside from income from work, the ADC family's financial situation is subject to sudden and unpredictable change. In part this results from the effect of appropriations upon payments.[43] Considerable current attention is being given to support payments. While the existence of a support order or agreement may reduce the grant, it is far from assuring regular income. During the month of the absent parent study, slightly fewer than a third of the families received the full amount of the father's payment. Over half received no payment at all.[44] It is hard to evaluate how much of a factor for how many families is change in administrative policies. Written reports give the impression that a great many clients are feeling the effects of welfare department restudy, but presumably reports are written by the departments that are in the process of change. *Future Citizens All* in 1950 noted that of those cases terminated but regarded as still in need, 2 per cent were terminated because of "change in agency policy." In 1951, the last year national statistics were collected on reasons for closing cases, 3.9 per cent of ADC cases were closed because of "refusal to comply with agency policy" and 3 per cent because of "change in law or agency policy." [45] All these are the changes which can be numbered and counted, however inadequately. Beyond this, one gets from the case reports an overwhelming impression of continual struggle and negotiation within the families and between the families and community agencies.

We have already said that we cannot know that this is more instability than would be found in any other comparably deprived and troubled group of people. What, then, is the direction in which ADC moves? Does it operate to aggravate change or to slow it down? The work dilemma is inherently unstable for the mother and, it may be added, for older children. That neither work nor failure to work can be genuinely satisfying is directly traceable to program operation. The absent parent provision can only mean family uncertainty for the young families who are the current and prospective case load. Those parents who are apart "for our benefit" do not constitute a stable situation. The need to establish that one meets the requirements of absence per se takes on a meaning of its own which may well be in conflict with a couple's struggle to resolve their own problems.[46] The point has already been made that this tends to divide parents; the point here is that, to the extent that division is different from the parents' impulse, irresolution and vacillation are promoted.

When one postulates that there is some virtue in a stable situation, unless change is for the better and gives at least some promise of being maintained, some of the published material about self-support and other demonstration projects raise serious questions of clarity. To begin with, change appears to be valued for itself without consideration of how lasting it is. For example, there is the observation that ". . . as soon as the parent has come to terms with the agency's requirements and has accepted assistance, she must be helped at once to face what is involved in moving toward giving up assistance." [47] What is of more concern, however, is the impression that two distinct developments are regarded as one in many welfare departments. One is the development to providing social services for rehabilitative purposes; the other is the trend to more rigorous exploration of the possibilities of support and work to hold down the cost of the program. While both objectives can often be pursued at once, it would be naive to suppose that they are identical. Projects directed to self-support, however, report their results in money saved and cases closed without meaningful evaluations of the consequences for families. Often there is also an attempt to show that closing the cases has benefited the families involved, but even in thoughtful departments this material is very far from convincing.[48] When there is evidence that in some cases the making of a support order almost immediately causes the father to return home,[49] the possibility must suggest itself that he is returning because he finds it cheaper.

This closes cases but hardly seems constructive for the family or promising of stability.

These comments are not directed to the need for better research; they add up to the observation that written material shows agency interest in closing cases as a primary end. Obviously, the propriety of a businesslike and economical operation of the program is not being questioned here. But general interest in reducing case loads, without attention to the effects on families or with the assumption that the family which leaves assistance is necessarily better served, adds to family instability. The mother who was not prepared to work will lose her job. The father will desert again. Some children will go to relatives and foster homes. The family may or may not reapply for ADC but, either way, they will have experienced another series of upheavals.

Fourth proposition: *In certain important respects, the ADC program operates to add to the instability which is characteristic of the troubled families who receive grants.*

SUMMARY

We have not tried to count the values of ADC—these have been profound—nor to say what may be done for troubled people in the day-to-day service caseworkers give, or can give. We have looked for major problems and we have found several. The program and its caseworkers continue to serve, but the forces that hamper them in being constructive are large, and conceivably unnecessary.

Nor have we sought solutions. For example, states that place a maximum on payments were used to estimate whether incentive influences women in taking work. The payment of grants which are lower than need, however, is not proposed as a solution to anything. Mainly, solutions were avoided in the belief that one may tend to see problems or fail to see them in the light of the ends one wishes.

Four interrelated propositions sum up the damage that is done to families by the operation of the ADC program: Social disfavor focused upon ADC families increases the pressure toward work, and, through regulation of the mothers' behavior, toward a maternal family. The work dilemma and the maternal family are important in producing instability. The maternal family and instability aggravate social disfavor. This is the problem spiral in which the ADC program and the three million children and adults it now serves are caught.

NOTES

1. Eleanor M. Snyder, *Public Assistance Recipients in New York State, January–February 1957* (New York: Interdepartmental Committee on Low Incomes, 1958).
2. Margaret Greenfield, *Self-Support in Aid to Dependent Children: The California Experience* (Berkeley: University of California, 1956).
3. Fulton County, Georgia, Department of Public Welfare and Division of Vocational Rehabilitation, *ADC VR Project: A Joint Project* . . . (Preliminary Mid-Point Evaluation), prepared by R. Winfred Tyndall, no date, multilithed, p. 6.
4. Mary M. Zender, *A Study of Public Assistance: Its Clients' Needs and Its Visitors' Skills* (Harrisburg: Department of Public Assistance, Commonwealth of Pennsylvania, February 1957), mimeographed.
5. Louisiana State Department of Public Welfare, "We Look at Our Aid to Dependent Children Program," *Louisiana Welfare*, XVII, No. 2 (April 1958), 7.
6. *New York Daily News,* October 1958–January 1959.
7. Two references which describe the effects of population trends on ADC are: Bureau of Public Assistance, "Public Assistance Trends" (Washington, D.C.: U.S. Department of Health, Education, and Welfare, August 1, 1958), mimeographed; and Saul Kaplan, "Support from Absent Fathers in ADC," *Social Security Bulletin,* XXI, No. 2 (February 1958), 3–13.
8. Gizella Huber, *Economic Indicators of Family and Child Dependency in the District of Columbia* (Washington, D.C.: Health and Welfare Council, 1958).
9. Snyder, *op. cit.*
10. Alan Keith-Lucas, *Decisions About People in Need* (Chapel Hill: University of North Carolina Press, 1957). *See also* Greenfield, *op. cit.,* and Mary Duren, "The ADC Worker's Task: An Approach to Definition," no date, mimeographed. (Duren is located at the University of California in Los Angeles.)

11. Gordon B. Blackwell and Raymond F. Gould, *Future Citizens All* (Chicago: American Public Welfare Association, 1952), p. 40, Table 14; p. 42, Table 16; p. 121.
12. *Public Assistance,* Report of the Advisory Council on Public Assistance (Washington, D.C.: United States Department of Health, Education, and Welfare, 1960). The other federally aided categories of assistance: Old Age Assistance, Aid to the Blind, and Aid to the Permanently and Totally Disabled.
13. *Ibid.*
14. Bureau of Public Assistance, *Money Payments to Recipients Under State-Federal Assistance Programs* (Washington, D.C.: United States Department of Health, Education, and Welfare, 1959).
15. *Public Assistance, op. cit.,* Appendix B. (See also Blackwell and Gould, *op. cit.*)
16. Fulton County, Georgia, *op. cit.*
17. Bureau of Public Assistance, *Handbook of Public Assistance,* Part IV (Washington, D.C.: United States Department of Health, Education, and Welfare, 1946), Sections 3401 and 3401.1.
18. Greenfield, *op. cit.*
19. The legislative design involved is in the provision of the Social Security law that all income must be taken into account in determining need. There is an identical problem in ADC for the adolescent child who wishes to work. To date, the child's problem has occasioned more interest than the mother's.
20. Bureau of Public Assistance, "Characteristics of Aid to Dependent Children Families, October–December, 1958," State Letter No. 392 (Washington, D.C.: United States Department of Health, Education, and Welfare, October 14, 1959), mimeographed.
21. Blackwell and Gould, *op. cit.;* Duren, *op. cit.;* Fulton County, Georgia, *op. cit.*
22. Rita L. Lynn *et al., Children in 104 Families Who Became Ineligible for ADC* (National Catholic School of Social Service of Catholic University, Washington, D.C., in co-operation with the District of Columbia Department of Public Welfare, 1956); and Rita L. Lynn, "Negro Families on Relief (ADC)," a research project at National Catholic School of Social Service (June 1953).
23. Richard A. Bittman, *Factors Increasing ADC Caseloads in New Mexico* (Sante Fe, N.M.: New Mexico Department of Public Welfare, 1956–1957).
24. Multnomah County, Oregon, Public Welfare Commission, *An Ex-*

periment in Administration: A Report on a Project Study of ADC Cases . . . *10–1–51 to 5–1–52* (Portland).

25. Lynn *et al., op. cit.*

26. Louisiana State Department of Public Welfare, "Report on Study of Orleans Parish Review Unit" (September 1954), ditto.

27. *Ibid.*

28. Elizabeth de Schweinitz and Elizabeth Ross, *Public Assistance and Children at Junior Village* (Washington, D.C.: Health and Welfare Council, 1958), p. 18.

29. Kaplan, *op. cit.*

30. "Ninety Day Ruling on ADC," Report of the FSS-DPW Project (New Orleans, La.: Family Service Society, September 1, 1959), mimeographed. This small study illustrates the hardship which results for the family from such a policy, and how it interferes with the family's struggle to resolve its problem.

31. Kermit T. Wiltse, *Social Casework in Public Assistance* (Berkeley: California Department of Social Welfare, 1952), p. 8.

32. Duren, *op. cit.,* p. 47.

33. Utah State Department of Public Welfare, "A Follow Up Report on the Outlook for Self-Support in Utah's ADC Cases," *Public Assistance in Utah,* XVII, No. 3 (March 1956).

34. New York State Department of Social Welfare, *Needy Non-Residents in New York State* (Albany: 1957).

35. E. Franklin Frazier, "The Cultural Background of Southern Negroes," *Institute on Cultural Patterns of Newcomers* (Chicago: Welfare Council of Metropolitan Chicago, 1957), p. 6.

36. Lynn *et al., op. cit.*

37. De Schweinitz, *op. cit.*

38. Eleanor E. Maccoby, "Children and Working Mothers," *Children,* No. 3 (May–June 1958), 82–89.

39. Blackwell and Gould, *op. cit.*

40. California Department of Social Welfare, *A Study of Marin County, California* (1957).

41. Kaplan, *op. cit.*

42. Bureau of Public Assistance, State Newsletter No. 392, *op. cit.*

43. Richmond, Virginia, Department of Public Welfare, *Project Assisting, Developing, Counselling* (September 1957).

44. Kaplan, *op. cit.*

45. Blackwell and Gould, *op. cit.,* p. 42, Table 16.

46. Duren, *op. cit.*

47. Esther Lazarus, "Social Casework Within the ADC Program," *Public Welfare,* IX, No. 8 (October 1951), 199.
48. Richmond, Virginia, *op. cit.*
49. Kaplan, *op. cit.*

3

ADC: What Direction?

"ADC: What Direction?" is an open-ended question, likely to stimulate the susceptible to fantasy. I want to consider first major possible internal changes in Aid to Dependent Children, and then consider the task, or mission, that is given ADC and ask if this program alone can be expected to discharge it. In both cases, I propose to be more specific about the condition that needs to be corrected or the gap that needs to be filled than about the remedy. In social policy perhaps more than in medicine, diagnosis is only the most general guide to the remedy.

Let us start with the problem of ADC that is the most familiar burden on a social worker's conscience—the absent-parent provision. The provision that ADC is available only if a parent is absent or incapacitated operates precisely counter to any cohesive forces in the family. When rent money is a week-to-week issue, the tentative inclination of partners to reconciliation, to live together, or to marry, tends to be deterred by the fact that, even if need continues, ADC will end. Caseworkers know this, if administrators sometimes seem doubtful. Some may feel that it demeans the clients to suggest that their marriages would be affected by money, yet it is the caseworkers who appreciate more than anyone

Reprinted from *Child Welfare*, XLI (1962), 72–78, 90, by permission of *Child Welfare*.

else how powerfully want may drive one. The studies of ADC that have addressed themselves more-or-less indirectly to this question usually find some number of parents who are "apart for our benefit," a phrase borrowed from a New Orleans study.[1] As future studies approach this question more directly, no doubt they will find a sprinkling of clients in any social worker's caseload who are deterred from reconciliation by the absent-parent provision.

This is the gross effect of the legislative provision; moreover, the provision has indirect effects that are likely to be diffused throughout the program's services. The focus of eligibility determination (unless there is disability) is on the father's absence. This can easily become—in some states, policy requires it to become—an attempt to establish that the father is permanently, not just casually, absent. The periodic review of eligibility focuses on the father's continued absence. From the point of view of the overloaded caseworker, this is the legal requirement, and it may set the tenor of discussion. Even if the caseworker avoids this trap, the client who risks mentioning that her husband has written to her must consider that doubt about her eligibility is as likely to result as is a thoughtful discussion of what is best for her to do.

This is not merely speculation. There is evidence that caseworkers do not see children's fathers even when they might be available. ADC checks are not usually written to the fathers even if disabled and at home. Caseworkers who are caught up in the children's needs, or what they regard as the mother's best interests, on occasion go so far as to advise a woman to get rid of her man. That voluntary agencies are able to hold interviews with men, and with women about their men, that usually do not take place with the regular ADC worker is often interpreted as a failure of the ADC worker. On the contrary, such interviews are stimulated by the very separation of the voluntary agency from the ADC program and the clients' conviction that they are separate. In truth, the Welfare Department stands more often than not in an adverse relationship to the ADC father, and a number of cities have institutionalized this relationship in special investigative units. If an investigator finds a man, "tag, and he is out," and so of course is the ADC payment to the mother and children.

I do not note these practices to say that caseworkers are inadequately trained, or not overloaded, or insufficiently understanding, but to say that an eligibility requirement based on the father's absence brings about this whole sequence of practices. Practice that is fine and dedicated will somewhat counteract this tendency, and poor practice will aggravate it, but the focus on separation is inevitable.

In general, three kinds of corrective or mitigating proposals are made; all appear in the recommendations of the 1960 Advisory Council on Public Assistance.[2] First is the proposal to merge all categorical programs into a single program for people in need, making no program distinction because of age or the reason for need. I have the impression that this proposal is regarded as not likely to be accomplished. Second is the proposal to drop the absent-parent provision from the ADC law, leaving a program that would serve all needy children in family homes. Such a change should effectively correct the problem that is built into the structure of the program. Third is the proposal to establish a federal-state program of general assistance. It seems likely that such a program would at least mitigate the effect of the absent-parent provision in ADC by making an alternative program available to the intact, needy family. It would also for the first time offer a program for the needy, though childless and able, adult. The choice between the last two proposals (and they are not mutually exclusive) involves judgments of political feasibility, cost, and the desirable long-range development of public welfare. At any rate, some change is necessary to meet the problem.

There are two other major internal problems that are perhaps less familiar and require, by way of introduction, that we pause to see the world as many ADC clients see it. Briefly, I suggest that the clients live in a state of despair to which, in its measure, the ADC program contributes.

Recent investigations of the poorest families yield a portrait that is entirely recognizable to an ADC worker. Called the lower-lower class by sociologists, these families are usually defined in terms of income or occupation, education, and area of residence. A substantial percentage receive public assistance at one time or another. Conversely the definition, since it is heavily weighted in terms of income, describes a large percentage of ADC families. The following is an outline taken from a paper by Martin B. Loeb:

> The family is a housekeeping unit and in general one of the parents, usually the mother, provides the basic continuity. The husband in such a case may seem to be a kind of male helper who may not even be seen as a provider. Children are members of the family unit to be fed, clothed, and housed, until they are old enough to fend for themselves. . . . There seems to be no real concept of leisure. Work is a burden and *not work* is a burden because it means one is not earning money. Simply staying alive is a major concern and keeps one pretty tired. . . . Income is sporadic. . . . They spend what they have when they have it on what they want immediately. . . . Education is just one more burden. It is a demand to be avoided if and when possible.[3]

Other material will lend emphasis to the description.[4] Lower-lower-class families live in a world that is hostile, barren, and arbitrary. They are powerless to control it—when they try at all, their thought mechanisms are magical. For example, a girl thinks she will not get pregnant if she has relations with a boy who has already made someone pregnant. Obviously some people in the world are well off; this is because of luck or "pull," another form of magic. It does not pay to make an investment in training or even in hoping—a turn of the cards may take it all away. The beatnik and the member of a fighting gang, like others of the very poor, share this fatalism. Though their behavior may appear otherwise—appearing otherwise is its function—the underlying feeling is one of impotence. Authority, including social agencies, is not to be trusted; at best it is whimsical, and at worst hostile.

This description of the world may be viewed as a static one, seeming to say that poverty is a character defect, and so perhaps several assumptions should be made explicit. First, this view of the world on the part of the poor is not pure fantasy. Usually the cards are stacked against them in any number of ways. Second, a profile gives no sense of the variety that exists. Some are on the way up and some have come down. Members of one family may have alarming moral standards, while their devotion to their children is unimpeachable. Third, social mobility is a promise that many of the lower class will follow, given reason to change their view of the world. This has been documented recently in *The Eighth Generation*.[5]

A program addressing itself to such fractured, beset, hopeless families faces a very difficult task indeed. It was put in a nutshell by a group of social scientists invited to advise the Social Security Administration on priorities to strengthen family life. Clients of some of our programs, they said, are "present-oriented"; we should help them to be "future-oriented." [6] That is, they should learn over time—possibly over generations, for it is uncertain what time span a fundamental change in values requires—to be willing to postpone present for future gratification, to plan ahead, and to strive. In short, they should behave as if the future is more important than the present, as do members of the middle class.

A caseworker approaches his client with a stubborn optimism that is not infrequently justified. Indeed, his confidence in human capacity to change and grow is one of the main contributions a caseworker can make. Nothing I have said would alter this approach to the client. But faith in human capacity to change, this faith that sometimes heals, need not blind us to the forces *on* the clients—which may in time become the forces *in* the clients—that work against change. Particularly, it becomes important to know these catabolic forces when we try to evaluate the program we have established to help. It is as if a tired swimmer is being swept out to sea on a strong tide. You encourage him to struggle and assure him he can make it. But safely on shore yourself, you raise hell with the management for letting anyone swim in such dangerous conditions.

I want to address myself to the management then. What are the qualities in a program that might encourage present-orientation among poor families? Two qualities are relevant: First, the program must reward effort. Promise of some future benefit barely helps—"that's for the birds!" There should be tangible reward, the more immediate the better. Second, the program must be dependable and predictable. Its rules must be clear and simple—any appearance of whim or discrimination is fatal.

Within the budgeting structure of public assistance it is extremely difficult to reward effort. Income is deducted from budgeted need to arrive at the amount of the ADC payment. To the client this means that if he earns ten dollars, he will lose ten dollars (less his carfare and so forth). To be sure, there are the prospects of earning far more than the ADC budget level and the emotional value of feeling self-dependent. However, for the families we are discussing chances of earning much are limited—the members lack training, their work histories are irregular, and the lone mother has a problem of child care that interferes with her work. The ultimate goal may be attractive but the immediate results are dollar-for-dollar reductions. And the satisfactions of feeling self-dependent must come hard to these people. What in their lives would give them experience with it or reason to think they could sustain it? The discontinuance of ADC and anxiety about whether it could be resumed, if needed, loom very large by comparison.

The previous chapter indicates the evidence that women tend not to work unless there is cash incentive despite the considerable pressure that may be brought to bear on them. For some years social workers have observed and been concerned about the effect withdrawing cash incentives has upon adolescents in ADC families. The effect upon adult men of their inability to contribute to their families must influence not only their feelings about work but about their masculinity. The problem of cash incentive must be one root of an agency's problems about securing support from absent fathers. As procuring support is the agency's problem rather than that of the ADC mother, she is likely to be concerned only when under pressure from the agency. Thus, procuring support changes from an internal family transaction to a problem of community enforcement, perhaps not always—but often—a shift that adds to community cost and personal pain. I am not saying that mothers *ought* to work, or *ought not* to seek support from their husbands on grounds of responsibility alone. I am saying that if their impulses lie in this direction they will find there is no cash gain. Ours is a society built on cash incentive; visible rewards are more, not less, important to ADC clients.

The Advisory Council on Public Assistance recommended

amendment of the social security law to allow states to experiment with permitting clients to retain and benefit from some portion of their cash earnings. They were joined by the American Public Welfare Association, who recommend, in *Federal Legislative Objectives—1961*, that the cost and policy implications of exemption of earned income should be studied. The problem of working out and testing a solution is a difficult one. The simplest type of income exemption—that the agency will disregard the first fifty dollars a month of earned income, for example—does not so much establish an incentive to self-improvement as it changes the point at which cash incentive vanishes. What may be needed, rather, is some type of escalator that provides continuing cash incentive up to a point at which the family may not, indeed, any longer require ADC. In any case, any type of exemption raises vexing problems of philosophy and cost. How is income exemption consistent with the philosophy that ADC is a "means test" program supplementing its clients' own resources? Where ADC payments are already inadequate (virtually everywhere), would the consequence be to favor some families by depriving others even more? Would exempt income in actual practice prove an incentive to ADC families? The answers to these questions are by no means plain. It is plain that we need to start to work on answering them.

Because the world appears bleak and arbitrary to many ADC clients, a program which is to help them must especially be dependable and predictable. Chapter 2, "Problems in the ADC Program," contains this proposition: "In certain important respects, the ADC program operates to add to the instability which is characteristic of the troubled families who receive grants." A review of studies confirms the impression that any group of ADC case records will give: the families are embroiled in a constant struggle, in movement. In itself this may say nothing of the program, for it may be only the disorganization that is characteristic of these families. There is intrinsic conflict, however, between the absent-parent requirement and the ADC mother's interest in her husband or in having a husband. There is intrinsic conflict between the lack of reward and the push to work that parents feel, out of their own need or out of a department's policy. These conflicts press a client to and fro, with no move quite satisfactory, and a pattern of relatively meaningless change is perhaps the abiding consequence.

Hastily considered intentions to help may even add to this uncertainty. There is an emphasis in programs that equates rehabilitation with closing cases. Where is the locality that reports a project as successful because it *kept open* some number of cases? There is some satisfaction in being able to say that the average ADC client receives assistance for twenty-four or twenty-five months. But how likely is he to reapply several months afterward? Social workers can understand how these emphases and the projects that result from them come about. The lower-lower-class client has a set of values that furnishes him with his own rather different interpretation.

These are problems for which the structure of the program is partly responsible, though even without structural change better work can probably be done. Specifically, casework should be meant to be sustained. A demonstration project tests something that is not yet settled—but the usefulness of skillful casework is hardly such an issue. The move off ADC must be considered as carefully as the move onto ADC. Neither a casework project nor caseworkers should be measured by "case closings" and "openings" but only by what happens within families. The transfer or turnover of personnel (every seven months in Chicago)[7] must be viewed in terms of its damage to clients. In a program that is basically intended to maintain income, the heart of the matter is the money payment. A payment that is less than genuinely adequate demonstrates less than genuine concern, not to speak of its results in food and shelter. One must move heaven and earth, and the accounting department, to see that payments are begun as quickly as possible. There can be no cheating of clients—I have in mind the intriguing fact that case audits uniformly discover more errors in favor of the agency than of the client.

Such a discussion leads to the needs for in-service training, for the development of technician positions, and for a considerable infusion of trained social workers. Yet improved administration and training alone, important as they are, are not sufficient.

I believe that in the past decade or two social workers have shifted from a position of partisanship with clients to a role of representing society to them. Professional literature and practice show at least the broad outline of this trend. Social workers are no longer chiefly protecting public assistance clients from society, but vice versa. I trust it is not heretical to emphasize that clients are victims of social and economic processes which they really cannot control. They are weak and require advocacy rather more than some larger concept of society, which has other and more powerful guardians. If we remember who is to be served, it will be easier to practice in and administer programs that provide dependability and predictability to the all-but-overwhelmed clientele.

Let me sum up so far. I have pointed to the problems in the absent-parent provision and named some alternatives that may correct them—an assistance program not limited by categories, a broader ADC program, and federally-aided general assistance. I have outlined the world in which many ADC clients live, and suggested that this makes the absence of cash incentive in the program and the absence of certainty and security in its administration particularly damaging. I have said that we need to study methods of providing cash incentive. As for certainty and security, these will follow to some extent from correction of these other problems. But some of the cure is in social workers' hands, in the conviction that ADC clients are not to be herded but helped, not to be badgered but protected.

A discussion of direction that stops at the confines of the ADC program inevitably burdens the program with a job it cannot perform. To discuss this, we move to the children of divorce, separation, and illegitimacy—the children one might call the socially orphaned, who share so many of the problems of the actually orphaned. By social accident, more than by design, ADC is given the mission of relieving need among these children and promoting their sound nurture. We note first that these children are a product of nation-wide family trends and widely endorsed personal impulses. The United States, as visitors from abroad frequently point out, is very much a marrying and a child-bearing country. We seem to be unaware that people have lived satisfying and fruitful lives without mate and child. The American marriage rate is among the highest in the world. Caught in a confidential mood, one's unmarried friends will testify warmly to the pressure put on them. Our birth rate is not quite pre-eminent, taking the world as a whole, but it commands respect in Europe. We require that marriage be personally satisfying; consequently one marriage out of four ends in divorce, and an uncounted number in separation. I shall not say that this divorce rate commands respect, for it has also been described as scandalous. It is not necessary to dwell upon the verve that is characteristic of American industrialization—spilling us together in cities, providing us with necessities that former generations did not know even as luxuries, and making use of the compact, movable family that we prefer. These, then, are the allegiances that shape us all—the orphaned and the intact: marriage, having children, and personal fulfillment for each person; ambition, mobility, and high levels of material satisfaction. If we make a mistake, often we start over. If divorce is not feasible or too expensive, many will separate.

What does this mean for children? At present, well over three million children have parents who have been divorced. At least an equal number are in families that have been broken by separation or desertion. We have as many illegitimate children each year as all the public institutional and foster-care programs count in their charge at a given moment. A divorce or separation in America means, on the average, one child of a broken home. For an overview, eight million children in our country; almost one in seven now live with one parent or with neither because of actual or social orphanage. Though the number of *actual* orphans is declining, the *socially* orphaned continue to grow in number.

On the whole, the main direction of recent activity on behalf of these children has been the enactment of reciprocal nonsupport laws and substantial activity to trace deserted parents. Such laws and activities are useful; parents have a responsibility to their children that ought to be compelled when it is not volunteered. But support can only be compelled when there is income upon which to call. Difficulties in compelling support are due not only to the ordinary orneriness of people. They are due to the fact that increasing numbers of fathers are being looked to for support by more than one family. For many fathers support of two families is not a practical expectation. This presents us with the alternatives of changing our marriage pattern—forbidding divorce or remarriage—or of providing basic security for many socially orphaned children in some other way. On the whole, we are not likely to change our marriage pattern.

The problem of socially orphaned children is compounded by a fact with which we have become familiar, but to which we have never been reconciled: family breakdown is bound to poverty in a cycle that is difficult to interrupt. Divorce, desertion, and illegitimacy occur in wealthy families, to be sure, and in middle-class families. But a poor family in prosperous times faces additional hazards in remaining whole. (Who is the failure? How meet the everlasting bills?) A broken family faces very difficult problems in sustaining income. (What arrangements can a working mother make for her children? How can she earn enough?) A study prepared for the Joint Economic Committee of Congress at the close of 1959 found that families headed by women constituted 25 per cent of the low-income families in the country. A fifth of the nation's children, it concluded, are being raised in "modern poverty." The disadvantage that families headed by women suffer in gaining income is not, under current conditions, expected to diminish. Thus it is plain that assurance of sustained income is as crucial to the socially orphaned as to the actually orphaned.

How might we approach the assurance of income to the socially orphaned? I have suggested implicitly by the manner in which I have presented this material, if not explicitly, that it seems worth asking whether we should address *only* a public assistance program to the need of these children. For the aged, orphaned, disabled, and unemployed we have a basic insurance or compensation program. These programs may be inadequate in some, or in many, respects, but the basic concept has been settled. For the socially orphaned, we have not as a nation accepted such responsibility. When their need becomes dire, we provide a measure of help from ADC. Nothing earlier, nothing more.

We are in need of a social invention—large in conception and cogent—that will meet the problem of the socially orphaned as survivors' insurance meets the problem of the actually orphaned

Such a program will meet these conditions: It will assure that no child is hungry or miserable because he was born illegitimate or his parents have parted. It will provide a moderate income during the time of the child's need, which is dependable and which terminates under more-or-less simple and predictable circumstances. It will operate to encourage regularity and cohesiveness in the family; certainly it will not discourage the family from remaining together or the father from returning home. Finally, it will meet the needs of the large numbers of socially orphaned children, relying on public assistance to help those who for special reasons require individual treatment.

Some adaptation of a system of family allowances may hold the answer. It is a drawback of most such systems that they pay a small amount to all children. Therefore, the payment that reaches the socially orphaned or the low-income children is greatly reduced—either that or the cost is greatly increased. Denmark meets this problem by relating the family allowance inversely to taxable income. As an indication of how this might apply to the United States, one-fourth of our children are in families with an income below the taxable limit.[8] Such a plan directs itself to poverty. The meeting of social scientists referred to above produced an idea more specifically designed for the socially orphaned—that families might be insured against breakup as they are against the death of a husband.[9] Mothers of young children, they said, stand as much chance of one as of the other. There may be other approaches, and this is really the point I seek to make. We are responsible for improving the ADC program we operate. But the program bears the burden of being America's basic program to meet the large, continuing, and, conceivably, growing economic risk of childhood. It was not designed for that problem and cannot meet it.

NOTES

1. Louisiana State Department of Public Welfare, "Report on Study of Orleans Parish Review Unit" (September 1954), ditto.
2. Advisory Council on Public Assistance, *Public Assistance,* United States Department of Health, Education, and Welfare, January

1960 (Washington, D.C.: United States Government Printing Office, 1960).

3. Martin B. Loeb, "Social Class and the American Social System," *Social Work,* VI, No. 2 (April 1961).

4. August B. Hollingshead and Frederick C. Redlich, *Social Class and Mental Illness: A Community Study* (New York: John Wiley & Sons, Inc., 1958); Walter B. Miller, "Implications of Urban Lower-Class Culture for Social Work," *Social Service Review,* XXXIII, No. 3 (September 1959); Lee Rainwater and Karol Kane Weinstein, *And the Poor Get Children* (Chicago: Quadrangle Books, 1960).

5. John H. Rohrer, Munro S. Edmondson, *et al., The Eighth Generation* (New York: Harper and Brothers, 1960).

6. This meeting is summarized in *Social Scientists' Advisory Meeting, Working Paper, June 20–21, 1960,* Division of Program Research, Office of the Commissioner, Social Security Administration, mimeographed, p. 4 and *passim.* For the formulation on which these terms are based, see Florence Kluckhohn and John P. Spiegel, "Integration and Conflict in Human Behavior," Report No. 27 of the Group for the Advancement of Psychiatry, August 1954.

7. *Facts, Fallacies and Future* (New York: Greenleigh Associates, Inc., 1960).

8. Leonore A. Epstein, "Some Effects of Low Income on Children and Their Families," *Social Security Bulletin,* XXIV, No. 2 (February 1961), 12.

9. *Social Scientists' Advisory Meeting, Working Paper, June 20–21, 1960, op. cit.,* p. 19.

4

The Socially Orphaned: The Next Step in Social Security?

This generation's orthodoxy was last generation's revolution. Those who are old enough may remember how visionary social security seemed when it was signed into law in 1935. "It would be a wonderful world," said a carpenter at the time, "if we could simply be secure and know that in our old age, particularly, we would not have to depend on anybody." Now social security has come to seem familiar and—with health insurance—even complete. But viewed in terms of 1965 rather than 1935, social security is far from complete. In a nation called the most child-centered in the world, the striking omission is children.

Eveline Burns made the point to Congress in 1955. "Of all persons affected by our income security and welfare programs," she said, "children are the least favored." [1] Robert Lampman, an early architect of the antipoverty program, made a similar observation to the American Economic Association in 1964. "We have done the least by social policy," he said "[in] family breakup

. . . and being born poor." [2] The words are circumspect but fellow economists understand that the victims are children.

The children for whom we have no protection similar to social security have been called the socially orphaned. They are those who live with only one parent or with neither. Between seven and eight million children in the United States—one out of nine—are socially orphaned. Most of them live with their mothers; perhaps a third live with grandparents or other relatives; about half-a-million live in institutions or alone. The income of socially orphaned children suffers just as if a parent had died. Their "encounter with poverty," writes poverty expert Mollie Orshansky, "can be predicted." [3] Children living with a mother and no father are three times as likely to be poor as other children. Such families have, on the average, two-fifths the income of intact families.

The plight of socially orphaned children is coolly summarized in ratios such as "three times as likely to be poor" and "two-fifths the income of intact families." The most primitive deprivations are involved. Children who are poor by the definition the government is using can spend less than 70 cents a day for food. Four million socially orphaned children live in families that choose every day between a decent diet and some other basic necessity. It does not follow that all these children are inadequately fed, of course. Studying poor families that spend too much for rent, a Chicago housing administrator discovered mothers who literally starved themselves so that their children could eat.[4]

In 1960, about ten million children lived in houses that lacked a proper toilet, bath, or hot water. About four million lived in houses that census enumerators called dangerous. If we may judge by surveys of Aid to Families with Dependent Children—the public assistance program originally designed for broken families—socially orphaned children live in the poorest of these dwellings. The state of Florida found they were paying "excessively high rents for unspeakably inadequate slum homes." [5] In Maine, most families had no central heating—not to speak of other necessities.[6] Even clothing may constitute a problem. Winter after winter in the nation's capital, some newspaper carries a pathetic story about children who alternate days at school because they share a pair of shoes or who stay away from school on "shower" days because they do not have underclothing.

A bit of modern folklore surrounds the prevalence of television sets in poor homes; certainly, television is widely regarded as a necessity. For example, a sociologist asked parents in desperate circumstances how they managed to have television. One had had her telephone removed but kept the television set. "You can count on TV any old time," she said, "but if you want to talk to somebody on the phone he's got to be there." A father of five sold most of his furniture but kept the bed, chairs, and television set. He said he felt he should have kept the books for his children but he decided that it was more important for them to have TV. Nevertheless, about five million poor children do not have television sets in their homes.

Before considering what is done and might be done for socially orphaned children we should understand why they are poor. Many intact families escape poverty because, although the husband earns little, the wife provides a second income. A divorced woman manages, perforce, with a single income. With the husband gone, a mother may decide to work. She has the problem of her children's care to solve. Even if these arrangements do not cost her too much, her children's demands on her energy and attention make her an erratic or weary employee. Women's wages are generally lower than men's and, on the average, women are less well trained for work. If a mother manages to work forty hours a week at the minimum wage, she will keep herself and two children just above the poverty line. Any illness, any upset with her children, any dip in the prosperity of her employer drop her into poverty. If she has more than two children, she both needs more income and has more difficulty in working.

What of the father who has left and his income? A carpenter provided an unwilling illustration of the limitations of divorced fathers. Years ago, he divorced his wife in Boston and subsequently remarried and moved to Maryland. Authorities in Boston corresponded with him for four years, asking that he support his school-age son. Finally, he was extradited to Massachusetts, tried for nonsupport, and sentenced to a year in prison. His second wife and their four children promptly became eligible for welfare payments—to the chagrin of authorities in Maryland. The carpenter's imprisonment may serve as a warning to errant fathers but, obviously, matters were not improved for the child in Boston or for the four in Maryland.

Three-fourths of all divorced persons remarry within five years. So, too, fathers of illegitimate children often enter into new families without great delay. Divorce or separation is, therefore, likely to mean that two families look to one man for support. A man needs at the very least income of $6,000 a year just to keep two small families out of poverty, but $6,000 is more than the average father's income. At the same time, divorce and separation are more prevalent among those who earn less than average. Besides, the fathers who might split their income equally are few; the second wives who would be amenable are fewer; and no court would enforce such a division.

The earning problem of a lone mother, or the limited support provided by a father with two families, may be all that deplete the income of some socially orphaned children, but for many the problem is a great deal more complicated. Family breakdown and poverty quite enclose their lives. A poor boy is likely to marry younger, diminishing his chances for completing education or job training. Children come sooner, adding to financial and marital strain. A family quickly finds itself in the situation Mirra Komarovsky describes in *Blue Collar Marriage:* "A 33-year-old man, a bottler in a beer company, struggles to support his wife and three children on $3,000-a-year pay. He does not like his job, but he also feels that he cannot risk giving up a secure job." [7] Though comparatively young, the family is trapped.

The man's alternative is to become what researcher Hylan Lewis has called a "marriage dropout." It becomes clear that the father can never earn enough, and things are not so sweet at home anyway. At the third or fourth pregnancy, he deserts, or his wife, conscious of his failure and her own misery, precipitates a divorce. (Lewis has pointed out that middle-class women, if they are not happy in their marriages, may settle for at least being kept comfortably. A poor woman does not have this to settle for.) [8] When each member of the couple remarries, they take trouble along—children already requiring support and, sometimes, the idea that escape is a solution for trouble.

This play back-and-forth—money troubles leading to marriage breakdown which adds to financial burdens—may produce the impression that a substantial minority of poor people are incapable of regular lives of any sort. With the situation of Negroes a national issue, it is beginning to be noticed how many Negroes have disorganized family lives as well as low income. But nine out of ten Negro children who are not poor are found in conventionally intact families, quite like white children who are not poor. For Negroes, as for whites, if *either* low income or family breakdown can be prevented for a time, both may develop toward regularity.

When we turn to the question of what is being done for children's income, we think immediately of the poverty program. However, the Economic Opportunity Act was not designed to provide support but to provide the equipment that is necessary for holding jobs. In its prescription for the war on poverty, the President's Council of Economic Advisers noted that poverty could readily be wiped out by providing money. "But this 'solution' would leave untouched the roots of poverty," they said. "It will be far better, even if more difficult, to equip and to permit the poor of the nation to produce and to earn the additional [income they need]." [9] Therefore, newly designed programs have emphasized education, training, and work, and the conditions— such as good health—that are necessary to them. Children and youths receive financial help if their parents are in work experience programs or if they are themselves in the Job Corps or Neighborhood Youth Corps, but children so aided are a very small proportion of those who need income.

The major national program that provides support to socially orphaned children is Aid to Families with Dependent Children (AFDC). Welfare departments provide assistance according to a "means test." That is, an investigator establishes family income and needs exactly in order to set the amount of the payment. Over three million children are being aided under this program, two-thirds of them socially orphaned and the others actually orphaned or with fathers disabled or unemployed. It is difficult to conceive how we might do less than this. On the other hand, as one federal official puts it, "the trouble with the means test is that it is so mean." Families receive an average of about a dollar a day per person; virtually all children remain poor while they are being helped.

Millions of socially orphaned children are not helped by AFDC because, although their families have only a niggardly income, it is above the prescribed minimum, or because for example, they fall afoul of other regulations. Families may not be eligible under a state's regulations because it appears that a man has been living in the house. (Despite federal encouragement, most states have not yet chosen to include families with an unemployed father in the program.) Families may not be eligible because the Welfare Department thinks that the mother or children ought to work, or because the mother refuses to sue the father for support. (She may be glad he is gone and reluctant to have him brought back, for all the good it will do her, or she may be afraid of him.) Indeed, families may be ineligible because it is assumed that the father is supporting, whether or not he is actually supporting. In short, although AFDC was originally enacted by Congress for socially orphaned children, the majority of them are not entitled to help under local regulations.

Although the restrictions applied to AFDC vary from state to state, to a large extent they represent the same underlying problems. The number of socially orphaned who seek help is increasing. The states with the largest proportion of poor people most lack the money to operate the program. Although AFDC is heavily subsidized by the federal government, poor states have difficulty in raising their share of the money. Regulations and paper work have multiplied to the point where no one will defend them. At least since World War II legislative and public attitudes to the program have been plainly unfriendly. Negroes make up a substantial portion (40 per cent) of beneficiary families, as they do of the poor; this contributes to unfriendliness in many places. Public unfriendliness is widely transmuted into private chivying of those who receive assistance. From these families through all the layers of professionals and officials who are concerned, no one regards AFDC with relaxed satisfaction. The United States Commissioner of Welfare, Ellen Winston, has criticized payment levels as "inadequate . . . to break the cycle of poverty and dependency." [10] The National Association of Social Workers has declared its "stand for the abolition of the means test in the archaic form in which it is applied." [11]

The problem of seven or eight million socially orphaned children calls for a federal, nonrelief solution, for they are a problem of national consequence. Cities and states lack the funds necessary to solve the problem. For example, if poor children were to be assured the extremely modest level of living that is provided in Old Age Assistance—the companion program to AFDC—the additional cost would approach five billion dollars. In any event, food and shelter for these children cannot long be left subject to local prejudices. As protection against all the other contingencies that interfere with family income—disability, unemployment, retirement, death of a husband or father—the government has provided social security or unemployment compensation. There is no reason why we should leave this last serious risk—loss of the father for social reasons—solely to an embattled program of public relief. Obviously all poor children deserve our concern and attention. I spotlight the socially orphaned because they represent a recognizable, nationally significant group who suffer income loss for reasons beyond their control. The problem shows no signs of diminishing; if anything, its impact on children is growing.

Nothing inherent in the situation of children makes it impossible to devise a nonrelief program for them. We are the only developed country in the western world without such a program. Most countries use children's allowances—monthly payments for each child to the father or mother, regardless of income. A family with four children receives $25.00 to $30.00 a month in neighboring Canada and about $100 a month in France. (The precise amount varies with the age of the children.) New Zealand and Australia have a program designed specifically for socially orphaned children. They receive social security payments, just as children whose fathers have died. Denmark ties a payment for children to the income tax return. Those who owe tax receive a credit against it. Those who do not owe tax, who are naturally poorer, receive a payment from the government.

It is difficult to compare these countries to the United States. None is as wealthy as we, and their programs were established for differing reasons. France was hoping to increase its birth rate; Canada was seeking to avoid a depression after World War II and to deliver on the promise of a better world. However, we may take two kinds of reassurance from the experience of western countries. First, there is no evidence that their programs lead to an increase in birth rate. Sweden has a lower birth rate now than it had when it began a program of children's allowances. The most remarkable quality about post-war birth rates in France and Canada is that they closely resemble trends in the United States. Second, a number of countries feared that children might not benefit from money paid out for them. Some, therefore, specified that the mother should receive the payment even when there was a father. The problem has turned out to be illusory. A microscopic proportion of families divert the money to personal or frivolous uses, but this is also true of families that receive income from work or from widow's pensions.

At least three types of programs are available that provide a federal, nonrelief solution for the problems of socially orphaned children. Two of them are suitable to the problems of all poor children; all have been tried out somewhere in the western world. We shall refer to them as the negative income tax, fatherless child insurance, and children's allowances.

1. A presidential task force in 1964 is said to have recommended a negative income tax. As in Denmark, families with income so low that they fail to benefit from the value of their income tax exemptions would receive a payment from the government. To some extent, the plan would correct an inequity in present tax law. That is, rich people—because they pay a higher tax rate—benefit more from the deduction for their children than do poorer people; poor people, paying no tax, do not benefit at all from their deductions for children. The plan seems simple and it could easily cover all needy children or all needy people. However, the sums of money involved in the income tax

deduction for children are small—around $100 a year for each child. A program that was limited to such sums of money would, like AFDC, leave most children who benefit still poor. It is a damaging drawback.

Schemes can readily be devised that would be administered in connection with the income tax but deal with somewhat larger sums of money. For example, Professor James Tobin has proposed a payment of $400 per person to families with no other income.[12] Payments to families who have other income would be diminished by a third of their other income. In effect, a family with three children would be assured a minimum income of $2,000 a year and at least some assistance up to an income of $6,000. Experts have so far seemed cool to this proposal, partly no doubt because it is expensive. More troublesome, although a man or woman would always stand to gain from working, the threat of stark privation would be eliminated for those who did not work —no matter what their reason. It is not clear that Americans are ready to take this step.

2. Fatherless child insurance was first proposed in the Beveridge Report,[13] which charted Great Britain's course in social security after World War II. Mothers divorced under circumstances for which they were not responsible were to be treated like widows under social security. Under such a provision, in the United States, a mother would receive benefits for her children until they were eighteen years old (or older, if in college). The mother would receive a small benefit for herself until the children grew up, unless she remarried or earned a moderate income. One advantage of such a program is that families would receive meaningful amounts of money. Establishing that mothers were not responsible for the divorce, as Beveridge proposed, would require a judge's opinion in each case. No doubt, this accounts for the omission from Beveridge's proposal of parents who were merely separated. Yet children whose parents are separated are a substantial proportion of the socially orphaned; a program that ignored them would be seriously limited.

3. Professor Burns and others have put forward proposals for a children's allowance. Lord Beveridge supported these, too. (He read an early book on the subject[14] in order to review it and was

forthwith a convert.) A government payment would be made to every father (or mother) for each child. It is possible to pay more for the first child than the third or fourth, or vice versa. It is possible to limit the allowance to preschool children or, on the other hand, to children in school. The payment would not be related to income. Undoubtedly, however, initiation of children's allowances would be coupled with reduction or elimination of the income tax deduction for children. As a consequence, higher-income families would suffer a tax loss in exchange for the payment. A program of children's allowances has much to recommend it. It is the simplest of all programs. The allowance would be welcomed even by families who are to have decent income later on, for it would come in the years when they need it most and have least. A program of family allowances has one major drawback: making a payment for every American child is very expensive.

Clearly, each program has advantages and disadvantages. The choice is not automatic and requires thoughtful debate. Cost might fall anywhere between three and ten billion dollars a year, depending on the program selected and how it is written. A program that costs less than three billion dollars is not likely to be worth the bother. At an average of even twenty dollars a month, fifteen million poor children in the United States require well over that amount. It is probably not necessary, in this age of the economist, to observe that this minimum amount of money is less than one-tenth of the amount that national production *increases* in a single year.

Funds for programs of negative income tax or children's allowances would come from the federal income tax. In announcing the 1965 income tax reduction, President Johnson observed that the next tax reduction would be for poor people. The next tax reduction must have seemed much closer at that time than events made feasible. In any event, the President's promise should not be forgotten when the time to deliver comes. A negative income tax would, obviously, represent a tax change for poor people. A program of family allowances carefully formulated to benefit poor families would not be far afield. Fatherless child insurance, as it represents an expansion of the social security system, would naturally be financed from the social security tax paid by employers and employees. However, the burden of the social security tax falls rather more heavily on low-income families than does the income tax. With health insurance in 1965, the precedent was established of a government payment to support social security. It would be possible, following this precedent, to finance fatherless child insurance by a government payment to the social security fund.

Whatever the mechanism, the nation must somehow bear the cost if socially orphaned children are to receive income. Against the cost, we balance the fact that many parents can do little to feed and clothe children that they are not already doing. Mothers will buy children what they need, but they cannot do it without money. The nurture of children is at stake. For want of nurture, all their future might be lost.

Frances Perkins has reported that the first reaction of Franklin Roosevelt to the idea of unemployment compensation was: "Oh, we don't want the dole; not the dole." [15] In 1935, the principle that a worker should be taxed so he could retire at sixty-five seemed quite possibly unconstitutional, even to proponents of social security.[16] These are the revolutions of a generation that is now growing old. Now, partly because we have solved other problems and partly because the problem of socially orphaned children looms larger every year, we confront an intrinsic irony in social security: It is far worse for children that their father should be separated from them than that he should die. We may be facing a national debate on the next stage in social security. Only in ten or fifteen years will the course that we take seem to have been inevitable.

NOTES

1. Eveline Burns, *Hearings before the Subcommittee on Low Income Families, Joint Committee on the Economic Report. United States Congress November 18, 19, 21, 22 and 23, 1955* (Washington, D.C.: United States Government Printing Office, 1955).

2. Robert J. Lampman, "Approaches to the Reduction of Poverty," presented at the Annual Meeting of the American Economic Association, Chicago, December 30, 1964.

3. Mollie Orshansky, "Counting the Poor: Another Look at the Poverty Profile," *Social Security Bulletin,* XXVIII, No. 1 (January 1965).
4. Elizabeth Wood, "Knowledge Needed for Adequate Programs of Public and Private Housing," in Donald J. Bogue, ed., *Needed Urban and Metropolitan Research* (Oxford, Ohio: Scripps Foundation and Miami University Press, 1953).
5. Florida Department of Public Welfare, *Suitable Home Law,* Preliminary Report (September 1960), mimeographed, p. 16.
6. John M. Romanyshyn, *Aid to Dependent Children in Maine* (State of Maine Department of Health and Welfare, June 1960), p. 10.
7. Mirra Komarovsky, with Jane H. Philips, *Blue Collar Marriage* (New York: Random House, 1964).
8. Hylan Lewis and Camille Jeffers, "Poverty and the Behavior of Low-Income Families," presented at the American Orthopsychiatric Association, Chicago, March, 19, 1964.
9. *Economic Report of the President, Together with the Annual Report of the Council of Economic Advisers* (Washington, D.C.: United States Government Printing Office, January 1964).
10. Ellen Winston, "Educational Approaches to Community Problems," presented at the Council of National Organizations for Adult Education, Washington, D. C., December 8, 1964.
11. Delegates' Assembly of the National Association of Social Workers, Chicago, November 1964.
12. James Tobin, "On Improving the Economic Status of the Negro," *Daedalus,* LCIV, No. 4 (Fall 1965).
13. Sir William Beveridge, *Social Insurance and Allied Services* (New York: The Macmillan Company, 1942).
14. Eleanor Rathbone, *The Disinherited Family* (London: Allen and Unwin, 1924).
15. Frances Perkins, speech to the staff of the Social Security Administration, Baltimore, October 23, 1962.
16. Thomas H. Eliot, "The Social Security Bill, 25 Years After," *Atlantic Monthly,* CCVI, No. 2 (August 1960).

PART II

---◆---

Filial
Responsibility
and Family Policy

AUTHOR'S NOTE

This section began as an attempt to evaluate the effect of social security programs upon the family relations of adult children and their aging or at least middle-aging parents. It was rapidly evident that this task could not be performed without setting forth what the relations of adult children and their parents generally are. The willingness of a son to contribute money to his indigent father, for example, depends for its significance upon what other sons are doing. As it turned out, information was more readily available about aging parents than others, and the work focused on them.

Chapter 5, "The Fifth Commandment," is a brief argument about the history of filial responsibility. It is not intended to cover the entire historical development but to clarify a specific point that is often heavily clouded with nostalgia. Chapter 6, "Current Practice," analyzes the responsibility actually exercised by adult children for their parents. Current practice is treated under three headings: financial support in separate living, living together, and the variety of other practices that reflect concern or affection. Though obviously interrelated, behavior about each of the three is quite different. Chapter 7, "Social Security and Filial Responsibility," comes to the point that touched off all the work, evaluating two social security programs and touching on two others.

The last two chapters are subsequent reflections on the forces that move government policy in the area of family relations. Chapter 8, "Beyond Pluck and Luck," recasts the material on filial responsibility to confront the primitive feeling that seems to sustain laws imposing financial responsibility on children, that is, the feeling that these laws are the last constraints on people who are already irresponsible. Chapter 9, "Family Policy in the United States," faces directly the question whether family policy can be dealt with rationally.

5

The Fifth Commandment

The term "filial responsibility" emphasizes duty rather than satisfaction and is usually connected with protection, care, or financial support. In law and in custom, filial responsibility is interwoven with parental, marital, and other kinship responsibilities. It is useful to separate it from "family responsibility" to try to see it more clearly. Filial responsibility is used broadly here, to cover the duties required by law, custom, or personal attitude. At points, as the contexts will make clear, legal responsibility is dealt with specifically.

It is a popular belief about filial responsibility that its origins are lost in antiquity, resting on even earlier if no more majestic sanction than the commandment, "Honor thy father and thy mother." This aura can make it difficult to get utilitarian answers to questions about present practices and their effects on families. Though there are old and honorable antecedents for the precept to render "offices of tenderness" to one's parents and household gods, the content of this precept changes with social change. The idea that the community is not responsible until children have made their maximum effort has developed since medieval times.

An excerpt from *Filial Responsibility in the United States,* United States Social Security Administration, (Washington, D.C.: United States Government Printing Office, 1960).

It is a modern situation, furthermore, that gives rise to the idea that a son ought to support his parent without economic force or benefit, out of more or less charitable impulse, and as likely as not from a distance. It is only in the last century that there has been opportunity to practice this idea widely.

Medieval church law held children to be responsible for their parents; the Church and the wealthy also had responsibility for those who were indigent. The emphasis on children's responsibility was addressed to the child, however. When the indigent parent sought help from others, he was viewed as having a moral right to it and could not be turned away unless he were a pagan or for a similar reason.* It may be that almsgiving was less discriminating in the thirteenth and fourteenth centuries; certainly it was less punitive than in post-Elizabethan times. But, for whatever reason, the examination of the child's responsibility was not generally thought to be an element in deciding whether to help a needy old person. Church concepts of relieving poverty were subjected to a variety of strains in the sixteenth century: the need to protect accumulated property, to suppress vagrancy, and to provide a new source of relief-giving. The Elizabethan Poor Law enacted a number of adjustments that had been developing. For the first time it established that the community would assist the indigent parent *only after* the means of his child had been called upon. This primary responsibility of the child had not existed in English common law, nor does it exist in American common law.[1]

The American colonies adopted the Poor Law whole, but from the beginning Americans held two ideas that were to prove antithetical to the strictest concepts of filial responsibility. First, children assumed an importance they had never had in Europe. "In a new world," wrote Calhoun in accounting for this, "men face the

---

* "The medieval canonists were entirely in harmony with the pioneers of the Charity Organization movement on at least this one matter, though they approached it from a different point of view. The canonists stressed the primary obligation of a man to relieve want in his own immediate circle. The Charity Organization movement insisted on the duty of a person in need to seek help from his family and neighbors before turning for assistance to public relief and organized charities." Brian Tierney, *Medieval Poor Law* (Berkeley: University of California Press, 1959), p. 65.

future and worship, not ancestors, but posterity." [2] Second, in an equalitarian atmosphere, every person is important in himself.[3] Once he reaches maturity, not even family ties interfere with the fullest exercise of independent choice. Although these principles formed the country, they did not immediately collide with the Poor Law principle that the needy parent has prior claim on his children. Pre-Civil War journals deal at length with many of the problems that upset us today—insolent children, loosening of sexual standards, and changes and uncertainty in the roles of husband and wife—but they mention rarely, if at all, problems of parents arising from the unconcern of grown children. On the contrary, there is marked and mounting emphasis on the struggle of youths to emancipate themselves—apparently in an atmosphere of considerable social approval.[4]

Major collision between the equalitarian, child-centered ethics of this country and the concepts of filial responsibility embodied in the Poor Law was postponed until nearly the twentieth century. The reasons for the postponement are common knowledge, but their full meaning is often overlooked. It is not simply that the family in an agricultural, frontier country was an economic unit, but that the parents owned the farm and equipment. In the early stages of industrialization the family—that is, the father—owned the machinery that was used at home; later it was the father who committed the family to work in a particular factory.[5] Though the mother was not the proprietor, so to speak, of the family economic unit, her situation as she aged was not very different from the father's. With the death of her husband, management might pass to a son, but not technical possession, and she continued with homemaking and other productive activities. Thus, the young adult was bound in an economic unit not merely by filial feeling or social expectation. When he left home, as he did increasingly early anyhow, he left behind the means of earning a living and had to develop new means for himself. It was both more difficult for him to leave than it is today and it was less of a blow to his parents.

Aside from parental ownership, our preindustrial economy tended in other ways to assure income to parents, without appearance or feeling that moral choice was involved. Income was family income, chiefly in subsistence items, which had been shared and continued to be shared. The spread of individually earned cash income was to dramatize a new ethical choice. The availability of free land reduced the scope of dependency. It also tended to support parental control over their own property, which did not need to be divided for the children. Finally, and perhaps most simply, there were not many retired people—as late as 1900, average life expectancy was forty-seven years and average *work* life expectancy thirty-two years.[6] There are more aged people living with children today than were alive as recently as 1920. Thus, there were undoubtedly some parents before the Civil War who relied on the voluntary help of their children. But they were few—by percentage or by number—compared with today.

Legislative history reflects the development that has been outlined: a perspective on filial responsibility that was borrowed from our English tradition, but that awaited industrialization to be actively tested. Early support laws were copied whole, their phrasing is vague, and they lack adequate provision for enforcement.[7] Courts have consistently held that ". . . the primary and essential objective of the legislation now in force still is, like that of chapter 2 of 43 Elizabeth, the protection of the public purse" (1941 New York State opinion).[8] In public assistance legislation, southern and western states tended much less than the states with a Puritan tradition to enact filial responsibility laws. Of all federal or federal-state programs, only public assistance with its Poor Law history placed first responsibility on adult children, even though others (for example, vocational rehabilitation) might also include a means test. With industrialization, the issue began to be joined. It was in 1868 that veterans' legislation included dependent fathers, though it had provided for dependent wives and children for some time. General liberalization of veterans' benefits after this time is attributed to the beginning of the breakup of farm family homes.[9] Similarly, the new State of Ohio omitted relatives' responsibility from its own 1805 law (though territorial law had included it) and enacted it only in 1898.[10]

In short, support of the aged did not become an issue until there were more old people and fewer were in control of their own situations. It was only when an economy that separated wages from ownership meant that the old person was no longer in control, that many adult children had reason to examine their willingness to help their parents. This material is often treated as if young people in the eighteenth and nineteenth centuries felt and discharged a duty to support their aged parents voluntarily, out of a sense of gratitude or obligation alone. Such a sense of filial responsibility, if it was widely felt, was only occasionally put to test.

It is in the twentieth century that the idea has achieved wide currency that an adult should voluntarily sacrifice his own, his wife's, and his children's resources to assist his parents before the community will assume responsibility. That it is novel does not mean it should be discarded, but frees us to see what current practice is and what are its effects.

NOTES

1. Richard H. Tawney, "Economic Virtues and Prescriptions for Poverty," from *Religion and the Rise of Capitalism,* reprinted in Herman D. Stein and Richard A. Cloward, eds., *Social Perspectives on Behavior* (Glencoe, Ill.: The Free Press, 1958), pp. 266–287. Stefan Riesenfeld with Richard C. Maxwell, *Modern Social Legislation* (Brooklyn, N.Y.: Foundation Press, 1950), pp. 692–700. *See also* regarding legal base of filial responsibility: *Corpus Juris Secundum,* LXVII, section 24, "Parent and Child," and LXX, section 60c, "Paupers" (Brooklyn, N.Y.: American Law Book Company, 1936); James Kent, *Commentaries on American Law,* II (New York, 1836); Brian Tierney, *Medieval Poor Law* (Berkeley, California: University of California Press, 1959), p. 65.

2. Arthur W. Calhoun, *A Social History of the American Family* (Cleveland, Ohio: A. H. Clark, 1917, 3 vols.), II, 51–54; III, 67–68; I, II, III, *passim.*

3. Alexis De Tocqueville, *Democracy in America* (New York: D. Appleton & Company, Inc., 1899), Introduction to Vol. I.

4. Calhoun, *op. cit.*

5. Calhoun, *op. cit.* Wilbert E. Moore, "The Aged in Industrial Societies," in Milton Derber, ed., *The Aged and Society* (Champaign, Ill.: Industrial Relations Research Association, December 1950).

6. United States Department of Labor, *Population and Labor Force Projections for the U.S., 1960–1975,* Bulletin No. 1242 (Washington,

D.C.: United States Government Printing Office, 1957). Work life expectancy data first presented in a paper by Seymour L. Wolfbein, July 1957.

7. Michael V. Hitrovo, "Responsibility of Relatives in the Old-Age Assistance Program in Pennsylvania," *Social Service Review*, XVIII, No. 1 (March 1944), 69 and 75.

8. Cited in Riesenfeld and Maxwell, *op. cit.*

9. The President's Commission on Veterans' Pensions (3 vols.), Vol. I, *Findings and Recommendations*, "Staff Report No. I: The Historical Development of Veterans' Benefits in the United States" (Washington, D.C.: United States Government Printing Office, 1956).

10. Edith Abbott, *Public Assistance*, Vol. I (Chicago: University of Chicago Press, 1940).

6

---◆---

Current Practice

FINANCIAL ASSISTANCE
IN SEPARATE LIVING

Although the aged (or those over sixty-five years old) do not include all the parents of adult children, they are the group whose income has been most carefully studied. On the whole, one may assume that the financial assistance they receive from their children is at peak level, for the need of the over sixty-five's is greatest and the earnings of their children has approached its highest level. Almost three out of five of those over sixty-five had less than $1,000 cash income in 1958.[1] When evaluating such a figure, one must take into account certain differences from younger people—income that is not in cash, for example, more home ownership, higher medical costs. The results of the Steiner and Dorfman analysis for 1951[2] are illuminating. It found that the following percentages of the aged were living below "subsistence budget" levels—27 per cent of the couples, 33 per cent of the nonmarried men, and 50 per cent of the nonmarried women. In any philosophy, these are large numbers of people who are in need of addi-

An excerpt from *Filial Responsibility in the United States,* United States Social Security Administration (Washington, D.C.: United States Government Printing Office, 1960).

tional income.* Roughly three out of four of the aged have living children.[3]

The attitudes that people express about financial support by adult children have been surveyed from time to time. The results that are produced are at least superficially confusing. For example, in answer to the general question of what a "good" son or daughter will do for his parents, more than 75 per cent of both parents and children thought he should provide financial assistance.[4] A National Opinion Research Center study, on the other hand, provides a brief story about a widower whose children, in modest circumstances, have families of their own.[5] Only 30 per cent of the over sixty-five-year-olds thought the widower should ask his children to help him. The results of some surveys suggest that old people assert a right to support that they will not voluntarily exercise. They make contradictory statements; they say children should support but when they are in need, do not ask for help.[6] When one inquires whether children should help a great deal or "some," only 5 per cent will take the former.[7] Cultural influence is evident in one set of findings:[8] 42 per cent of Negroes thought that children should help their parents and 37 per cent of Caucasians, but only 24 per cent with Spanish background. The low figure for people with Spanish background is interesting for, in fact, theirs is much more deeply an extended family culture;[9] however, they do not share Anglo guilt at seeking public assistance.

It is difficult to summarize the results of opinion surveys in the area of filial responsibility. The better surveys are so carefully sampled and analyzed that they produce a wholly misleading sense of precision, for the values they seek to measure are in con-

---

* In the material that follows, figures and percentages about nonmarried men and women refer to current status. That is, the divorced and widowed are included in the nonmarried.

It will be evident that this article was completed before data from the 1960 census were available and before the subsequent series of studies on poverty. In 1963, aged people living in poverty—defined differently from those living below subsistence budget levels—came to higher percentages: 24 per cent of the families with an aged man at the head, 43 per cent of men, and 65 per cent of women living alone. Mollie Orshansky, "Who's Who among the Poor: A Demographic View of Poverty," *Social Security Bulletin*, XXVIII, No. 7 (July 1965).

flict and colored by deep feeling. In general, surveys yield respectable percentages in favor of filial responsibility as long as the question is put quite simply and in ethical terms. But responses may be manipulated almost at will by framing questions that introduce the responsibility of the adult child to his wife and children, his responsibility for his own advancement, choice between the adult child and other sources of assistance, choice between money and other things children can give, and the sense that one speaks of oneself rather than in general. Many surveys introduce one or more of these considerations, with the result that a majority oppose and a fairly large minority (a third or more) affirm the responsibility of children to support. There is little doubt that a question heavily stacked with these conflicting values would produce a smaller percentage (perhaps 5 to 15 per cent) of aged people who would say their children should support them. Then one recalls that in many areas Americans do not feel constrained to practice what we profess, and it becomes important to turn to what is our actual practice.

The percentage of aged people who receive cash contributions from one or more children is probably between 5 and 10 per cent (that is, about 1 to 1.5 million parents); the proportion may be lower but it is not higher. There are studies that arrive at lower percentages.[10] Other studies arrive at figures up to 20 or 25 per cent,[11] but higher figures invariably include help from other relatives or friends, or the estimated value of free rent and other help in kind. Both are apt to add materially to percentages. Though there is some impression that children who do not ordinarily contribute will pay for emergency or special needs, in a given year 10 per cent or fewer of the aged report doctor bills paid by a relative.[12] Presumably, if data were available for younger (that is, less than sixty-five years old) parents of adult children, all these percentages would be lower.

In short, the pattern of cash contribution by adult children is not significant in terms of numbers. For the 5 to 10 per cent who receive some contribution, the amount is meaningful. For example, a national study[13] found in 1957 that the median yearly contribution for those aged people who received contributions from a child or other relative was $300 for couples ($150 per person) and $240 for nonmarried individuals. As the median total money income was, respectively, $2,250 and $1,070, these contributions take on importance. (Contributions that are not made in cash are treated in the next section, below.)

In general, contributions by children are more often made to nonmarried women, less often to nonmarried men, and least often to couples. Undoubtedly this difference reflects the circumstances of each group. Married couples have higher incomes, their health is likely to be better, and various studies have indicated that they are in a more favorable state of mind. The nonmarried women, on the other hand, are likely to be the group with the lowest earnings and the poorest health. Their average age will be higher and their chances of remarriage not so favorable as for the men. It has been observed, further, that personal relationships are easier when mothers get help from married daughters than from married sons.[14]

The percentage who contribute to parents increases regularly with the income of the giver. Conversely, it is the parents in the lowest income group who more often receive contributions.[15] That those who have most should give most often to those who have least could, perhaps, have been predicted. But it is inconsistent with the observation in a number of sociological studies[16] that working-class mores require help to parents and other relatives in a way that middle-class mores do not. Cash contribution is not the complete story, however, as financial help may be given in other forms, notably living together.

It is interesting that investigations of filial contributions treat them as if the flow were one way, from the adult child to the parent. Perhaps this is in the nature of studies that focus on the income of the aged and, after all, are not concerned with the income of younger groups. Or perhaps we assume, because we are acutely conscious of the problem of the aged, that what flows the other way will be insignificant. Where the question has been asked, however, the balance of financial aid proves to be "greater in the direction of helping children." [17] Moreover, this held true in each income category. While one must suppose that there is a decrease of assistance from parent to child with decreasing income, individuals and two-person families in the lowest income categories still show small percentages making contributions for someone else's support.[18]

One has only to reflect on how students attend college to appreciate the extent to which parental financial assistance operates beyond children's minority. Seventy-four per cent of unmarried full-time college students received assistance from their parents in 1952–1953, in a median amount of $764.[19] Two out of five college students are twenty years of age or older.[20] Though parental help may be concentrated among the younger students, obviously a substantial number of older students are also being helped. Other areas that might reflect similar investment are cash contributions when young adults establish a home and are rearing children. It is entirely representative of these developments that a scale developed to measure performance in the parent role[21] rates highest the parent who "had no need to give [adult children] everything. If he supports them financially, does so unobtrusively and in a matter-of-fact way. . . ." Here is a development that may represent more change in voluntary patterns than the contributions up the age ladder that we have been discussing—that is, the extension of parental support into their children's majority.

LIVING TOGETHER

A special survey,[22] which provides the most usable information for our purpose, indicates that 33 per cent of the aged in the country in 1952 were living with children. Fifty-eight per cent were living alone or as couples only; the remaining 10 per cent had other shared living arrangements. Higher percentages of aged living with others are provided by measures that combine other relatives as well as children in one figure. Such figures are roughly a third higher than those that count only aged people living with children. Lower percentages are provided if one counts as living together only the aged who are not heads of households.[23] Who is named head of the household may reflect courtesy, however, more than the actual circumstances.[24] The long-term trend appears to be toward a declining percentage of aged people living with children.[25] By 1957, about 28 per cent were living with children.[26]

It is the currently nonmarried and especially the women who are most likely to share living arrangements. The third who lived with children in 1957 include the following: 23 per cent of all aged couples, 27 per cent of the nonmarried men, and 37 per cent of the nonmarried women.[27] Other factors that increase the likelihood of living with children are advancing age, poor health, and low income. Obviously these factors are interrelated and, as has been indicated, they are related to sex and marital status as well. Nevertheless, one should not conclude that only poor, sick, old widows live with children, for though the numbers of men, of couples, and of well-to-do who live with children are smaller, they are noticeable. Women prove to be pivotal in live-together arrangements. Aged parents are more likely to live with their daughter and her husband and children, if any, than with a son and his family. Young couples starting out are more likely to live with the wife's family than with the husband's.[28] Aged women with low incomes will tend, if they have children, to live with them. Men's choices are apparently dependent on other factors; they are as likely to live alone, whether or not they have children.[29]

It has been noted that cash contributions are more frequently given by those with higher incomes, and more frequently received by those with lower incomes. This, as far as it goes, is inconsistent with sociological and anthropological studies that conclude that working-class, but not middle-class, mores require assistance to relatives beyond husband and children. Living together is somewhat more in accordance with this expectation, as Table 6–1 indicates.

Thus, among the families with less than $2,000 income, there is substantially more living together (this includes other relatives as well as children) than their representation in the population. Conversely, families with more than $2,000 income tend less to have aged relatives living with them.

How is one to interpret this? The more that people have, the more likely they are to give in cash. But having more will not lead them (except perhaps in the highest income brackets) to share their living quarters more readily. The overrepresentation in the lowest income brackets must be a result, at least in part, of the need of the parent rather than the income of the family. For example, a retired laborer is five times as likely to live with rela-

Table 6–1

DISTRIBUTION BY INCOME CLASS OF ALL FAMILIES COMPARED WITH FAMILIES
THAT INCLUDE AN AGED MEMBER, 1951

| | | Families that include aged member | |
Money income class	All families in United States (per cent)	Families with aged couples (per cent)	Families with aged nonmarried individuals (per cent)
All income	100.0	100.0	100.0
Less than $2,000	20.5	27.0	31.8
$2,000 to $2,999	15.4	14.5	12.3
$3,000 to $4,999	35.3	27.1	29.3
$5,000 or more	28.7	31.3	26.5

Sources: U.S. Dept. of Commerce, Bureau of the Census, *Current Population Reports*, Series P–60, No. 12, June 1953, Table 1; Lenore A. Epstein, "Economic Resources of Persons Aged 65 and Over," *Social Security Bulletin*, June 1955, Table 8.

tives as a retired corporation executive.[30] Undoubtedly, family income among the laborers' families is lower, but the retired laborer's own income is lower than the retired executive's. The laborer's need for a living arrangement that will in part support him presents the question of help to his family. The executive's family is less likely to have a question to consider. Thus, the fact that more low-income families live together is, to some extent, simply a reflection of the fact that more of these parents need help. Why does not starker need of their parents also produce more cash contributions from the lowest-income families? Presumably because their own plight is so difficult that they must select the most efficient way of sharing, which is living together. Possibly, too, the reciprocal services that the parent may offer—babysitting, housekeeping—are more meaningful to the low-income families. To summarize, perhaps oversimply, the giving of cash reflects a feeling of having some excess that may be shared (a feeling, apparently, that few Americans at any income level have). Living together reflects much more simply a response to the need of the parent.

Aside from sheer need, there may be a degree of readier receptivity to living together among lower-income families, but such a statement must be used guardedly. Recent English exploration of the relationship between kinship intimacy and class concludes that class is not determining. Rather, certain factors are determining that may be (or may not be) associated with class: economic ties within families (helping one another get a job in the same factory, for example), whether their neighborhood tends to throw them together, social and geographic mobility, and opportunity to make other contacts.[31] Moreover, it seems possible that it was not so much a working-class as an immigrant characteristic that older studies reported. It has been observed that loyalty to an extended family is an immigrant tradition, particularly among those from eastern and southern European countries.[32] That working-class and immigrant groups were in many places identical would make such confusion unavoidable. There is an ironic note here: As immigration declines and Americans become more thoroughly Americanized, alarm arises that a tradition of extended family solidarity (thought by some to be American) is vanishing. That such a development is in fact involved tends to be indicated by findings that the lower their socioeconomic position, the more likely aged people living alone are to become isolated with advancing age *except where immigrant cultural traditions intervene.*[33]

Obviously, it is more difficult to assess the value of living together than of cash contributions. An estimate based on 1951 data found 10 per cent of the aged couples and 38 per cent of the nonmarried living without payment in quarters that they did not own. The guess was made that the value of free quarters to the old person was $360 a year,[34] a substantial addition to his income. In addition to free rent, 3 per cent of the aged couples and 8 per cent of the aged nonmarried said that they contributed less than their full share to household expenses, or had bills paid for them by relatives or friends. In any case, value cannot be measured in financial terms alone. The relationship of advanced age and poor health to living together strongly suggests that protection or nursing care is often involved. Less tangible factors, such as attention and company, are certainly involved too.

There are also the possibilities that living together is for the children's benefit, for mutual benefit, or for no benefit at all, but simply the way family living is working out. These are possibilities that, as with cash contributions, are often obscured by the assumption that living together is for the parent's benefit. Upward of a third of the aged who live with children or other relatives own their own home.[35] Though this means that the parents are giving something, one can only conjecture how many are therefore contributing more than their share. When they are specifically asked for whose benefit they are living together, the majority of parents say they are helping the children.[36] The Rhode Island Governor's Commission[37] concluded that "in many instances the arrangement is undoubtedly one of mutual economic necessity." Aside from occasional wry observations that the positive attributes of parents in their families "must be taken as a possibility also," [38] the literature of aging has little more to contribute. It is curious that one must turn from the field of aging, where one is so often urged to stress the positive, to other technical fields in the United States and to English research for evidence of the utility of living together to adult children.

To begin with, the living together of parents and adult children is influenced by parental concern about children just as is parental contribution of cash. In 1951, one in five married couples postponed setting up a separate home during the first year of marriage, one in eight for three years. Though the housing shortage may have been involved at that time, three years later 12 per cent of couples under twenty-five did not have their own households.[39] In 1959, one out of four or five couples in their middle years had a young adult child living with them.[40] That parents are turned to in later years in the face of emergencies—death, divorce, desertion, and migration—has also been noted[41] but not counted. In 1950, 4.8 million people twenty-five years and over were living with parents who were the head of the household, accounting for about half the living-together households.[42] We have noted, of course, that who is head is an uncertain indication of actual circumstances.

To turn to nonmonetary services to adult children, Dr. Ernest Burgess has described contributions that are well known in folklore, basing his comments, however, on studies of engagement and marriage.[43] "Where both parents and children elect to live together," he writes, "the arrangement may work out more or less satisfactorily. Where the wife is working, the mother-in-law often takes on the major charge of the household responsibilities. She may be very happy to function as a babysitter. . . . Although there may be some disagreements, these tend to be minor, and both generations report the relationship as satisfying." A survey of working mothers documents the role of grandparents in caring for children.[44] The major role of aged parents in household help has also been verified.[45] Finally, disaster and stress studies, which have been carried on since World War II, find uniformly that families which include grandparents are more flexible and resilient in the face of the father's induction into the Armed Forces, and of flood, fire, or other disaster than are parent-child families.[46]

It is unfortunate that description and documentation appear to segment the relations of adult children and their parents, as if living together were separate from the giving of cash and as if the benefit of the parent were separate from the benefit of the adult child. Actually, as Dr. Burgess' statement suggests and as studies in England make clear, at least for England, the dominant note is one of "reciprocal services being freely performed." [47] In view of this and of the fact that so many adult children and parents do live together, it is important to examine the general opposition to this arrangement. From half to 90 or 95 per cent of the population will say that it is better for parents and children to live separately.[48] The smaller percentages are produced when the query is addressed to a group such as aged nonmarried women who, it may be assumed, do not see the question as entirely abstract.[49] Even so, the percentage opposed to living together is high. Though there is some dissent in the general population, specialists in family relations and in aging are nearly unanimous. "It is impossible to say," reads a typical statement, "that with us it is 'natural' for any other group than husband and wife and their dependent children to maintain a common household. . . . It is, of course, common for other relatives to share a household with the conjugal family, but this scarcely ever occurs without some important elements of strain. For independence is preferred. . . ." [50]

It must be noted, without implying that this is the reason social scientists hold it, that such a point of view serves several functions in our society. It has been amply demonstrated [51] that the conjugal family, permitting emphasis on individual merit and mobility, is the most suitable for an industrial society. It also seems clear, or at least it is widely believed,[52] that young adults in our society need support in making a clean break from their parents. This emancipation function is evident as one follows the later phases of child-parent relationship—children break away in late adolescence or early adulthood, only to reestablish ties with parents after marriage and particularly after their own children arrive.[53] Finally, the American ethic that the individual (and his child) comes first has been supported in the face of the poignant appeal that growing numbers of retired people were bound to exercise. The type of sweeping endorsement of separate living that has been cited has served these functions, and it has the advantage of simplicity. It is time to recognize, however, that the evidence for such a statement is entirely anecdotal and a priori.

At the moment, clinical and theoretical evidence is virtually all we have and it is not to be disregarded; but we do not have field studies such as the English have conducted (which imply rather different conclusions*) and we do not have sufficiently deep and adequately controlled studies of living together. Possibly we have been too much involved with schedules and questionnaires, which by their nature simplify, and too little involved in direct observations of living patterns. Pending better evidence, we must retain perspective. The anecdotal evidence is made up of repeated reports of the problems that occur when parents live with children.[54] "Severe family tensions," these say in one way or another, "most painful conflicts to old and young, are reported by psychiatrists and caseworkers when families are trying to combine arrangements satisfying for two or three generations in the same home." [55] More recently, people reporting strain have been asked to define the chief problem in living together, and they frequently speak of privacy, space, and conflict over raising chil-

* For example: "It seems to me that many clinical workers, doctors, and family research workers take it for granted that [the conjugal family] is the natural and normal form for familial behavior to take. Advice based on the assumption must be rather bewildering." [Elizabeth Bott, *Family and Social Network* (London: Tavistock Publications, Ltd., 1957), p. 218.]

dren.[56] The consistency with which such reports appear makes it quite clear that the sharing of households by parents and adult children may cause problems. They do not establish that it necessarily causes problems.

Theoretical evidence moves beneath the complaints that are voiced, to indicate the tensions that modern psychology recognizes in the living together of adult children and parents. Otto Pollak, in a brief review of this evidence,[57] touches on the added financial burden a parent represents, the possibility that a child may be caught with an unresolved need to be dependent on his parent, or that the parent may resent being dependent on a child whom he has never really wished to see adult. He points out the possibilities for working out forgotten resentments between parent and child, the consequent guilt, and the possibility that either parent or child will find himself with less status in this new situation than he has had. "The economic and psychological mining of such situations leads easily to explosions for reasons implied in our culture," Dr. Pollak concludes. There can be no question that there are potential strains when parents and adult children live together. But potential strains are inherent in any living situation—in work, in rearing children, in marrying. If technical and popular literature confined themselves to the strains intrinsic to each of these activities, would we conclude that we should give them up?

An analogy may make this point clearer. One may suppose that a visitor from Israel in the year 2000, third or fourth generation of a line of children raised communally in a kibbutz, would inquire whether Americans find it a strain to raise children in the family home. Do they not interfere with their parents' privacy; are they not insensitive and demanding; they must be an enormous physical and financial drain? Does not rearing children provoke unresolved conflict about dependency, and so forth? What can one answer to these questions but "yes," adding if we will that we find compensating satisfactions or that we do not like the alternative of raising our children communally. Moreover, a healthy family organizes itself so that these strains do not mount up as much as, to the uninitiate, it might seem. The useful questions about raising children, as about living together, are not categorical (Is there strain? Are there failures?) but discriminatory: When is strain greater and lesser? How are strains handled by those who handle them? What are the situations in which they cannot normally be handled?

We have looked into these questions very little indeed. Dr. Burgess has noted that in-law conflict is almost always with the mother-in-law,[58] and we have seen that in living together families prefer to organize themselves around a mother-daughter tie. There has been some speculation about this, but we hardly know, for example, whether we may say that such arrangements do often work out well. Havighurst has suggested that constructive plans for living together may be made if, first, parents have truly freed their children.[59] It is in England that the mechanisms of intergenerational living have begun to be identified. In a major step forward,[60] it is concluded that when the mother is related to the adult son, living together is workable if she can yield authority to her daughter-in-law. With unmarried children, a mother may without special difficulty retain more authority. People seem willing to acknowledge a special bond of mother and daughter, though too close a tie of father and daughter or son and mother seems to create a problem. This work also describes the manner in which husbands and wives segregate certain financial and domestic roles so that one or the other is shielded from relationships that may be painful. This material points, of course, to the importance of further research, but more than that it indicates that living together may be workable and, indeed, satisfying in certain circumstances. The significant point appears to be not that parents and children should or should not live together, but that they should know whether they can and select whether they wish to.* It is now a decade since Dr. Burgess wrote[61] that "particularly significant is the hypothesis that mutually satisfying relations are

---

* Recent writing for lay audiences presents such a point of view somewhat more than technical material, perhaps because the writer must face the fact that a third of his audience does live with children. For example: "For one reason or another it may be best to live with your married children. This need not be the fate above all to be avoided that folklore says it is. It may work out very pleasantly for all of you. Of course, it may be unbearable." [Evelyn Millis Duvall, *In-Laws—Pro and Con* (New York: American Book–Stratford Press, Inc., 1954), p. 363.]

much more likely to be maintained where living with or away from parents is a matter of choice and not of necessity both for the elderly and for the younger couple." Since then, in this country, the significance of choice has received inadequate attention.

CARE AND AFFECTION

Many older people say, often when their financial means are modest or less than modest, that the important thing they wish from their children is affection. If they are asked to rank material and affectional support to indicate importance, material help turns up a poor second.[62] They want to live alone but at the same time they want to be close to their children.[63] Adult children make complementary statements.[64] The Havighurst scale for role of adult child of aging parents[65] which, in its own way, states a consensus, rates highest the child who "keeps in close personal touch . . . by visits, letters, or actually living together." Ranked high is the child who "has no responsibility for caring financially for parents but feels a real responsibility for maintaining satisfactory relations with them—visiting them, keeping in touch. . . ." The adult child is rated medium who "feels that their lives are fairly separate from his."

There has been widespread alarm, though in recent technical material there is effort to dispel it, that older people are isolated from their children and other relatives. The stereotype is abroad that the aged person is a lonely old woman, querulous or embittered, needy, and either demanding or overly proud, with no one to care for her. It is suggested occasionally that this stereotype springs from the guilt of the young who write about the aging. Possibly it is a result of strenuous efforts to create interest in a growing problem in which there was, for a time, no interest. Unquestionably, also, there has been a tendency to assume that physical isolation means social isolation. For example, analysis by Talcott Parsons[66] demonstrated that the effect of conjugal family living, of an economy that maintains a man at full employment and then abruptly retires him, and of the connection between work and where one lives—the effect of these forces is physically to separate the aged from the families of their children. It was more or less assumed that physical separation meant that the children no longer cared about or kept in touch with their parents. A body of material has accumulated that makes it clear that in England this assumption is quite inaccurate. The United States has substantial social differences from England, but our recent investigations yield findings that are consistent with the English. In general, their studies find that old people prefer to live alone, but they live near to children or other relatives, whom they see quite frequently. Paying special attention to feelings of loneliness, the English found that four out of five made no complaint and only 8 per cent were very lonely. Moreover, it was not those who had lived alone all their lives (the "isolated") who were lonely. It was those who had lost a spouse (the "desolated") who felt lonely, and with time their grief might diminish. There were single men who "lived completely lonely lives without any trace of loneliness." The parents got a great deal of help from their children, and they reciprocated to a marked degree.[67]

Similarly, studies at Duke University and the National Opinion Research Center find that "while some older people are isolated from their families, most older people are a part of family configurations." [68] Upward of two-thirds of aged parents see their children at least weekly.[69] Even when there are not visits, there may be daily telephone contact.[70] Study of middle-class families concludes that the generations "have a desire to help one another . . . parents had established a pattern of giving moderate help and service . . . parents and children take care of one another during illness regardless of distance. . . ." [71]

In an area of give and take, where intangibles are the chief currency, it is particularly difficult to say that parents or children have, in general, the net advantage. Deeper attachments are involved than may be understood in remaining overly focused on "responsibility" in filial relations. For example, although isolation of parents from adult children is frequently attributed to children's ambition to move into a higher social class, there is evidence that parents will say they are closer to children who have been more successful.[72] This can be puzzling unless one realizes that parents too are ambitious for their children. Thus one sees that parents take pleasure from the success of adult children, and find in it a means of continued expansion of their own lives, even if its visible result is to reduce physical contact between parents and children.[73]

Similarly folklore recognizes, though middle-class mores may reject, a tacit tie between grandparents and grandchildren,[74] which is the reverse face of the common complaint that grandparents interfere with the raising of children. Grandparents do often seem to mitigate parental anger at children, in the course of which naturally they may become the object of anger themselves. Grandparents may indulge their grandchildren in a way parents cannot—in a way, in fact, that parents cannot approve. But grandparents get satisfaction from this relationship, and it may serve salutary purposes for the grandchildren. Moreover, the relief that the parents, the middle generation, may find in the mediating influence of grandparents has been less adequately explored than the resentment that they express. The outward evidences of this tie of alternate generations—babysitting, child care, and nursing—have been noted.

To give recognition to the positive tone of filial relations for so many people is not to imply that there are not aged people in need of protection, care, and social contact. We know that when a retired person is incapable of handling his insurance benefit, it is often difficult to find someone who will help him.[75] That there is conflict between generations, particularly when circumstances thrust living together upon them, has been noted above. Further, there are old people who do not have and who miss social contact.[76] To many the advance of years unavoidably brings illness, declining income, death of contemporaries, senility, or declining responsibility and status. For the three out of four who have grown children, they are often a satisfaction and a support. When they are not, this may be particularly disappointing.

CURRENT PRACTICE IN CLOSING

Adults with children of their own or only with personal wants of their own face now for the first time, in substantial numbers, the free choice of sacrificing these to the needs of their parents. We deal with this in the abstract by expressing allegiance to all moral values at once—that is, to the rights of children, the independence of adults, and responsibility to parents.* Our practice in relation to cash, however, is tersely described by an old German proverb: "One father takes better care of ten children than ten children take care of one father." When parents' need is stark, and often then for protection and care as well as for income, adult children do in substantial numbers live together with their parents. As for the intangibles—attention, affection, and so forth —there is no value conflict, or at any rate less, for the giving of these things to parents does not diminish what remains for a spouse and children. On the contrary, a warm relationship with grandparents may mean more to be shared by everyone. The evidence is that these ties are usually to some extent satisfying, though unquestionably there are also lonely and isolated parents.

Two key points are implicit in the material that has been reviewed. First is the reciprocal nature of filial relations. In the net, parents may give more to adult children in cash, though less in living together. Living together is frequently a situation in which both parties benefit, though a set of scales would tip one way or the other. And whatever the material balance, the receiver often renders service or repays with fondness, an important coin in itself. Conflict between such drives as advancement of one's own family and ties to the older generation is not necessarily intergenerational conflict; parents are as much wedded to their children's advancement as are the children. Though to the onlooker, on occasion, adult children may be living disproportionately well compared with their parents, it may be that the parents would not have it otherwise and take pleasure in their children's success.

The other key point is the spontaneous nature of filial relations. What children and their parents give to each other has little connection with law or compulsion. The money contribution, which is the only gift that can actually be compelled, is a

---

* For example, two quotations from a single book: "It is not the function of children of small families to support the older members of families in which they were reared. That the parent and child families are related by blood and bound together by one common member is more or less immaterial." "One of the deep-seated traditions in this country is that adult children will care for their aged parents when necessary." [Joseph T. Drake, *The Aged in America's Society* (New York: Ronald Press Co., 1958), pp. 32, 327.]

relatively unimportant pattern. Helping each other with chores, visiting, and showing concern, which cannot be compelled, is the dominant pattern. Moreover, it is not only children but other relatives and friends who engage in these activities. We have noted that other relatives and friends add materially when they are included in the statistics of cash contributions to the aged, and these groups add about 25 per cent when they are included in statistics of living together. They illuminate a point about filial responsibility that is perhaps elementary—the help or exchange that takes place between people is a function of the way they feel about each other. In the presence of fondness or gratitude, the exchange will take place even if individuals are not thought to be responsible; in their absence, it is unlikely to take place.

That this is the pattern of filial relations should be useful to us. Many have confused the family support that was assured by the pre-Civil War economy with the voluntary support that they wish would be forthcoming today. They have equated the absence of filial contributions with the absence of filial ties. In consequence, they point to general deterioration of filial relations. This exaggerates the problem and, in any case, it is inaccurate; we should take heart. On the other hand, pointing to deterioration may be a way of evading problems that need to be faced. (Since this is an evasive course that often invokes the Fifth Commandment, one might label it as "taking the Fifth. . . .") Plugging up the gaps in our income-maintenance programs, voluntary protective agencies for the aged,[77] and the homemaker services that have seemed to move so slowly are among the needs that may be faced. The need for broader counseling and research activities is implicit in our discussion. We have dwelt here particularly on the need to deal realistically with living together, which has so far been treated as if it were a very poor arrangement indeed. We are old enough as a country and in our social sciences to take a more sophisticated position. It appears that children should, at some point, live independently. Later on, if it suits them and if it suits their parents, perhaps they can satisfactorily share a household again. The task before us is to learn when this may be sound and when it may be disastrous, and the techniques that work in living together, so we may equip our families to make sound choices.

NOTES

1. United States Department of Health, Education, and Welfare, Division of Program Research, *Family Status of the Aged in 1959 and Money Income in 1958,* Research and Statistics Note No. 5 (Washington, D.C., January 25, 1960), mimeographed.

2. Peter O. Steiner and Robert Dorfman, *The Economic Status of the Aged* (Berkeley: University of California Press, 1957), pp. 68–85, 109–111.

3. Saul Kaplan, *Technical Supplement to Old-Age Assistance: Children's Contributions to Aged Parents* (Washington, D.C.: United States Department of Health, Education, and Welfare, Bureau of Public Assistance, July 1957), mimeographed, p. 1. Ethel Shanas, "The Living Arrangements of Older People in the United States," *The Gerontologist,* I, No. 1 (March 1961), 27–29.

4. William M. Smith, Jr., Joseph H. Britton, and Jean O. Britton, *Relationships Within Three-Generation Families,* College of Home Economics Research Publication No. 155 (University Park, Pa.: Pennsylvania State University, April 1958), p. 7.

5. Ethel Shanas, "Some Sociological Research Findings About Older People Pertinent to Social Work," *Toward Better Understanding of the Aged* (New York: Council on Social Work Education, 1958), p. 52.

6. Gordon F. Streib, "Family Patterns in Retirement," *Journal of Social Issues,* XIV, No. 2 (1958). A special issue on "Adjustment in Retirement," edited by Gordon F. Streib and Wayne E. Thompson, with Ernest W. Burgess, Edward A. Suchman, and Ethel Shanas. Smith, Britton, and Britton, *op. cit.* Floyd A. Bond *et al., Our Needy Aged* (New York: Henry Holt and Company, 1954), pp. 256–259.

7. Bond *et al., op. cit.*

8. Bond *et al., op. cit.*

9. Lyle Saunders, "English-Speaking and Spanish-Speaking People of the Southwest," from *Cultural Differences and Medical Care: The Case of the Spanish-Speaking People of the Southwest,* reprinted in Herman D. Stein and Richard A. Cloward, eds., *Social Perspectives on Behavior* (Glencoe, Ill.: The Free Press, 1958).

10. Rhode Island Governor's Commission to Study Problems of the

Aged, *Old Age in Rhode Island* (Providence: July 1953), p. 7. Steiner and Dorfman, *op. cit.*

11. Bond *et al.*, *op. cit.*

12. Health Information Foundation, "Use of Health Services by the Aged," *Progress in Health Services* (New York: April 1959). Rhode Island Governor's Commission, *op. cit.*

13. United States Department of Health, Education, and Welfare, Bureau of Old-Age and Survivors Insurance, *Adults Who Are Incapable of Handling Their Own Benefit Funds or Who Are Marginally Capable of Doing So* (Washington, D.C.: May 1958), mimeographed.

14. Allison Davis, Burleigh B. Gardner, and Mary R. Gardner, *Deep South* (Chicago: University of Chicago Press, 1941). Peter Townsend, *The Family Life of Old People* (Glencoe, Ill.: The Free Press, 1957), p. 165.

15. United States Department of Labor, Bureau of Labor Statistics, *Study of Consumer Expenditures, Incomes and Savings, Urban United States—1950*, Vol. XI (Washington, D.C.: 1957). Bernard Kutner *et al.*, *Five Hundred Over Sixty* (New York: Russell Sage Foundation, 1956). Gordon Streib, *op. cit.* United States Department of Health, Education, and Welfare, Bureau of Old-Age and Survivors Insurance, "National Survey of OASI Beneficiaries" (Washington, D.C.: 1957), unpublished tables.

16. August B. Hollingshead, "Class Differences in Family Stability," from *The Annals of the American Academy of Political Science* (November 1950), reprinted in Stein and Cloward, *op. cit.* Davis, Gardner, and Gardner, *op. cit.*

17. Marvin B. Sussman, "The Help Pattern in the Middle Class Family," *American Sociological Review*, XVIII, No. 1 (February 1953), 23, 25. Streib, *op. cit.*

18. United States Department of Labor, Bureau of Labor Statistics, *op. cit.*

19. Ernest V. Hollis, *Costs of Attending College,* United States Department of Health, Education, and Welfare, Office of Education Bulletin No. 9 (Washington, D.C.: 1957).

20. United States Department of Commerce, Bureau of the Census, *Current Population Reports,* Series P–20, No. 101 (Washington, D.C.: May 22, 1960).

21. Robert J. Havighurst, "Research Memorandum . . . ," in John E. Anderson, ed., *Psychological Aspects of Aging* (Menasha, Wis.: George Banta Company, Inc., 1956), pp. 294, 296.

22. Steiner and Dorfman, *op. cit.*
23. Henry D. Sheldon, *The Older Population of the United States* (New York: John Wiley & Sons, Inc., 1958).
24. Lenore A. Epstein, "Economic Resources of Persons Aged 65 and Over," *Social Security Bulletin,* XVIII, No. 6 (June 1955). Steiner and Dorfman, *op. cit.*
25. William F. Ogburn, with Clark Tibbitts, "The Family and Its Functions," *Recent Social Trends in the United States,* Report of the President's Research Committee on Social Trends (New York and London: McGraw-Hill Book Company, Inc., 1933). Paul C. Glick, *American Families* (New York: John Wiley & Sons, Inc., 1957).
26. Ethel Shanas, *op. cit.*
27. *Ibid.*
28. Glick, *op. cit.* Hope J. Leichter, *Kinship and Casework,* presented at Groves Conference (Chapel Hill, N.C.: April 6, 1959), mimeographed.
29. Ruth Shonle Cavan, "Family Life and Family Substitutes in Old Age," *American Sociological Review,* VIII, No. 4 (August 1943).
30. John J. Corson and John W. McConnell, *Economic Needs of Older People* (New York: Twentieth Century Fund, 1956).
31. Elizabeth Bott, *Family and Social Network* (London: Tavistock Publications, Ltd., 1957), p. 218.
32. Oscar Handlin, *The Uprooted* (Boston: Little, Brown and Company, 1951). Kutner *et al., op. cit.* Ruth Shonle Cavan *et al., Personal Adjustment in Old Age* (Chicago: Science Research Associates, 1949).
33. Kutner *et al., op. cit.*
34. Epstein, *op. cit.*
35. United States Department of Health, Education, and Welfare, Bureau of Old-Age and Survivors Insurance, "National Survey of OASI Beneficiaries" (Washington, D.C.: 1951, 1957), unpublished tables. Rhode Island Governor's Commission, *op. cit.*
36. Streib, *op. cit.*
37. Rhode Island Governor's Commission, *op. cit.*
38. Smith, Britton, and Britton, *op. cit.* Streib, *op. cit.* Belle Boone Beard, "Are the Aged Ex-Family?" *Social Forces,* XXVII, No. 3 (March 1949), 274–279.
39. Glick, *op. cit.*
40. United States Department of Commerce, Bureau of the Census, *Current Population Reports,* Series P–20, No. 100 (Washington, D.C.: April 13, 1960).

41. Hans Von Hentig, "The Sociological Function of the Grandmother," *Social Forces,* XXIV, No. 4 (May 1946).

42. Sheldon, *op. cit.* Rhode Island Governor's Commission, *op. cit.*

43. Ernest W. Burgess, "Family Living in the Later Decades," *The Annals of the American Academy of Political Science,* CCLXXIX (January 1952), 111–112.

44. Henry C. Lajewski, "Working Mothers and Their Arrangements for Care of Their Children," *Social Security Bulletin,* XXII, No. 8 (August 1959).

45. J. H. Sheldon, "Social Aspects of the Aging Process," in Milton Derber, ed., *The Aged and Society* (Champaign, Ill.: Industrial Relations Research Association, December 1950). J. H. Sheldon, "Old-Age Problems in the Family," *Milbank Memorial Fund Quarterly,* XXXVII, No. 2 (April 1959), 123. Catherine Varchaver, *Older People in the Detroit Areas and the Retirement Age* (Grand Rapids, Mich.: Wm. B. Eerdmans Publishing Company, 1956).

46. Helen Swick Perry and Steward E. Perry, *The Schoolhouse Disasters* (Washington, D.C.: National Academy of Sciences, 1959). Michael Young, "The Role of the Extended Family in a Disaster," *Human Relations,* III (1954). Reuben Hill, *Families under Stress* (New York: Harper, 1949).

47. Townsend, *op. cit.*

48. Smith, Britton, and Britton, *op. cit.* Kutner *et al., op. cit.*

49. Bond *et al., op. cit.*

50. Talcott Parsons, "Age and Sex in the Social Structure of the United States," *American Sociological Review,* VII, No. 5 (October 1942), 604–616.

51. Harold L. Wilensky and Charles N. Lebeaux, *Industrial Society and Social Welfare* (New York: Russell Sage Foundation, 1958). Wilbert E. Moore, "The Aged in Industrial Societies" in Derber, *op. cit.* Alvin L. Schorr, "Families on Wheels," *Harper's Magazine,* CCXVI, No. 1292 (January 1958).

52. Arnold M. Rose, "Acceptance of Adult Roles and Separation from Family," *Marriage and Family Living,* XXI, No. 2 (May 1959), 120–126.

53. Bott, *op. cit.*

54. Robert M. Dinkel, "Parent-Child Conflict in Minnesota Families," *American Sociological Review,* VIII, No. 4 (August 1943). Ruth Shonle Cavan *et al., op. cit.*

55. Hertha Kraus, "Housing Our Older Citizens," *The Annals of the*

American Academy of Political Science, CCLXXIX (January 1952).
56. Kutner *et al., op. cit.* Anthony Lenzer, with Adele S. Pond and John Scott, *Michigan's Older People, Six Hundred Thousand Over Sixty-Five* (Ann Arbor: State of Michigan Legislative Advisory Council, 1958). Smith, Britton, and Britton, *op. cit.*
57. Otto Pollak, *The Social Aspects of Retirement* (Homewood, Ill.: Richard D. Irwin, Inc., 1956), p. 13.
58. Ernest W. Burgess and Paul Wallin, with Gladys Denny Shultz, *Courtship, Engagement, and Marriage* (Philadelphia: Lippincott, 1954).
59. Robert J. Havighurst, "Social and Psychological Needs of the Aging," *The Annals of the American Academy of Political Science,* CCLXXIX (January 1952), 11–17.
60. Townsend, *op. cit.*
61. Burgess, "Family Living in the Later Decades," *op. cit.*
62. Streib, *op. cit.* Shanas, *op. cit.*
63. Townsend, *op. cit.*
64. Kutner *et al., op. cit.*
65. Havighurst, *op. cit.*
66. Parsons, *op. cit.*
67. Sheldon, "Old-Age Problems in the Family," *op. cit.* Michael Young, "The Extended Family Welfare Association," *Social Work,* XXVII, No. 2 (London: January 1956), p. 150. Bott, *op. cit.* Townsend, *op. cit.* Sheldon, "Social Aspects of the Aging Process," *op. cit.*
68. Shanas, *op. cit.*
69. Streib, *op. cit.* Rhode Island Governor's Commission, *op. cit.*
70. Leichter, *op. cit.*
71. Sussman, *op. cit.* Marvin B. Sussman, "Family Continuity: Selective Factors Which Affect Relationships between Families at Generational Levels," *Marriage and Family Living,* XVI, No. 2 (May 1954).
72. Streib, *op. cit.*
73. Streib, *op. cit.* Raymond G. Kuhlen, "Changing Personality Adjustment during the Adult Years," in John E. Anderson, ed., *Psychological Aspects of Aging* (Menasha, Wis.: George Banta Company, Inc., 1956).
74. Davis, Gardner, and Gardner, *op. cit.* Edna C. Wentworth, "How Persons Receiving Social Security Benefits Get Along," Address to American Library Association (Washington, D.C.: June 23, 1959).
75. United States Department of Health, Education, and Welfare, Bureau of Old-Age and Survivors Insurance, *Adults Who Are Incapable*

of Handling Their Own Benefit Funds or Who Are Marginally Capable of Doing So (Washington, D.C.: May 1958), mimeographed.

76. Kutner *et al., op. cit.* Streib, *op. cit.* Cavan, *op. cit.*
77. Charles W. McCann, "Guardianship and the Needy Aged," *Public Welfare,* XVI, No. 3 (July 1958).

7

Social Security and Filial Responsibility

OLD AGE, SURVIVORS, AND DISABILITY INSURANCE

Old age, survivors, and disability insurance (OASDI), itself a consequence of ethics and social forces that have been described, has in its turn become a major social force. When a program develops concurrently with spectacular increases in national wealth and in the numbers of its potential beneficiaries, it is difficult to disentangle the changes the program causes from coincidental changes. Nevertheless, certain observations are possible about its overall effect on filial relations.

It is commonly observed that reliance on one's own income, even if it provides only partial support, contributes to an aged person's sense of dignity and self-respect. When his relations with his children are based on at least partial independence, warm and spontaneous relations with his children are promoted.[1] Abraham Epstein estimated in 1928 that one-third of the aged, a bit less than two million people, were substantially dependent on their relatives or on organized charity.[2] In the intervening years, the aged population has tripled and employment opportunities for

An excerpt from *Filial Responsibility in the United States,* United States Social Security Administration (Washington, D.C.: United States Government Printing Office, 1960).

them have shrunken. The number without income from earnings
or social insurance in 1959 was not inconsiderable (2.8 million)
and is perhaps a measure of the distance we have yet to travel.
Nevertheless, the contribution of OASDI is evident in the number of aged people to whom it provided independent income in
1959—ten million.[3] OASDI is providing income to almost twice
as many aged people as were living in 1928.

We have dwelt on the significance of choice in living arrangements. If many aged parents prefer their own living arrangements, as they say, and if increased income facilitates separate
living, as we have said, OASDI ought to affect the living arrangements of recipients. In 1951 the percentages of OASDI beneficiaries living with children were as follows: 26 per cent of the couples, 32 per cent of the nonmarried men, and 39 per cent of the
nonmarried women.[4] This was less, though not by much, than
the percentages for the total aged population in 1952. From 1951
to 1957 the average monthly old age benefit increased from $42
to $65.[5] By 1957 the percentages of beneficiaries living with
children had dropped to 17 per cent of the couples, 26 per cent of
the nonmarried men, and 31 per cent of the nonmarried women.[6]
Table 7–1 will make it easier to compare the trends for all aged
people and for OASDI beneficiaries.

Table 7–1

PERCENTAGE OF AGED LIVING WITH CHILDREN

	Total aged population		OASDI beneficiaries	
	1952	1957	1951	1957
Couples	26	23	26	17
Nonmarried men	31	27	32	26
Nonmarried women	45	37	39	31

Sources: For the total aged population: Peter O. Steiner and Robert Dorfman,
The Economic Status of the Aged (Berkeley: University of California Press,
1957), and Ethel Shanas, "The Living Arrangements of Older People in the
United States," *The Gerontologist*, I, No. 1 (March 1961). For OASDI beneficiaries: United States Department of Health, Education, and Welfare, Bureau of Old-Age and Survivors Insurance, "National Survey of OASI Beneficiaries" (Washington, D.C.: 1951, 1957), unpublished tables.

Thus we observe that increased independent living has accompanied increased income for all the aged, and the rate has been
faster for OASDI beneficiaries.

From certain points of view, geographic mobility also reflects filial relationships. Although younger age groups move chiefly for occupational advancement, it is fairly well established that the aged move chiefly to be near their children or other relatives or friends.[7] This is true even of Florida[8] and California[9] where, as none will dispute, aged people may have other reasons for wanting to go. No doubt, moving for this purpose in part explains the surprisingly high percentage of aged in our country—well over a majority[10]—who do live near a child. In the general population, 1.1 per cent of the aged move across state boundaries in a year.[11] Of the aged OASDI beneficiaries, between 1.5 and 2 per cent move across state boundaries in a year.[12]

Perhaps this adds up to what is in any case obvious: a program that is planned to insure aged people against loss of income succeeds at least partially in doing this. In the process, it contributes to spontaneous family interchange on a basis of equality, it assists people to make the living arrangements they prefer, and to live near relatives when they prefer. A relatively small segment of the program makes specific provision for the dependent aged parent of a wage earner. This segment will repay closer examination.

Upon the death of a worker, benefits are available to his dependent parent or parents. The history of the Social Security Act shows a progressive liberalization of the definition of dependent parent. Dependency was introduced into the program in 1939; in order to qualify, parents had to be *"wholly* dependent upon and supported by." In 1946 this was changed to *"chiefly* dependent upon and supported by." In 1950 the law was amended to require only that the parent must have been receiving at least one-half his support from the worker. Subsequent changes made it possible to pay benefits even if support had been discontinued during a specified period of disability and also even if there were other survivors. By January, 1960, 35,000 dependent parents were receiving benefits.

We note the implicit recognition that parental dependency is not typical; if benefits are to be paid there must be proof that there really was dependency. "One-half support," like prior provisions, is a yardstick to establish a loss of support; in consonance with its objectives, the program seeks to replace the loss, at least in part.

Although relatively easy to understand and explain, "one-half support" has produced vexing problems of administration. It requires proof of payments that may be difficult to prove, particularly as one party is dead and the other old. In living together (which we have seen to be more common than cash payment), it may involve exact calculation of who paid the bills, who bought the food, and what should be charged to whose account. Moreover, the rule may give results that seem unfair in principle. For example, a parent who is supported equally by three children would not be eligible on the death of any or all of them. A parent receiving public assistance and receiving somewhat less from a child would not be entitled to benefits if the child died.[13] Presumably, one might find difficult examples in the administration of any rule, but in 1957 two out of five applications for parents' benefits were denied, the majority of them for failure to establish "one-half support." Apparently, many parents think they are dependent whom the rule rejects.

If we refer back to current practice in the United States, we shall understand why parents think themselves dependent who are receiving less than half their income from a particular child. In lower and moderate income groups, cash contribution, infrequent as it is, almost surely represents a sacrifice by the adult child to assist his parent. We have seen that the median amount of the child's contribution to parents living elsewhere is between $150 and $240 a year. Let us take as an example the parent who receives contributions of $400 a year. To meet the definition of dependent parent, if he lived alone, he can have had no more than $800 income, in total. He would very likely have had to supplement such an income with public assistance. Thus, the $400 that parent and child regard as significant, both in giving it and accepting it, is insufficient by this rule to constitute a loss of income that ought to be replaced.

The most difficult applications of the rule are to the situations in which, as we have said, most dependent parents live—that is, living together. To begin with, the burden of establishing one-half support is on the parent in a situation where separate accounts may never have been kept. No evidence may, in effect, be negative evidence. Further, as the calculation goes where two people were living together, half support of the parent is three-quarters support of the joint household. (That is, the child must have paid for his own share plus half of his parent's share.) It requires very little income of his own, therefore, to put a parent over "one-half support" in a modestly budgeted household. Yet, with the death of the child, his own income may not be enough for rent and utilities, let alone food and other needs. The situation need not be this desperate to make the point. We have seen that illness and incapacity lead to shared living arrangements. Consequently, the death of the child may present, as financial costs, needs that were not previously financial—housekeeping, transportation, nursing. The parent may be able to get along after the death of the child, but one can hardly maintain that he has not suffered a significant financial loss.

To conclude, 35,000 people benefiting as dependent parents seems an insignificant figure for a program making payments to 10 million. What accounts for this? In part, 35,000 is a residual figure. That is, an untold number who would meet the definition of dependent parents are insured in other ways and receive their benefits as retired wage earners, their wives, or their widows. Thus, as more people become entitled to benefits based on their own or their spouse's earnings, fewer of them will show up as dependent parents. For the present, however, the more telling question is how 35,000 dependent parents compare with the 2.8 million aged people who are without income from earnings or social insurance. Most of these are, in fact, dependent on some person or agency, though it must remain speculative how many have lost a child who had attained coverage under OASDI.

We do know that cash contribution is barely a pattern of filial support in American life. Living together is more the way in which adult children assist their parents. But "one-half support" does not test either in the ways in which they are typically practiced.

OLD AGE ASSISTANCE

Old age assistance (OAA), like OASDI, owes its existence to new forces and conceptions affecting the aged. For many whom opportunities or other programs have failed to make secure, it provides maintenance and some dignity. Despite the growth of social insurance, 2.4 million aged people look to OAA for minimum support.[14] That such support enhances parental relationships with children has also been observed.[15] We only mention, without examining, that the effect of a measure of security and independence upon filial relations must be constructive. We shall look more closely at the area in which the program concerns itself directly with filial relations, that is, the policies governing filial support. These policies are established by the various states.

State laws regarding the obligation of adult children to support their parents in general affect only the families of public assistance applicants. The parent with income in excess of public assistance standards is not likely to be able to compel support from his wealthy son, no matter how disparate their circumstances.[16] It has been indicated that filial support statutes have been on the books in many states from the time of their admission to the Union, but with more or less desultory enforcement. During the first decade of the Social Security Act these statutes were under substantial professional attack, and, being difficult to administer besides, their enforcement was neglected. At the close of World War II there was renewed interest in the enforcement of filial support, stimulated, there is general agreement, by sharply rising public assistance costs.

The results of renewed interest were not entirely uniform. A trend to liberalize these laws, particularly by dropping the responsibility of more distant relatives such as grandchildren, continued into this period. Nevada abolished filial support in 1943, the State of Washington in 1949, and Alabama in 1955. On the other hand, Washington subsequently restored filial responsibility, Montana in 1953 enacted a law requiring filial support, and Florida applied filial responsibility in establishing aid to the permanently and totally disabled, though it was not applicable to the older categorical programs. Aside from basic legislation, however, the postwar period has been characterized by clarification of law and policy to facilitate enforcement. There is a subsidiary trend to eliminate peculiarly offensive situations that arise, for example, the obligation of a child to support the father who deserted him at birth.

Filial support policies vary a great deal from state to state, both in rigor and in the methods of their application. To begin with, the majority of states have legislation requiring support that has been made clearly applicable to OAA. Seven states have general legislation that does not specifically apply and twelve states have no legislation at all that requires support.[17] However, the legislation alone does not determine the states' practices. Tennessee, for example, has no support legislation, but nevertheless assumes that children contribute to their parents. It is more useful to describe states' actual practice, whether prescribed by law or by administrative policy. Because several detailed studies in 1952 and 1953 permit special analysis, data about state practices are reported for those years. More recent reports[18] do not show marked departures from state practice in 1952.

In general, in 1952, sixteen states made no support requirement of adult children. Contributions would be taken into account if they were made but they were voluntary. Twenty-one states required a contribution by law or policy, but did not make assistance contingent on the contribution. That is, a contribution from children is required, but OAA is given even if the child avoids his responsibility. Fourteen states require a contribution from children and, in addition, will withhold assistance or reduce the payment on the assumption that the expected contribution is income.* In general, children living outside the state are not held

---

* This summary of state policies relies heavily on an article by Elizabeth Epler, "Old-Age Assistance: Plan Provisions on Children's Responsibility for Parents" [*Social Security Bulletin*, XVII, No. 5 (May 1954)].

The sixteen states that made no support requirement: Arizona, Colorado, Florida, Idaho, Kansas, Louisiana, Missouri, New Mexico, North Carolina, Oklahoma, South Carolina, South Dakota, Texas, Utah, Washington, and Wyoming.

The twenty-one states that required support but would not deny assistance: Alaska, Arkansas, California, Delaware, Georgia, Hawaii, Indiana, Maryland, Massachusetts, Minnesota, Montana, Nevada, New Jersey, New York, North Dakota, Oregon, Pennsylvania, Rhode Island, Virginia, West Virginia, and Wisconsin.

The fourteen states that required support and adjusted assistance even if support was not provided: Alabama, Connecticut, the District of Columbia,

responsible, though they may be encouraged to contribute. (Reciprocal nonsupport laws may apply, but they have rarely been used for filial support.) The determination of how much adult children are responsible to contribute is a difficult one; increasingly, states have relied on a scale that adjusts for number in the family and income, with special expenses calculated separately. In 1953, twenty-seven of the thirty-five states requiring a contribution used an income scale or similar method.

Most administrators agree, regardless of their position on requiring filial support, that it is difficult and painful to administer.[19] For reasons that the foregoing material on "current practice" ought to illuminate, many parents resist the requirement and adult children resent it. The legislator enacting filial responsibility envisions a wealthy son whose father ekes out a desperate living on old age assistance. But caseworkers and administrators see a different picture, as we shall observe. Though income scales help to achieve a degree of equity, their application in varying situations and to families whose filial feelings may range from love to hatred may easily seem unjust to parent or child, client or caseworker. If, in the end, the agency must have recourse to the courts, prosecutors and judges are reluctant to bring these cases to trial. Even then, it frequently turns out that the child does not contribute the specified sum and the entire procedure begins again.

The roles of welfare department, court, and legislature in states that require filial support are not the straightforward ones taught in high school civics books. They are symptomatic, rather, of the conflict of American and Poor Law ethics. The reluctance of prosecutors and judges to bring filial support cases to trial is most often attributed to the political damage it will do them.[20] The well-to-do have influence and the knowledgeable know how to list special expenses that excuse them. Suing the poor or uneducated for support does not bring acclaim. Legislators may be as vulnerable as prosecutors, but no one charges that they are deterred from passing support laws. This suggests that legislators act in terms of the general ethical principle of filial obligation—a principle that

---

Illinois, Iowa, Kentucky, Maine, Michigan, Mississippi, Nebraska, New Hampshire, Ohio, Tennessee, and Vermont.

few dispute in general. But prosecutors and judges act in relation to individuals and must therefore in each case balance the conflicting values we have described. When courts hand down their decisions, it is evident that a man's right to his own advancement and his children's has weighed heavily against his responsibility to his parent. That this difference in point of view is not necessarily unconscious or uncalculated is illustrated by the Secretary of Public Assistance in Pennsylvania, who asked a member of a legislative committee dealing with relatives' responsibility, "Why do you make laws which you don't expect, and don't want, us to enforce?" [21]

The role of welfare departments in this situation can only be difficult. If they also overlook the law or interpret it generously, they must of course find a philosophy of administration that justifies this. In addition, they may suffer legislative displeasure—a situation that occurred in Maine.[22] They risk not only more exacting legislation regarding filial responsibility, but irritated restriction of unrelated aspects of the program—risks that may not be taken lightly. Many welfare departments take an alternative position, requiring filial contributions on a scale that they know courts will not support.[23] That this does not result in clogging agencies and courts with numerous appeals is a result only of the children's reluctance or financial inability to go to court.[24] This alternative resolves the dilemma for the department, but patently raises the question whether legal rights are being infringed upon simply because they will not be defended. The role of departments should not be left resting entirely on the basis of expediency, however. Quite possibly courts have a broader, more liberal view of family income out of their experience than welfare departments which, however much against their impulses, may come to regard inadequate income as normal. Obviously, welfare boards and administrators incorporate their own views of what is proper in the policies they establish.

As the legal reason for requiring filial support is the saving of tax funds, the most cogent question is the magnitude of the saving. If one examines the case loads of states that require filial support, they turn out to be markedly lower than in states that do not.[25] As these tend to be the wealthier states that would in any case have lower case loads, however, the saving is only in part a result of filial support. Among people receiving assistance, thorough exploration of filial support does not usually, in agency experience, produce a great deal more than is already being contributed.[26] It appears that the savings might be balanced by the cost of administration. Studies in New Jersey and New York, both states that are very careful about support, indicate how expensive exploration of children's resources can be. For New Jersey in 1958, investigation of filial support represented 13.5 per cent of the total cost of administering the OAA program; for New York the percentage was 11.8 per cent, or about 1.5 million dollars.[27] In both states, the cost was substantially more than that for social services (aside from those involved in eligibility and medical care).

On the whole, it appears that substantial saving lies not in what is contributed to OAA recipients, but in the effect that filial requirements have in deterring old people from applying—either because they would be ineligible or because they are not willing to have their children's resources looked into. This seems evident from the experience of states that have revised their support requirements. Repeal of relatives' responsibility in Washington and Texas, for example, was followed by a large increase in case loads.[28] Upward revision of the income scale for relatives in California resulted in a "sharp spurt" of OAA applications.[29] The "very rough" estimate has been made that if public assistance replaced children's contributions to all aged people in 1953, the cost would be 200 to 300 million dollars.[30] However, this figure lumps voluntary contributions and the value of all shared space and so forth together with support that is produced by legal requirements. One indication of the saving involved in deterrence is provided by the experience of Maine, which revived filial support in 1948—making more than ordinarily strict requirements of children. The new requirements resulted in the closing of 2,150 cases; about 200 were subsequently reopened, having been closed in error.[31] If the cases closed were receiving average payments, in 1948 Maine saved about $800,000. Similarly in 1951, a year after Alabama enacted filial responsibility, it was spending at the rate of one million dollars a year less for OAA.

More than half the states provide for recovering any amount paid in assistance from the recipient's estate after his death. Usually his estate is the home he has lived in. Many states take liens on the property of recipients. To some degree the state's practice on recovery may affect its practice in enforcing support from children. On one hand, many who oppose enforcement of filial support feel that it would be unreasonable for children to inherit their parent's estate after the state has supported him. On the other hand, states that are firmly convinced of the importance of enforcement may apply both kinds of provisions. In practice, the majority of states that do not require support do not have recovery requirements either. Most that require support also recover from the recipient's estate. A few have one requirement but not the other.

Review of substantially the material we have covered, administrative problems, financial savings, and questions of equity, leads people to very different conclusions. Some conclude that it may be time to abandon compulsory support,[32] others that it is worth enforcing support despite the problems,[33] and not a few manage to find a position in between.[34] Basically, difference of opinion revolves around two questions: first, the relative weight given to the difficulties as against the savings; and second, a question that we have not so far discussed, the effect of requiring filial support on families. Those who would continue or strengthen filial support see its damage as minimal. More than this, they believe that filial relationships are deteriorating and that states should not be in a position of hastening this deterioration by wiping out the legal basis for filial responsibility. A representative statement of this point of view: "There is a moral responsibility, even higher than the legal, for children to help their needy parents. The forces tending toward the disintegration of strong family bonds are already too numerous; for the state deliberately to add to them by removing any filial obligations would be to weaken still further the most basic and revered of all our social institutions." [35] We have discussed at length the point of view that filial bonds are deteriorating, and have seen that it represents a confusion about the meaning of past practices and a mistaken identification of cash with other expressions of love or gratitude. However, we are left with the question of the effects of filial requirements on families. In a sense, this is the crucial question. At some expense of equity and of feelings, both clients' and administrators', there is net saving in enforcing filial support; opinions divide on whether it is worth while. The question that remains is: What is the human cost of the saving? We shall discuss three kinds of human cost: the perpetuation of poverty, the substitution of enforcement for incentive, and the domination of family arrangements by considerations that are secondary, and often inimical, to family cohesion.

PERPETUATION OF POVERTY. Welfare department administration of filial support operates in a variety of ways to reduce the income of people who have little. It leaves parents with less income than is regarded as adequate by their own state's standards. And it takes from adult children money that, by their own families' standards, they cannot spare. There are two issues. The one more often dealt with is that some people go in need. The second, which is less often recognized, is that in this area the administration of public assistance not only fails to assist in rehabilitation but actively interferes with whatever potentialities children and young adults may have for self-advancement.

The key factor has already been alluded to, that is, that the children of indigent parents are generally in modest circumstances; not infrequently, they are indigent themselves. Studies in Pennsylvania that predate the Social Security Act established that "in the great majority of cases, children can ill afford to support their parents," [36] and social workers have been remarking this ever since.[37] The State of Maine has found families expected to make substantial contributions, who had minus income by Internal Revenue standards.[38] When Florida looked into the reasons that children terminate support to their parents, they found death or similar crisis in many cases. Of the remaining 37 per cent, they concluded: The children "never were able to support their parents, but simply were doing the best they could. . . ." [39] A Pennsylvania study indicates that half the support contributions to clients were from children whose family income was less than $2,400 a year. In no case was there a contribution from a child whose family income was over $5,400 a year.[40] (However, this study was limited to children who live with their parents, a point we shall touch on below.)

The income scales that states use to determine ability to support are perhaps the clearest indication of the income of families whom filial support laws reach. These scales cannot be set higher than the state regards as proper; yet they must be applicable to a reasonable number of adult children or they are meaningless. In general, states establish a base sum, which they regard as the minimum families require and below which they can afford no contribution. In addition, they usually allow for special and unusual expenses. Of the amount that remains, 20 to 100 per cent may be expected as a contribution.

Twenty-four states used income scales in 1952; it is useful to appraise them against a yardstick. Epler compared them with the Bureau of Labor Statistics' city workers' budget for four persons, which is regarded as a modestly adequate budget.[41] Seven states had base sums higher than the highest city workers' budget figures. Ten states were in approximately the same range, and in seven the base sums were lower than the lowest city workers' budget figures. Thus in ten states support requirements would tend to keep net income down to the city workers' budget level, and in seven income would be reduced below this level.

This material deals with support where the child and parent live separately. The expectation for support is likely to be different if they live together. In part, this results from dealing with two calculations at once—the support calculation, and the calculation of the child's share of household expense. The difference results in part also from the belief that living together shows added ability or willingness to support parents. Thus, some states assume a contribution from children if they are living with their parents, and do not assume it if they are living separately.[42] Though state support requirements in combined households have not been compiled, they would equal and in some states exceed the requirements that have been cited.

We are now in a position to consider what the filial support requirement does to the income of parents and their children in these circumstances. There are, first of all, the parents who do not apply. Either they genuinely do not wish to deprive their chil-

dren or they hesitate to risk their anger.* [43] These parents continue to live on less than a public assistance budget. Those who
apply and receive an OAA grant, in addition to an amount of
support that has been established or agreed upon, may find that
the contribution is erratic or does not come at all, and often they
will not report this fact.[44] In the fourteen states that assume a
contribution, it does not matter whether parents report failure to
receive an expected contribution; in any case they will not receive
a larger grant. Those who do apply, then, may also live on less
than a public assistance budget. These are the private faces of
deterrence: to some extent, people who will get help from their
children rather than apply and to some extent people who will
live on less than the state regards as adequate rather than apply
or complain. The Maine experience cited earlier provides some
indication of the magnitude of reluctance to apply. Two-fifths of
the cases closed were because of failure to submit income statements; only three-fifths were because of a finding that there was
adequate income.[45]

Aside from the reluctance of parents to seek support or touch
off someone else's seeking of support for them, there may actually
be no legal measures open to them or legal redress may be difficult.
In three of the fourteen states where assistance may be denied
because of children's ability to support, there is no legal remedy.
(Two of them, Mississippi and Tennessee, may reverse their denial of assistance, if, after three months, it can be demonstrated
that the old person has been dependent on an unrelated person
or has suffered privation.) In two states only criminal action can
be taken, and in nine the parent can sue in civil court.[46] In assess-
ing the consequences of these policies, one must bear in mind the
common diffidence that so many poor people feel in facing legal
process, and their inability to sustain its cost. One must bear in
mind also that whatever the eventual outcome, privation for
twelve, six, or three months is consequential to the person who
bears it.

We have discussed deprivation among old people. To the ex-

---

* "If you want to start us on the road to hell," said one old man, "just force
relatives to support us." [Mabel J. Remmers, "Meditations of a Visitor En
Route," *Kansas Welfare Digest* (May 1945), p. 2.]

tent that support is actually compelled from people with low incomes, it is likely to interfere as well with the advancement of adults and the nurture and education of children. If one asks not whether a base sum is enough to live on, but whether there is enough to spare so that in time a man might make a downpayment on a small business or help to send his two children to college, one perceives a different dimension in filial support. Many of the studies already cited picked up this additional element. For example: "Children can ill afford to support their parents without depriving their own families of necessities and their children of opportunities." [47]

This effect may be felt particularly by children growing to maturity in public assistance households. In living together, we have noted, the state's expectation for sharing income may be highest. In Pennsylvania in January, 1958, 5,180 children in ADC homes were regarded as legally responsible relatives.[48] Most of them are children just beyond eighteen, who are now expected to devote a portion of their income to the support of their mother and brothers and sisters. We have touched on the cost of going to college and noted that it usually involves help from parents. Can these children, assuming they have the capacity, really accumulate any funds toward higher education, particularly since they are not going to have help from their parents? Higher education is used as an example, of course; not all advancement involves college education, but it does frequently involve some expenditure, if only for better clothes. Though state practices on this point have not been collected, it is clear that Pennsylvania is not unique. North Carolina, for example, assumes a contribution from any employed child over eighteen—50 per cent of his net income or $75 a month, whichever is smaller. Utah assumes a contribution from any child earning more than $75 a month—50 per cent of the amount over $75.

These, then, are consequences of support requirements: they impose on some old people a standard of living lower than public assistance levels. Where support is procured, the deprivation is shifted to the adult child and his family. One effect of this deprivation is to handicap him and his children in their own struggle for a better standard of living.

INCENTIVE AND SUPPORT REQUIREMENTS. As support requirements are applied within the structure of public assistance, they take on a special problem that arises from the nature of the budgeting process. They operate to compel support by adult children but not to encourage it. Where support is not forthcoming, it may be exacted in court or by withholding assistance from a needy old person. But there is no incentive for a child to contribute to his parent; generally speaking, it will not improve his circumstances. Consequently, less is contributed or the form of the contribution changes.

The problem of incentive arising from the practice of budgeting in public assistance has its counterpart in every categorical program; in old age assistance the problem is seen particularly in connection with filial support. Generally speaking, the payment to the aged person is determined by subtracting the money and other resources available to him from what the agency determines to be his monthly needs. Consequently the contribution that a child makes simply diminishes the payment that his parent receives. (There is the qualification that many states pay the old person less than he has been determined to need. In these states, his income may equal this deficit without reducing his payment.) Permitting the parent to retain his child's contribution, or some part of it, in addition to his payment, might raise other serious problems: It has been argued, for example, that the result would be that one needy person would have more income than another. That there are issues to be resolved should not prevent us, however, from seeing the effects of compelling support within the present budgeting framework.

We have noted that, aside from the substantial effect of deterrence, the tax money that support requirements save is modest. Or, to translate this in terms of what people do: Relatively few children contribute to parents who are OAA recipients. State reports confirm this. We have estimated that, for the general population, between 5 and 10 per cent of aged adults receive cash contributions from children living separately from them. Among the states with support requirements in 1953, 7 per cent of the old age assistance recipients were reported as receiving cash contributions from children. (The OAA figure includes contributions from children *in* the home and is, if anything, overstated in relation to the general population figure.) Only eight states (Alabama, California, Connecticut, Michigan, Massachusetts, Nebraska, North Carolina, and Tennessee) had more than 10 per cent receiving contributions.[49] Five of these were states that report a contribution whether it is actually being made or not; one was California which, as we shall see, managed to provide a degree of incentive for contributions. It is necessary to provide the qualification that public assistance recipients are not directly comparable to the general population; their families have less to give. But at any rate we observe that if their contribution rate is not lower, neither is it higher. Very likely two forces operate in different directions on the public assistance contribution rate. What can be compelled adds to the rate; what cannot be compelled but might otherwise be volunteered is dried up as a source of funds.

The social security law does not permit contributions to be ignored, either entirely or in part; consequently we have no experience with what would happen to contributions if they truly raised the standard of living of the recipients. However, in 1953 California's law did offer some incentive. California established a number of special needs that might be budgeted. These were not met by the OAA payment, but the recipient who received outside help might retain that money for special needs that he had established. In that year, 50 per cent of all OAA recipients in California had allowable special needs. However, 83 per cent of the recipients who received help from relatives had allowable special needs, and special needs absorbed 89 per cent of the money received in contributions. Moreover, only half of what relatives contributed was in satisfaction of legal liability; relatives were not liable for the other half of what they contributed.[50] The conclusion seems inescapable that the honey of accomplishing something for one's parent is more effective than vinegar in producing a contribution.

Although the dollar value of what is contributed is the main point here, we should not lose sight of the effect of the support requirement on the form of the contribution or its meaning to the family. Depending on the state's policy, or on the caseworker's willingness to undervalue contributions in kind (out of his own mixed feelings about filial support), a premium may be placed on giving in kind or the direct payment of bills. Giving in kind may be advantageous to the parent if it is undervalued or if policy ignores it. All families exchange gifts in kind, of course, but the giving of assistance in kind by welfare departments was prohibited by the Social Security Act for reasons that apply to encouraging it as a practice within families. Overused, it reduces the aged person's sense of being competent and independent in a cash world. The direct payment of bills by adult children contains somewhat the same element; moreover, it is likely to be intended to evade the requirement that recipients report income. Finally, there may be less satisfaction in a compulsory contribution, a point we shall treat further.

To review, we have seen that filial relations in the United States are, in general, characterized by a spontaneous exchange of help and services. The nature of the exchange shows little influence by support laws. When one looks into the operation of support laws in old age assistance, it appears that no more is contributed than in the general population. Such effect as compulsion may have would be equaled or exceeded if a contribution could bring advantage to the needy parent. Moreover, compulsion may change the meaning of the contribution.

How is this consistent with the previous conclusion that most families are too poor to contribute? Some who escape compulsory contribution, because they are knowledgeable, will evidently make a contribution if it is useful to the parent. Moreover, children *will* deprive themselves for their parents, particularly in living together. Only the concerned family can judge, however, which deprivation is keenest—the parents', the adult child's, or his child's. The income scale has yet to be devised that can weigh this as delicately as the people who are making the sacrifice.

FAMILY COHESION. The support requirement is an irritant to families in several ways. It goes to the core of family relations, moreover, in influencing the decision of parents and children about their living arrangements. This effect has been reported as pressure on parents and adult children to live together, but this is only a partial statement of the problem. Fundamentally, the support requirement (with an assist from residence requirements) reduces choice about living together. It strengthens economic necessity as the determinant of living together or, in some cases, separately.

The irritants to families that compulsory support creates are the feelings that surround most of the issues we have discussed. In deciding on an application for public assistance, the parent is caught between his own need and the problem he may create for his children. If he applies, furthermore, they may be annoyed or bitter.[51] The son who contributes may be angry about the one who does not; one or both of the children may feel the parent is at fault. Often, father and child are in agreement about an application. It is when the parent gets caught up in the application process and finds himself needing to make distasteful allegations about his child that they find themselves at odds.[52] In some states the responsibility for suing for support is placed with the parent. Though he may be extremely reluctant, he finds himself facing his adult child in court, not as a witness, but as accuser. These roles take on meaning for people; they cannot easily be explained away as something the agency required but that the parent did not really mean. To be sure, the parent may feel himself that his son should support—mixed feelings of this sort are familiar—but the mechanics of establishing support leads easily to expression of feelings that would not otherwise have been expressed, or expressed quite differently. Want is a powerful driving force; yet we have seen that parents say other needs their children can meet are more important to them. In being forced to take a position that he and his child think hostile, a parent may sacrifice a great deal for the financial support that he also needs. Thus the support that is presumably sought as an expression of filial solidarity occasions anger, hurt, and, no doubt, guilt.[53]

Perhaps this oversimplifies. An official statement of an expected contribution may be helpful to the son who wants to give, but is uncertain about how much. Only a guide, however, not a requirement, is essential to this purpose. The skillful caseworker will see in the conflict that arises an opportunity to bring parent and child together, gently perhaps but with candor, about issues they have been unwilling to face. There is no doubt that these policies may serve such a purpose (in the presence of well-trained staff), but two points need to be made. First, in using the policy for this purpose, the caseworker is arriving at a secondary goal. The policy must be applied whether it accomplishes such a result or not, and frequently it will not. Second, the difficulty in administering filial responsibility that we noted earlier not only creates problems for administrators, who are appointed to work out these problems and to suffer what they cannot work out, but is also reflected in the service that caseworkers are able—or rather, unable—to give to their aged clients. It has been observed that, because caseworkers themselves often have doubt about requiring filial support, in self-protection they become angry at the clients who resist them.[54] Further, the compulsion to focus on the mechanics of filial support, along with other aspects of eligibility, "has encouraged a paucity of interest, imagination, and constructive work in our dealing with the aged. Some caseworkers even regard assignment to an old age assistance case load as a form of punishment." [55] When, as a logical development, separate business units are established to do more effectively the job of collecting support that caseworkers dislike anyway, one consequence is that neither staff sees the relationship of parent and adult children as a proper field of interest.[56] The business staff is not concerned with feelings and the social work staff is not concerned with adult children. Between them the whole vital and sometimes painful subject is ignored.

The heart of the problem is living together. A number of early studies[57] report that support laws force parents to live with their children. In general, this is the current assumption. (There have been few, if any, recent studies of the question.)

Data on the living arrangements of OAA clients do not lend themselves to a conclusion on this point. In 1953, fewer OAA recipients (26 per cent) lived with children[58] than the one-third we have estimated for the general population, although approximately the same percentage had living children. This probably means simply that those who live with their children are less likely to be eligible for OAA. The percentage of parents living with their children was approximately the same in the states that required filial support as in those that did not. However, the two groups of states differ in wealth and urbanization, as well as filial

support, and it is difficult to untangle their effects on living arrangements. Moreover, if filial support requirements tend to force
joint living arrangements, this result may be seen not within
OAA but among the parents who are, because of the requirements, not eligible for assistance.

How much living together results from financial need may be
inferred from the finding, in 1952, that "those of the aged living
in a family as parent or other relative of the head were very frequently without a major source of receipts and a low percentage
had earnings, in sharp contrast to the group not living with relatives." [59] Obviously the first exigency, so to speak, is lack of income. When public assistance is therefore sought, choice about
living arrangements may nevertheless be hampered because
budget standards are low or payments limited. When this is not
in itself determining, the states we are discussing move precisely
to strengthen the role of necessity at the expense of family choice
about living arrangements by requiring that children support.
We have seen that cash contributions are infrequent in any income class, and particularly in the lower-income groups. The
characteristic way to help, if help is going to be provided, is to
share living quarters.

But the support requirement may operate to prevent living together among families that otherwise would. In those states that
treat differently the income of a son who is living with his parent,
there may be a substantial financial disadvantage in living together. More may be expected by way of contribution, or the contribution may be assumed rather than negotiated. Similarly, the
eighteen- or nineteen-year-old is likely to be at considerable advantage if he can live away from home. Living alone will cost him
more, but he will at least control his own income. Financially
speaking, though there is no evidence that youngsters discover
this, his best bet is to find a relative out of the state with whom he
can live. It is this aspect by which the English remember their
own late filial support laws. (The English gave them to us but
have not thought it necessary to retain them.) "Children," writes
Michael Young, "were forced to leave their parents to escape the
Means Test man." [60]

The residence requirements that states establish for old age assistance are another matter than filial support* but also operate to reduce choice in living arrangements. Nineteen states require five years' residence, the maximum the social security law permits, to be eligible for old age assistance. Five states require slightly less, and twenty-four require one year's residence. Only five states accept residence at the time of application as qualifying.[61] This might not deter movement if the state of residence were willing to pay old age assistance outside its boundaries but, generally speaking, only eighteen states will do this for more than a year.[62] A figure is not available for mobility among OAA recipients, but it seems plain that, when moving means giving up assistance, it is difficult for them to join children who are living in other states. It is ironic that this may restrict moving not only to a strange place but to a state that the old person regards as home. A Pennsylvania study indicates that, of applicants for public assistance who were rejected for lack of residence in January, 1959, only one-third had never been state residents. One-fourth had been residents of Pennsylvania within the past five years.[63]

What is alarming, then, is not simply that parents may be forced to live with children or with others. It is that they may find they must live together when they would rather live apart, that there is advantage in living separately when they might prefer or need to live together, and youths may leave home or resent what is required of them at home. We have noted indications that living together may be more or less successful depending on the age of the adult child, whether there are grandchildren, the sex of the child and parent—not to mention the past relationship and present inclination of the people involved. Support policies cannot concern themselves with subtleties such as these. On the contrary, they introduce considerations extraneous to family cohesiveness. Often the results are damaging and contrary to what the people involved would choose.

OLD AGE ASSISTANCE, IN CLOSING. Nothing in this review appraises, or lessens, the meaning to old people of having

---

* The connection of filial support and residence requirements is a negative one. As support laws usually do not apply to children living outside the state, the state's interests would lie in making it relatively easy for parents to move near their children. Residence laws have the opposite effect.

a measure of support from OAA. We have seen that thirty-five states expect adult children to contribute money to their parents, an expectation that differs from customary American family practice and from the assumptions underlying other programs. In focusing on filial support requirements in these states, we have noted administrative difficulties, grave questions of equity, and financial savings. People weigh these differently. But there is a high human cost to support requirements. They tend to minimize opportunity for those to whom it is most important. They wield the power of the law where encouragement would be more acceptable and effective. And, aside from putting other strains on family relationships, they reduce families' area of choice about their living arrangements.

BENEFITS FOR PARENTS OF SERVICEMEN AND VETERANS

Several programs of military benefits bear on the relations of adult children and their parents. During World War II an allotment, in which the government shared, might be made to dependent parents if the serviceman could show that he had contributed "substantially" to their support. Currently, to make the same allotment, the serviceman must show that he has contributed more than one-half the parent's support for a period of time. One bears in mind that in peacetime the typical serviceman is young; his parents are normally not aged. Medical services are available to dependents of servicemen, using the same test of dependency. Servicemen also are covered under old age, survivors, and disability insurance; consequently their surviving dependent parents may be entitled to applicable benefits.

Dependent parents of veterans may be entitled to compensation if the veteran's death is determined to be related to his military service. The test of the parent's dependency is different from that for an allotment. Currently, he must establish that his income is less than a specified amount; the time when this occurs is not an issue. A parent may not be dependent at the time of his son's death, but be entitled to benefits subsequently if his income falls below the amount that tests dependency. The amount of the benefit varies with the parent's income. The number of parents receiving death compensation has risen steadily from 86,000 in 1940 to 318,000 in June, 1959.

Eligibility and the amount of the dependent parent's compensation are determined by the scale (in 1960) given in Table 7–2.

Table 7–2

Annual income	1 dependent parent	2 dependent parents living together (each)
$750 or under	$75	$50
$751 to $1,000	60	40
$1,001 to $1,250	45	30
$1,251 to $1,500	30	20
$1,501 to $1,750	15	10
Over $1,750	0	0

This sliding scale is an innovation; before 1957 eligible dependent parents received a flat amount. In explaining an early proposal for a sliding scale, a House select committee in 1956 wrote: "The purpose of relating the amount of payments to the income from other sources is to provide an incentive for gainful employment." [64]

In these programs, as in old age, survivors, and disability insurance, the implicit assumption is that parents are not ordinarily dependent on their children. If they seek benefits, they must demonstrate that they are in fact dependent. This is in contrast to widows and children, for whom there is a statutory presumption of dependency.[65] The implicit assumption that parents are not ordinarily dependent on their children is, we observe, in accordance with the facts. Dependency in death compensation is defined generally and currently, in contrast to old age, survivors, and disability insurance where specific dependency on the covered wage earner before his death is the issue. The income test establishes that the parent is dependent on someone or on society, not that the veteran would be assisting if he were alive. The assumption is that he would wish to assist, even though he could not or might not.

The basic philosophy of military benefits rests on compensation for loss and removing deterrents to enlistment in time of war, and poor relief concepts have on the whole not been involved. That a number of other adult children may be living, in whatever circumstances, does not affect the determination of dependency. State laws requiring support are taken into account only when their application has produced a contribution that alters the total income. The effect of different standards of dependency for servicemen's allotments and death compensation has been that many parents are classified as dependent after a serviceman's death who were not while he was serving. "It hardly seems appropriate," comments the President's Commission on Veterans' Pensions, "for the government to have two different definitions of dependency applicable to the same persons." [66]

VOCATIONAL REHABILITATION

Certain services are available from state rehabilitation agencies without a test of economic need—diagnosis, counseling, placement and, in most states, training. A test of economic need is required, however, to receive maintenance, medical and hospital services, prosthetic appliances, training materials, and the equipment or licenses necessary to start an enterprise. The test of need applies to receiving these free or with part payment; people are not excluded from the program who may pay the cost themselves. In fiscal 1957, roughly half the rehabilitants reported to the Office of Vocational Rehabilitation had received services subject to a test of economic need; in the great bulk of cases there was some cost to the state-federal program.[67]

Two kinds of questions involving filial relations may arise in the application of a needs test. First, the disabled person may have a parent dependent upon him; the question is whether this claim upon his resources is properly taken into account. Federal standards recommend that obligations to legal dependents and others living in the home be considered as a necessary expense. They permit the inclusion also of support to parents living separately.[68] Second, the disabled person may have adult children; the question then arises whether these children have an obligation to contribute to the cost of his rehabilitation. Federal recommendations distinguish between spouses or minor children, where the rehabilitation agency "has an obligation . . . to secure cooperation," and other relatives such as adult children, where the agency should solicit the permission of its client and ask the adult child whether he is "able and willing" to contribute.[69] States may apply stricter standards of filial responsibility than these, but in fact no state policy does. No state law applies filial responsibility to the rehabilitation program, and no state policy construes general law to have this application.

These standards are generally in accord with filial responsibility as it is practiced in the United States. They do not require from the family of the disabled person contributions that few Americans render. They recognize that some families do provide a contribution, particularly in living together. In these cases they adjust the determination of economic need in accordance with what families are actually doing. In some cases this adjustment makes clients eligible and in others it makes them ineligible. The standards make possible discussions that may bring families together around a rehabilitation plan without enforcing discussions where they seem undesirable or wasteful. Little is remarkable about these policies except their radical difference from public assistance. Speculation about the reasons for the difference might touch on the short-term nature of the rehabilitation program, on the conviction that disability is not an individual's fault, that he desires rehabilitation and need not be compelled, and that in the end it saves money to rehabilitate people. Are these not a variety of ways of announcing that "no Poor Law principles need apply?"

NOTES

1. Esther Lazarus, "Economic Functioning of Older People: Implications for Social Work," *Toward Better Understanding of the Aged* (New York: Council on Social Work Education, 1958), pp. 98–99. Peter Townsend, *The Family Life of Old People* (Glencoe, Ill.: The Free Press, 1957), p. 65.
2. Abraham Epstein, *The Challenge of the Aged* (New York, The Vanguard Press, 1928).
3. Lenore A. Epstein, "Money Income Sources of Aged Persons," *Social*

Security Bulletin, XXIII, No. 7 (Washington, D.C.: July 1960), 14–15.

4. United States Department of Health, Education, and Welfare, Bureau of Old-Age and Survivors Insurance, "National Survey of OASI Beneficiaries" (Washington, D.C.: 1951), unpublished tables.

5. United States Department of Health, Education, and Welfare, *Trends* (Washington, D.C.: 1959), p. 55.

6. United States Department of Health, Education, and Welfare, Bureau of Old-Age and Survivors Insurance, "National Survey of OASI Beneficiaries" (Washington, D.C.: 1957), unpublished tables.

7. Janet Pleak, "Reports of Payments to Out-of-State Recipients," *Public Welfare,* IX, No. 5 (May 1951), 122–123. Zane M. Polemis, "Public Assistance Payments to Out-of-State Recipients," *Public Welfare,* XIII, No. 4 (October 1955).

8. Florida Department of Public Welfare, Division of Research and Statistics, "Effect of the Migration of Oldsters to Florida on the OAA Program," *Florida Public Welfare News,* XVIII, No. 2 (February 1955), 4.

9. Floyd A. Bond *et al., Our Needy Aged* (New York: Henry Holt and Company, 1954), pp. 256–259.

10. Ethel Shanas, "The Living Arrangements of Older People in the United States," *The Gerontologist,* I, No. 1 (March 1961).

11. United States Department of Commerce, Bureau of the Census, *Current Population Reports,* Series P-20, No. 73 (Washington, D.C.: March 12, 1957).

12. United States Department of Health, Education, and Welfare, Bureau of Old-Age and Survivors Insurance, *Interstate Mobility of Aged Beneficiaries Under OASI in 1957, . . . in 1958* (Washington, D.C.: 1958), mimeographed.

13. United States Department of Health, Education, and Welfare, Bureau of Old-Age and Survivors Insurance, "Dependency Requirements for Auxiliary Beneficiaries," *Program Simplification Memorandum* (Washington, D.C.: November 24, 1958); also *Report of the Work Simplification Group* (August 1959).

14. United States Department of Health, Education, and Welfare, Advisory Council on Public Assistance, *Public Assistance* (Washington, D.C.: January 1960), Appendix A.

15. James West, *Plainsville, U.S.A.* (New York: Columbia University Press, 1945), pp. 58–59.

16. Stefan Riesenfeld with Richard C. Maxwell, *Modern Social Legisla-*

tion (Brooklyn, N.Y.: Foundation Press, 1950), pp. 692–700. *See also* regarding legal base of filial responsibility: *Corpus Juris Secundum*, LXVII, section 24, "Parent and Child," and LXX, section 60, "Paupers" (Brooklyn, N.Y.: American Law Book Company, 1936).

17. United States Department of Health, Education, and Welfare, Advisory Council on Public Assistance, *op. cit.*, Appendix H.
18. *Ibid.* Florida Legislative Council and Reference Bureau, *Florida Welfare Services: A Research Report of the Select Committee on Welfare* (Tallahassee: 1959).
19. Harold L. Wilensky and Charles N. Lebeaux, *Industrial Society and Social Welfare* (New York: Russell Sage Foundation, 1958). Minnesota Commission on Aging, *Minnesota's Aging Citizens* (January 1953). Riesenfeld with Maxwell, *op. cit.* Bond, *op. cit.*
20. Wisconsin Legislative Council, *Problems of the Aged,* Vol. I, Part 2 (Madison: 1953). Margaret Greenfield, *Administration of Old Age Security in California* (Berkeley: University of California, May 1, 1950). Eveline M. Burns, *Social Security and Public Policy* (New York: McGraw-Hill, 1956). United States Department of Health, Education, and Welfare, Bureau of Public Assistance, *Study of Special Support and Services, Office of Public Assistance, Pennsylvania Department of Public Welfare* (Washington, D.C.: 1959).
21. Michael V. Hitrovo, "Responsibility of Relatives in the Old-Age Assistance Program in Pennsylvania," *Social Service Review,* XVIII, No. 1 (March 1944), 69, 75.
22. David H. Stevens and Vance G. Springer, "Maine Revives Responsibility of Relatives," *Public Welfare,* VI, No. 7 (July 1948).
23. Minnesota Commission on Aging, *op. cit.* United States Department of Health, Education, and Welfare, Region II, *Study of Special Support and Services, Office of Public Assistance, Pennsylvania Department of Public Welfare* (New York: 1959).
24. Edith Abbott, *Public Assistance,* Vol. I (Chicago: University of Chicago Press, 1940).
25. Bond *et al., op. cit.*
26. Riesenfeld with Maxwell, *op. cit.* Bond *et al., op. cit.*
27. United States Department of Health, Education, and Welfare, Region II, *Administrative Study of New Jersey Department of Institutions and Agencies* (New York: 1958). United States Department of Health, Education, and Welfare, Region II, *Administrative Cost Study, State of New York Department of Social Welfare* (New York: July–October 1959).
28. Wisconsin Legislative Council, *op. cit.*

29. Greenfield, *op. cit.*

30. Saul Kaplan, "Old-Age Assistance: Children's Contributions to Aged Parents," *Social Security Bulletin*, XX, No. 6 (June 1957).

31. Stevens and Springer, *op. cit.*

32. Burns, *op. cit.*

33. Bond *et al.*, *op. cit.*

34. John J. Corson and John W. McConnell, *Economic Needs of Older People* (New York: Twentieth Century Fund, 1956). Hilary M. Leyendecker, *Problems and Policy in Public Assistance* (New York: Harper, 1955).

35. Bond *et al.*, *op. cit.*

36. Hitrovo, *op. cit.*

37. Otto Pollak, *Social Adjustment in Old Age,* Social Science Research Council Bulletin No. 59 (New York: 1948). Bond *et al.*, *op. cit.* Edith Abbott, *op. cit.*

38. State of Maine, unpublished studies (1956 and 1958).

39. Florida Department of Public Welfare, *op. cit.*

40. Pennsylvania Department of Public Welfare, *Composition of Shelter Groups, Latter Half of January 1958, Special Analysis* (Harrisburg: June 9, 1958), mimeographed.

41. Elizabeth Epler, "Old-Age Assistance; Plan Provisions on Children's Responsibility for Parents," *Social Security Bulletin*, XVII, No. 4 (April 1954).

42. Gladys O. White, *Methods Used by States in Determining Need and Amount of Payment for Assistance in the Aid to Dependent Children Program* (Washington, D.C.: United States Department of Health, Education, and Welfare, Bureau of Public Assistance, October 1959), p. 24.

43. Edith Abbott, "Abolish the Pauper Laws," *Social Service Review*, VIII, No. 1 (March 1934). Ethel J. Hart, "The Responsibility of Relatives Under the State OAA Laws," *Social Service Review*, XV, No. 1 (March 1941). Anthony Lenzer with Adele S. Pond and John Scott, *Michigan's Older People, Six Hundred Thousand over Sixty-Five,* (Ann Arbor, Mich.: State of Michigan Legislative Advisory Council, 1958). Bond *et al.*, *op. cit.*

44. Bond *et al.*, *op. cit.* State of Maine, *op. cit.*

45. Stevens and Springer, *op. cit.*

46. Epler, *op. cit.*

47. Hitrovo, *op. cit.*

48. Pennsylvania Department of Public Welfare, *op. cit.*

49. United States Department of Health, Education, and Welfare, Bu-

reau of Public Assistance, *Recipients of Old-Age Assistance in Early 1953* (Washington, D.C.: 1953) Part 1, state data, tables 8 and 18.

50. Bond *et al., op. cit.*

51. Bond *et al., op. cit.*

52. Hart, *op. cit.* Bernard Kutner *et al., Five Hundred over Sixty* (New York: Russell Sage Foundation, 1956).

53. Greenfield, *op. cit.* Lazarus, *op. cit.*

54. Elizabeth Wickenden, *The Needs of Older People* (Chicago: American Public Welfare Association, 1953).

55. Elizabeth Breckenridge, *How Public Welfare Serves Aging People* (Chicago: American Public Welfare Association, July 1955), p. 11.

56. United States Department of Health, Education, and Welfare, Region II, *Study of Special Support and Services, Office of Public Assistance, Pennsylvania Department of Public Welfare* (1959).

57. Robert M. Dinkel, "Parent-Child Conflict in Minnesota Families," *American Sociological Review*, VIII, No. 4 (August 1943).

58. United States Department of Health, Education, and Welfare, Bureau of Public Assistance, *op. cit.*

59. Peter O. Steiner and Robert Dorfman, *The Economic Status of the Aged* (Berkeley: University of California Press, 1957), pp. 68–85, 109–111.

60. Michael Young, "The Extended Family Welfare Association," *Social Work* (London), XIII, No. 1 (January 1956), 150.

61. United States Department of Health, Education, and Welfare, Advisory Council on Public Assistance, *op. cit.*, Appendix G.

62. Florida Department of Public Welfare, *op. cit.*

63. Pennsylvania Department of Public Welfare, *Effect of Length-of-Residence Requirement on Eligibility for Public Assistance in Pennsylvania* (Harrisburg: March 5, 1959), mimeographed.

64. The President's Commission on Veterans' Pensions, *Survivors Benefits for Service-Connected Deaths and Veterans Insurance* (3 vols.), Vol. 1, "Findings and Recommendations," Staff Report No. 7, May 22, 1956 (Washington, D.C.: United States Government Printing Office, 1956), pp. 30, 49.

65. *Ibid.*

66. *Ibid.*

67. United States Department of Health, Education, and Welfare, Office of Vocational Rehabilitation, *Facts in Brief,* Rehabilitation Service Series, No. 40 (Washington, D.C.: May 1958).

68. United States Department of Health, Education, and Welfare, Office

of Vocational Rehabilitation, *Measuring the Disabled Individual's Economic Need,* Rehabilitation Service Series No. 248 (Washington, D.C.: 1956), mimeographed, 15.

69. *Ibid.*

8

Beyond Pluck and Luck

Attitudes about the responsibility of adult children for their aging parents are rooted in personal ideas about family relationships and social goals. This broad frame of reference is seldom clarified in discussions of filial responsibility. It is possible, even likely, that differences such as those about the administrative difficulties in enforcing children's responsibility arise from deeper differences. Let us examine the underlying frame of reference with some care.

IMAGE OF THE FAMILY

Two kinds of things must be said about the frame of reference into which we fit filial responsibility. The first has to do with our image of the American family. The term "image" is used with premeditation to suggest a perception that may or may not be accurate, that is manipulable, and that is used by a profession or a business to advance its own interests. We have possibly become too charmed with images. The great danger lies in dealing with them as if their tie to facts is not consequential; what matters is

Reprinted from the *Social Security Bulletin,* XXV, No. 5 (May 1962). Originally presented at the National Biennial Conference of the American Public Welfare Association (November 30, 1961).

whether an image serves our purposes or someone's else's. The image of the American family that is commonly held is an example of this separation of image from fact. Though fantasy can be pleasant, in this case it may be a major single factor in perpetuating relatives' responsibility laws.

What shape does this image take? *The American family is deteriorating! In what was once a family-centered society, industrialization and urbanization have separated our old people from their children and everyone from his home. Margaret Mead announces the end of the war of the sexes—women have attained emancipation and need not struggle further. Suffragists may applaud, but equality leaves men and women uncertain about sex roles. The age of permissiveness was ushered in by Freud. We pay for its glories with character disorders in adults and—who knows? —delinquency in children. Our civilization has become so complex that each of us feels adrift, uncertain of our purposes, unable even to achieve genuine intimacy. The man who survives the driving thirties, the dangerous forties, and the frantic fifties may live to be sixty-five—and aged! What awaits him? His children— anxious, ambitious, and hedonistic—have neither time nor material support to offer.*

This description is a bit of a caricature but with small changes it would make a sober, persuasive, and typical description of the American family. Though each of the parts of this description contains an insight that is valid, much as the whale contained Jonah, in sum it is chiefly interesting for clinical purposes—as a symptom of the anxiety with which we view ourselves and of the ease and inaccuracy with which we generalize. The flat statement that the American family is deteriorating cannot be supported. The family is *changing*. Some of the changes may be bad, and others are all to the good. As far as the relations of older men and women and their children are concerned, to say that the net effect is on the debit side is a distortion.

A review of some of the changes in the American family should be helpful. The greatest change of all, of course, is that so many persons live to be old. It would be a rash man who would suggest that this is a change for the worse. At the same time, it must be apparent that the doubling or tripling of the aged population creates a problem of income maintenance, even if nothing else in family relationships changes.

This growth in the number of the aged has been going on for the past century or longer. So, too, there has been a steady, long-run shift from a property-centered to a wage-centered economy. When a parent owned his handicraft tools or farm he had an income, whoever did the work, but gradually his income has become dependent on selling a marketable skill that can evaporate. Here is a change that has produced a new problem of support and that one may evaluate as unfortunate. (A rural, handicraft society would be a lot further from reaching the moon, to be sure.) On the other hand, it may not be said that the adult child once supported his father because he cared for him and that today he does not. It is more exact to say that it was, many years ago, in the nature of the situation of many aged people that they commanded support. Today this is less often the case. If feelings or morality have much to do with the change, the evidence has yet to be presented.

A third change, considerably related to the shift to wages, is the ascendancy of the nuclear family. The nuclear family—a man, his wife, and their young children—is becoming as well known as nuclear fallout and, to judge from the tone in which it is discussed, as unpopular. It is sometimes said that the larger families, including several generations and degrees of relationship, became obsolete in response to the requirements of industrialization. One must be wary of reading this kind of direct purpose into our preference for nuclear families, but it is clear that small, mobile families work well in an industrial society.

Now, the argument goes, since grandpa and grandma are no longer part of their children's family, they are forgotten, frequently lonesome, and in any case not supported. The main thing wrong with this argument is that it is not in accord with the facts. Part of it does appear to be true; adult children in the United States do not habitually make cash contributions to their parents. Perhaps 5 per cent—certainly not more than 10 per cent —of the aged get cash contributions in a given year from children with whom they do not live.

Money is more likely to flow in the opposite direction.* Marvin Sussman and Lee Burchinal, in reviewing available studies, concluded that "financial assistance appears generally to flow from parents to children." [1] It seems likely that it is chiefly the middle-aged parents who are giving to their children, but the reason that they give continues into their old age. In other words, an American parent is ambitious for his children and grandchildren, as they are for themselves. He is reluctant to take money from them if he believes that it interferes with their meeting their own needs. Even when the parent is less ambitious for his children, he may prefer to do without such contributions and make some sacrifice in his standard of living so that he may keep his feeling of independence.

The older and younger generations are usually in agreement that if a choice is to be made, the cash must be spent on the children. The aged do not, however, go without help. For obvious reasons, those who are most in need of help usually turn to adult children who have comparatively little to spare. The preferred method of helping that these families use is to share living quarters. For one thing, it leads to the most efficient use of money. For another, living together may provide the older person with natural ways of reciprocating—babysitting, help with housework, and so on. Often, the old people are also in need of nursing care or of benevolent supervision. Indeed, living together is more common with the parents' advancing age and ill health.

If the giving of cash is not a common pattern, living together is. Of the old people who have children, more than a third live with one child or another.[2] (It should be noted that helping the old person is only one reason for a family to live together; sometimes help goes the other way. Others live together simply because they always have.) More old people live with their children today than the total number of old people who were alive during World War I. This is something of a blow to the theory that nuclear families

---

* There was speculation about this as long ago as 1940. Barkev S. Sanders wrote then that "As a group, the aged may spend as much from their own resources for the support of younger persons as is spent, in the aggregate, by younger persons toward the support of the aged." ["Economic Status of the Aged in Urban Households," *Social Security Bulletin,* III, No. 10 (October 1940).

spin off their aging parents, careless of love and heedless of responsibility.

The intangibles that are exchanged between parents and their children—the feeling, the visiting, the marketing—are as important as the material exchanges. It is a common concept that the old are lonely, uncared for, and, in fact, alone. Public welfare workers may have some excuse for thinking this, since the lonely and deserted loom larger in their case loads than elsewhere.

Nevertheless, there is a growing body of solid evidence that this view is wide of the mark. As Ethel Shanas has observed, only 15 per cent of all aged parents live more than a short ride from some child.[3] About half live within walking distance or a short ride, and about a third live with a child. These figures are especially impressive if one considers the rate at which Americans move about and the fact that young families move most rapidly of all. Physical proximity aside, an exchange of services between the parents and their children—an exchange that is typically spontaneous and reciprocal—is noted in a number of studies. More than two out of three aged parents see their children at least weekly. When there are no visits, they keep in touch—perhaps daily—by telephone. What of the help that children and parents give each other in emergencies? Enrico Quarantelli writes that disaster studies lend little support to the notion that the extended family is now of little importance. This group, he says, "is the preferred, sought, and major source of short and long term help in time of crises." [4]

One must conclude that the view that the American family is deteriorating is oversimplified and in error, at least so far as it concerns parents and their adult children. Obviously, this is not to say that there are no needy or lonely old people. The case for filial responsibility laws rests most firmly on a powerful feeling that frequently goes unstated. It is the feeling that families are falling apart and that somehow limits must be established. It is the feeling that morals and responsibility are dissolving everywhere and that somehow a halt must be called. It is the feeling that the government is being expected to do everything and that it cannot. The image of the American family described earlier, unreal though it is, aggravates these feelings. As long as this inaccurate, popular image of the family and this general, semiconscious feeling of deterioration support each other, no change is likely to occur.

THE CONCEPT OF POVERTY

Filial responsibility has been discussed so far in the frame of reference of the American family. Let us shift now to consider filial responsibility in the context of poverty. There was a time not so long ago when poverty might have been defined as the absence of money. This definition is influenced perhaps by the Horatio Alger notion that if money is lacking, with work and determination one provides it. Another definition of poverty may be more useful; a point about Horatio Alger will serve to introduce the definition.

The Alger heroes had a lack of money that impresses one from the first pages of their story. Luke Larkin swept out his school twice a week to earn money to attend it. Ragged Dick shined a gentleman's shoes but couldn't make change for a quarter. There was a lack of money! It would be hard to be worse off than these street boys, but one should pause to count their blessings. They were white, these heroes of Horatio Alger. They came from homes with a proper, legal view of what a family is. Sometimes, if their fathers had died, they were left with anonymous but well-heeled guardians, who came through at crucial points. Because of their early training and associations, our heroes were polite and well-mannered. Only Phil the Fiddler was an Italian immigrant and could not even manage English. (By then some social workers had been talking to Horatio Alger and spoiled the purity of his story line, but only for one book.)

Horatio Alger's heroes had a solid early education. They had a degree of ambition that suggests they had seen the last pages of the book. As if this cornucopia of blessings were not enough, in the last act fortune favored them with a rich little girl to rescue from runaway horses or a river in flood. Take nothing away from Horatio Alger—he figures in our country's adolescence and gave us what we needed, or wanted—but these street boys did not know poverty. They knew an episode when money was less plentiful, so they could enjoy it when it became more plentiful. That is not poverty in our country today.

A definition of poverty more appropriate to the present day would go like this. Poverty is a complex set of circumstances, each caused by and in turn reinforcing the others, that combine to keep a person without money despite such energy or hope as he is able to muster. It may be exact to say that in our country today those people are poor who can least afford it.

If a person is poor, there is a fair chance—one chance in five—that he is Negro, or Puerto Rican, or Mexican, or Indian.[5] There is a better chance—one in four—that he is in a home where there is no father. (The average income in such cases is one-third the average for intact families.) [6] If he is poor, he is relatively uneducated (two chances out of three), and his cultural equipment is meager. One may think that therefore he needs better schools, but on the whole the schools he attends are poor. (On this point, Dr. Conant's conclusion will serve: "The contrast in the money available to the schools in a wealthy suburb and to the schools in a large city jolts one's notion of the meaning of equality of opportunity.")[7] The poor person is not necessarily a child; if not, the chances are good that the person is the mother in such a home as has been described or is old.

Where does he live, this non-Alger hero? In Chicago today, half the poorer, broken families that include children live in housing that is seriously crowded, dilapidated, or lacks central heat, electricity, or plumbing.[8] The aged do not fare so badly in terms of housing. If they live with relatives, they share their fortunes so far as housing is concerned. Of those living alone or with nonrelatives, from a fourth to a third are in substandard housing.

Poverty means other things. For many, it means living in a state of despair or bitterness that, if it represents a realistic and even necessary reaction to their experiences, in itself becomes a barrier to improving their circumstances. Poverty means that a man's family is not likely to be able to help him get ahead. Not only are they not able to help, but they may turn to him when they are in such desperate need that he must share with them anything extra that he has managed to scrape together.

The point of this catalog of the elements of poverty has now been reached. Filial responsibility legislation is not examined realistically when it is examined in isolation. Taken as an abstraction, the requirement to support may be a small, not to say reasonable, requirement to make of a person. Its appearance may be different if it is seen as one element in a network of circumstances that combine to handicap a person at every turn.

It would be another matter if people of average means or better were being considered. The fact is that those with good income tend to have parents with adequate income. The fact is that persons with good income do not need to be required by law to help their parents when they are in need; they tend to do it voluntarily. The fact is, finally and ironically, that those with good income know best how to evade the law if this is what they want.

One might grant the thesis that many factors in a poor person's situation interact to keep him poor and yet doubt whether support requirements are in themselves a significant handicap. As far as is known, the matter has never been studied in just these terms. Yet, one must take note of the extent to which the self-improvement of adults is subsidized by their parents today. Marvin Sussman and Lee Burchinal observe, for example, that we are well on our way to a new norm, that parents should, if at all possible, provide a college education for their children.[9] College education is not the only subsidy; middle-class parents make substantial contributions at marriage, in connection with grandchildren, and so on. The adult children being considered here not only fail to get this assistance; they are required to give assistance.

Visualize a child on the aid to dependent children rolls reaching the landmark of his eighteenth birthday. Obviously, his family is not going to be able to help him toward the goal of self-improvement—financially, at least. Much less than that, the child is now a legally responsible relative. North Carolina assumes a contribution from an employed child over age eighteen—50 per cent of his net income or $75 a month, whichever is smaller. Utah assumes a contribution from any child earning more than $75 a month—50 per cent of the amount over $75.

Not all of these children, or even most of them, will achieve earnings that bring these requirements to bear on them. Nor are all of those who do achieve such earnings striving for self-improvement. What of those who are? Shall we debate how to provide specialized services to encourage self-improvement while we require them to give up the means for it?

Filial responsibility and poverty can be viewed in two ways. One can put the emphasis on support and consider questions of justice and reasonableness. Using this approach, it is possible to establish a definition of moderate income and to require that all or part of any sums above that amount be contributed to the needy parent. Some states set this level low indeed. In addition, one's concept of justice must somehow encompass the fact that most Americans, of any income level, do not make cash contributions.

At least implicitly, a second approach is being proposed here. This approach puts the emphasis on poverty and asks at how many points and how substantially it is possible, within the framework of the public assistance programs, to interrupt the cycle that keeps people poor. Interfering with poverty is, it must be apparent, far from a simple thing to do. It requires change on a variety of fronts—education, race relations, employment, family relationships, and so on—many of them outside the reach of a public welfare worker. One small area can lie within his reach: if he deals with an old man, his children may be included in the goal of fostering independence.

With respect to the points made so far, a few qualifications are necessary. Why, for example, so much talk about children when the subject is filial responsibility and the aged? The reason has already been stated in another connection: The welfare of the aged and their children and their grandchildren is indivisible. It is not possible to have old people comfortable at the expense of their children. No one wants it that way, but in any case it could not be achieved.

Second, it is not intended to give the impression that parents and adult children are necessarily distinct groups of people. A great many people are parent and child at once. It has been noted, for example, that support requirements may be a handicap to the child after he is dropped from the rolls of aid to dependent children because of his age. Similarly, a youth may be handicapped because support for an older relative is required from his forty-year-old father. Further, increasing numbers of aged Americans are finding that they have even older relatives who might be considered to be dependent on them. The proportion of those just over age sixty to the really old—over age eighty—is now about three to one; in a generation or so, the proportion should be three to two.[10] Thus, contributions *to* the aged might have to be enforced *from* the aged.

There is a third qualification: In speaking about poverty, human spirit and drive have been referred to only negatively—that is, in terms of despair and bitterness. This is not to say that the human spirit will not assert itself despite all obstacles. The human drive toward self-respect may surmount decades of repression and indignity. It does seem clear, however, that poverty will be left behind only bit by bit, here and there, unless we create the conditions for leaving it behind.

Finally, it may seem that it is being suggested that children should not help their parents but should think only of themselves. Far from it. Evidence that children freely and spontaneously help their parents has been noted. It is the effect of the legal requirement that has been discussed specifically, in particular its effect on adult children who are being denied the right to the smallest surplus income that may be applied to self-advancement. These are not the people upon whom one should choose, as the law chooses, to enforce support.

CONCLUSIONS

To sum up: Filial responsibility laws cannot be considered alone, for they should have some rational relationship to the way families live. These laws do not represent the normal pattern of American family life, nor are they likely to be enforced except on public assistance families. In fact, a case for the repeal of these laws can be based solely on their effects on family relationships. Support laws appear to be intimately related to vague, though powerful, fears about the deterioration of families. The anxiety may be real, but it is not tied to objective trends in family life.

Filial responsibility laws must also be considered in relation to poverty. The requirement to support is one of the network of handicaps that surrounds a poor family; it may, on occasion, be the crucial handicap that persuades a person that improvement is not in the cards for him. Earlier in this article images and their dangers were discussed. Visions merit rather more respect. We have had the vision from time to time of so organizing public welfare, and our society, that we shall wipe out poverty as we know it today. Eliminating support requirements in public assistance is only one element in this program, but it is an element.

NOTES

1. Marvin B. Sussman and Lee Burchinal, *Parental Aid: Prospects and Implications for Family Theory* (Cleveland: Western Reserve University, September 1961), processed.
2. Ethel Shanas, "The Living Arrangements of Older People in the United States," *The Gerontologist,* I, No. 1 (March 1961).
3. *Ibid.*
4. Enrico L. Quarantelli, "A Note on the Protective Function of the Family in Disasters," *Marriage and Family Living,* XXII, No. 3 (August 1960), 264.
5. Robert J. Lampman, *The Low Income Population and Economic Growth,* Study Paper No. 12, United States Congress, Joint Economic Committee (Washington, D.C.: December 16, 1959).
6. Lenore A. Epstein, "Some Effects of Low Income on Children and Their Families," *Social Security Bulletin,* XXIV, No. 7 (February 1961).
7. James Bryant Conant, *Slums and Suburbs* (New York: McGraw-Hill Book Co., 1961).
8. Beverly Duncan and Philip M. Hauser, *Housing a Metropolis— Chicago* (New York: The Free Press of Glencoe, 1960).
9. Sussman and Burchinal, *op. cit.*
10. United States Senate, Committee on Labor and Public Welfare, Subcommittee on Problems of the Aged and Aging, *The Aged and the Aging in the United States—A National Problem* (Washington, D.C.: January 27, 1960).

9

Family Policy
in the United States

The United States does not come readily to a national family policy. To be sure, many, if not most, national decisions and activities influence family relationships. "Family policy" is used here, however, to mean consensus on a core of family goals, toward the realization of which the nation deliberately shapes programs and policies. The United States may now conceivably be in the first stages of development toward having a national family policy. First, we shall note the conflicting goals or traditions that the country has had. This will provide a basis for proposing and illustrating some generalizations about the development of national policies affecting families in the United States. Finally, we shall come to the forces that may be making for change.

It should be borne in mind that national policy applies itself to citizens who, whatever course they may expect from their government, regard family living as a most desirable state. The marriage rate in the United States is among the highest in Western industrial countries; the median age at first marriage (22.8 for grooms and 20.3 for brides) is the youngest.[1] Remarriage, upon death or divorce, also takes place at a high rate. Though a mobile nation, Americans move as families rather than as individuals. Home

Reprinted from the *International Social Science Journal,* XIV, No. 3 (1962), 452–467. UNESCO.

ownership, which is likely to reflect a family interest, has always been highly valued; at present three out of five dwellings are owned by their occupants. Family goals may be pursued by voluntary organizations, such as the Family Service Association of America, and by state and local governments. Marriage and divorce, legitimacy and inheritance, and family responsibility are subject to state law. Thus, the discussion that follows examines national policy but is not fully descriptive of family relationships in the United States, of the efforts to enhance them, or even of their official regulation.

THE GOALS DETERMINING POLICY

Three major traditions of the United States have had special influence upon the development of its policies toward the family. First, its goals are individualistic. For the early colonists, a family spirit that was brought from the old world combined with the isolation that was enforced on the frontier of the new world to continue the feeling that the family was primary. But it was "the democratic disposition to deal with individuals, not families." [2] The primacy of the individual became evident as beginning industrialization freed him from locality and family—evident to visiting Europeans, among others, who recorded it with satisfaction or alarm.[3] The subsequent emancipation of women and securing of the rights of children were further evidences of prime interest in the individual; in their turn, these developments tended further to subordinate the interests of families. The individual—his achievement, his development, or his happiness—is the desired end implicit in American tradition; his family is regarded by his country, and by himself, as a private venture for the sake of personal satisfaction.

This distinction may readily be observed at the level of formal federal activity. There has been a White House Conference on Children each decade since President Theodore Roosevelt called for the first one in 1909. The first—and only—National Conference on Family Life was held in 1948; nor was it held at the call of the President. The federal government contains a Children's Bureau and a Women's Bureau, each with concern for the family as it relates to its work; but there is no bureau for families as such.

Looking to the principles that underlie this structure, one finds the President's Commission on National Goals affirming that "the family is at the heart of society." The report addresses itself, however, "to the citizens of this country, each of whom sets his own goals. . . ." More explicitly, "All our institutions—political, social, and economic—must further enhance the dignity of the citizen, promote the maximum development of his capacities, stimulate their responsible exercise, and widen the range and effectiveness of opportunities for individual choice." [4] However far behind us the "old frontier" may be, it leaves individualism stamped in our personal and national images.

Perhaps even more striking than official statements is the tendency among clinicians and social scientists to focus upon the individual—more striking because the tendency is apt to be unconscious and, on occasion, to be denied. Psychiatrists have notably been concerned with individuals; it is only in the past few years that formulations have been attempted that in any way add to the notion that a family represents the sum of several two-way relationships. (Role theory has been significant in this attempt.)[5] Perhaps one would expect a psychiatrist to become lost in the individual, but it is only recently that social work agencies have attempted similar formulations.[6] Interviewing of several family members at a time is now being examined as a novel technique in the more sophisticated agencies,[7] though undoubtedly it was once more common. A recent study shows that a family agency has been encouraging nuclear families to maintain some distance from parents and in-laws.[8] It appears that, in learning from psychology and psychiatry, social work has lost a family orientation which it is now deliberately seeking to regain.[9] Nor have social scientists escaped the effect of their own culture upon the manner in which they investigate families. After a conference on family research several years ago, the interpretive summary observed: " 'Family' research becomes research into courtship, into marital interaction, or into parent-adolescent relationships, and seldom do families come through." [10] During 1960, a group of social scientists was called together to advise the Commissioner of Social Security on "priorities for sustaining and enriching family life." They dealt specifically with the question of seeing the family as an end in itself, but serving the individual in the context of a family turned out to be the framework of the majority.[11]

If an individualistic tradition had not tended to subordinate family goals in the national ethos, dedication to PRIVATE EN-TERPRISE (written large) and government (written small) would in any case have made family goals difficult to achieve. One might regard the United States as a vast experiment in which two variables have been economic development (including industrialization and urbanization) and the structure and internal relationships of families. It is apparent that, in the United States as elsewhere, the family has been the dependent variable— stripping itself of kin, yielding one institutional function after another (economic, educational), and deepening its personality functions as the economy required a more compact and mobile unit.[12] Though the family has also influenced the economy, the main direction of change—from economy to family—has nevertheless seemed clear. The achievement of family goals would, therefore, have required a degree of government intervention in the economy that would not have been regarded as acceptable until the comparatively recent past.

Apart from loyalty to individualism and free enterprise, the nature of the political process in the United States has not lent itself to a monolithic statement of goals to which the nation would more or less consistently adhere. "The essence of American democracy is that it isn't anybody's exclusive right to tell us what it is," said Harlan Cleveland, Assistant Secretary of State.[13] Our origins are plural and, in contrast to other western countries, relatively recent. Although families of various national, cultural, and economic backgrounds appear to be converging toward common patterns, negotiation and compromise among diverse interest groups nevertheless continue to characterize our political process. This "infra-structure . . . beneath the constitutional frame of the state"[14] approaches an identity of values only on certain core concepts—the importance of the individual, of children, and of free choice. (Differences are submerged only in the face of national crisis.) The absence of agreement on family goals would appear with greater clarity if it were not masked by a tendency to broad moralizing. Thus, all groups hold the family to be of primary importance if one goes by statements of principle. It is in the market place of political decision making that it becomes clear how diverse are the definitions of family and how different the goals for it.

For example, specifying family goals would go to the heart of differences between religious groups, Catholic, Jewish, and Protestant, and of differences within these groups. Tacit agreement to let each prevail in the city and state where it is strongest would become difficult in the face of an explicit national policy. On the national level, compromises are feasible in practice that might not especially be defended as matters of principle. Thus, federal funds may be spent for contraceptive devices and advice in those states that wish it, and not in others, with no federal direction in either case. We observe that, because the need for assistance to education has assumed critical proportions, this issue involving religious differences has had to be joined on a national level. Questions of family policy have not so far assumed such dimensions. It should be noted that, although salvation is individual, marriage is a sacrament in Catholic and some Protestant thought; in other churches the family is at least regarded as consecrated to the service of God. Consequently, all religions are more or less united, as a formal matter and increasingly in their pastoral practice, in attending to the family as a family. They are led, therefore, to an interest in national family policy, but not to agreement on what such policy should be.

Not only does diversity have political effect, but national policies must serve a variety of types of families. It may be safe to suggest that the most common concept of family in the United States is the intact nuclear family—a man, his wife, and three or four children. Yet the inevitable passage of time transforms them into new nuclear families and a couple living alone. The death of one leaves a widow living alone or with the family of one of her children. Furthermore, the extended family is favored by some ethnic groups—from eastern and southern Europe, for example. A death or a divorce may produce a broken family, one parent with children—the United States has about three million of these. It has been suggested, further, that in an integrated lower-class culture in the United States, the single-parent family and serial mating are the norm.[15] This wide variety presents the problem of formulating broad policies in a manner that best serves all families. The problem is to arrive at policies that support the broken family without excluding the intact family, that assist the old person who wants to live with his children without enforcing this if he would rather live alone.

THE COURSE OF POLICY

Under the influence of these traditions—individualism, minimum intervention by government, and negotiation among diverse interest groups—national planning that meets family goals in the United States has taken its particular course. I should like to offer the following propositions as descriptive of this course. In this discussion, "family" is used most broadly to mean the related group of people who live together, whether the unit is intact or broken, nuclear or extended.

1. *The Principle of Coherence.* The family is an instrument, sometimes an indispensable one, in the maturation and satisfaction of individuals. The outline of a core of beliefs about family goals will be most readily discernible where they are necessary to or at least consistent with the needs of individuals.

2. *The Pickaback Principle.* Change to achieve family goals is most likely to occur when it is coincidental with other developments, for example, resolving some serious social issue or meeting an economic crisis. (Partly this reflects the fact that there are no organized efforts in the interests of the family. Groups organized for other purposes promote the interests of the family when this advances or is at least consistent with their own aims.)

3. *The Principle of Direct Response.* Action taken explicitly in pursuance of family goals tends to occur on issues that are narrowly defined. It is on such issues that agreement can most readily be reached. Not infrequently such action is taken to correct the inadvertent effects on families of programs designed for quite other purposes. It may tend to be regulatory rather than preventive.

These propositions will be illustrated chiefly with material about housing and standards of living. Adequate housing is, of course, a central consideration in any body of policies concerned with families. In a "Declaration of National Housing Policy," Congress records its intention to ensure "a decent home and a suitable living environment for every American family." [16]

Apart from a temporary program during World War I, the federal government's debut in the housing field came with the depression of the 1930's. Social research in this period was largely concerned with "social bookkeeping." That is, research demonstrated the high financial cost and low tax return of slum dwellings; it demonstrated their high correlation with rates of death, disease, and social pathology.[17] Though it was shortly pointed out that a correlation is not a causal relationship, the weight of the data was convincing to many researchers and there is indication that it was convincing to congressmen. In the development of federal programs in this period, however, the "principal emphasis was upon the stimulation of residential construction as a cure for the depression." [18] It has been argued that the need to provide housing was not incidental in political effect to the economy's need for stimulation. Rather, there had been a long-term change in the public view of housing which awaited this opportunity to be realized.[19] Even if this had been the case, housing was not provided solely because it was needed but waited upon other national needs of considerable force.

It was assumed that these were housing programs for families— one could hardly conceive of anything else. Having helped to carry the day, researchers turned their attention to new issues that seemed significant—consumer attitudes to housing, effects of mixed racial occupancy, and the effects of housing patterns upon social relationships. Losing interest in the earlier issues was symptomatic of the assumption that families are served if people are served, and it was unfortunate. In their dissatisfaction with social accounting, researchers had been calling for more sophisticated designs that would undoubtedly have begun to clarify the reciprocal effects of housing and family patterns.[20] At the critical time when post-war building was about to be undertaken, such research was postponed for perhaps a generation.

The questions on which we do not have substantial information have since become apparent to all—builders, planners, owners, and officials. Though gifted insights are not lacking, we do not know whether high-rise housing damages families, or is unsuitable for certain kinds of families. Many Americans do not like row housing, but we do not know its effects. We have a variety of assumptions about privacy and family interaction in the use of internal space, but our information about actual use patterns comes mainly from attitudinal questions, with all their limitations. (Observes one researcher, illustrating at least the debatability of present assumptions: "The only privacy that is wanted by the poor families we are studying is to be protected from the designs of middle-class architects.")[21] Researchers are just now beginning to return to an exploration of family patterns and how they alter when housing alters.[22]

Federal activity in the housing field after 1940 tended also to be connected with the needs of the economy, of prosecuting a war, or of assisting veterans.[23] Former Senator Ralph Flanders, recalling hearings in the United States Senate in 1947 and 1948, observed:

> When we were discussing the housing bill . . . I supported public housing, but all of the time the thing which fundamentally worried me was: Why are there so many people with such low incomes that they cannot afford to pay economic rent? It seemed to me that we ought to know more about who they are, and how many there are, and what kind of industries they are working in, and where they are, and what is the cause for these unsociably low incomes of people who cannot pay their way. I have had no success in finding out very much about these people. . . .[24]

Because programs were not primarily designed to meet such questions, the relocation of families who would be displaced received little attention at first. It soon became evident, however, that redevelopment would be slowed to a snail's pace by families' refusal to move. *Then* attention focused on the people who were involved—programs demonstrating the effects of counseling with families and studies to examine their attachment to their houses and neighborhoods.* Urban studies prior to 1950 might be said to

* The first redevelopment proposal in the city of Milwaukee, announced in 1947, was defeated by residents. The following reaction is more heated than

have been considering the spatial mobility of families;[25] after 1950, a growing number of demonstration projects and studies focussed on spatial inertia.[26]

In an attempt to meet the problem of relocation, the Housing Act of 1949 gave priority in public housing to families displaced by urban redevelopment. Public housing had originally served families who voluntarily sought to improve their housing but could not afford private rentals. During World War II public housing was largely reoriented to the families of war workers. With the Housing Act of 1949, its character was entirely changed by the depressed, untutored, and frequently dependent families who were now concentrated in its projects.[27] By and large, after the war public housing employed no social workers to aid in planning, design, or management. Despite its new clientele, so to speak, management was viewed in the traditional real estate terms of rent collection and property protection. An income test required that those who increased their earnings, and incidentally might provide the best example to their neighbors, must leave public housing. As a consequence, some number of poor people prefer substandard housing to public housing. They see the tenants as undesirable, and the management as overly controlling. These problems are not by any means simple to solve, but they were predictable if attention had been focussed on them. They are cited here to indicate that the main movement of the programs comes in response to other than family pressures.

It has been suggested that policies in the interests of families would be most perceptible where consistent with policies that enhance individual welfare. Steadily rising standards of living may be the conspicuous illustration of this point. It is not necessary to enumerate the devices that the government has used to encourage expanding production, a rising wage rate, and sustained income to those who, for one reason or another, cannot work. (The instrument that is conspicuously absent from this arsenal is family

---

most, but contains a lesson that had to be learned. " 'Slums,' one woman shrieked. 'Slums, they call us. Why that's a terrible word—those are our homes, our shrines. We live there.' " [The *Milwaukee Journal* (November 9, 1948), quoted in Coleman Woodbury, ed., *The Future of Cities and Urban Redevelopment* (Chicago: University of Chicago Press, 1953).]

allowances, a device that has been regarded, at least until recently, as "a considerable departure from the traditional American concept of the living wage.") [28] National policies in this area have been notably successful, increasing family income by 45 per cent in the last decade[29] and reducing the number of families defined as "low income" from 27 to 20 per cent of the United States total.[30] It goes without saying that the remaining low-income families, not to mention a far larger percentage of low-income "single individuals," provide cause for continuing concern and national attention.

The order of development in social insurance and public assistance programs has, on the whole, been to legislate for individuals and to follow this, sooner or later, with amendments that include family members. For example, the Social Security Act was enacted in 1935 and family benefits were added in 1939; disabled workers were covered in 1956, and their dependents in 1958. In the Aid to Families with Dependent Children program (AFDC) federal participation was at first available only for the children in a family home; participation in aid to mothers was added fifteen years later. Fathers in need because of unemployment were added after another eleven years, in circumstances consistent with two of the propositions that have been advanced. First, they were added in connection with legislation designed to meet an economic recession. Second, they were added after two Secretaries of the Department of Health, Education, and Welfare had defined the precise issue that exclusion of fathers from the *program* might be leading to the exclusion of some fathers from their *own families*.[31] The clearest element of a family policy has appeared in national agreement that children are best cared for by their own families. This has been clear in AFDC, as in survivors insurance. In the end, the net effect of these programs has been to promote family goals, because these have been seen to be consistent with and, indeed, necessary to, individual satisfaction.

An illustration has been noted, in AFDC, of the tendency to deal narrowly with issues posed as issues of family policy. Here a legislative corrective was provided for a problem that legislation produced. The tendency to respond narrowly applies as well to the family difficulties that are produced by the profound social and economic changes the country experiences. For example, on occasion there has been concern in Congress and the administration about the failure of some fathers to provide support for their children when they divorce or separate from their wives. A large element in the problem is the deep-rooted American interest in satisfaction in marriage (that is, in the individual's need) which contributes to comparatively high divorce and remarriage rates. At the same time, low-income fathers are patently unable to support two families. Thus, the roots of the problem reach into the American concept of marriage and the persistence of inadequate income. The decisions of public bodies so far, however, have been essentially regulatory—concerned with methods of bringing fathers to proper judicial attention or with other ways of requiring them to meet their responsibility.[32] Such decisions require only the common-denominator agreement that fathers should be responsible; broader differences about marriage need not be resolved. On the other hand, and this may be one of the forces leading to change, such an approach has not been notably successful.

The evident impotence of regulation alone has led to recent emphasis on family responsibility to control and satisfy its members, but this emphasis has been largely hortatory. (Probably, too, it suffers from the familiar difficulty that those who need instruction are not within earshot.) To some extent, public bodies are beginning to go beyond this point (in relation to juvenile delinquency, for example) to challenge social welfare and the social sciences to elucidate the connection of delinquency with broader issues of social and family policy. This is a road from which—for those who are asking the questions and for those who must answer them—it may be difficult to turn back. The tendency has been, as Alexander Leighton writes, to use "social science as the drunk uses the lamppost, for support rather than illumination."[33] When the questions about family needs are asked and answered, however, this will be more difficult to do. As for the professionals, they are called upon now to produce the answers they believe they have the techniques to find.

Can we say what the net effect of government activity is (as it is described by the "coherence," "pickaback," and "direct response" principles) on family relationships and structure? On the one hand, the main movement of government policy would be consistent with its other economic and social policies and with the movement of nongovernmental forces. Thus, the retirement provisions of the Old Age, Survivors, and Disability Insurance program appear to contribute to the ability of old people to live separately from their children, and to relationships with the children that are warm and spontaneous.[34] As we have noted, economic forces have resulted in small families, living separately, with close family ties nevertheless preserved.[35] On the other hand, because family policy is neither the foremost consideration nor even formulated, family effects that are damaging may inadvertently be produced. For example, state requirements that children support their aged parents, applied within the federally-aided old age assistance program, may induce old people and their children to live together even when this is contrary to their wishes and to their best interests. These effects, one way and the other, have not been examined systematically so far.

These observations—about housing, standard of living, and certain related matters—are illustrative of the propositions that have been offered. They are not, by any means, an exhaustive treatment of the national policies that affect families, and may seem to understate national interest in families. For example, income tax laws provide special benefits to families with children. In immigration laws, the spouse of an American citizen is given preferred treatment. The Armed Services give special recognition to families, both in the selection of servicemen and in their treatment. (In establishing wartime compensation for servicemen, the United States has come closest to the concept of family allowances.) The thesis that is being advanced is that citizen interest in families, which is real, receives expression on the national scene in succession to other interests. In consequence, a national family policy has not developed, and the de facto policies that, taken together, meet family goals may be described in terms of the "coherence," "pickaback," and "direct response" principles. Certain policies have been used to illustrate the thesis; other policies affecting families might have been selected.

FORCES MAKING FOR CHANGE

The relationship of the American family to current problems appears to be due for more attention. Indeed, it is possible that contemporary developments may be pressing the nation to the point at which the elements of a national family policy will be formulated more deliberately. The need for such a policy has been urged with increasing frequency of late: at the White House Conference on Children and Youth, at the Advisory Meeting to the Commissioner of Social Security, by the National Association of Social Workers, and in professional literature.[36] These statements reflect current forces that lead to increased emphasis upon families as such, and that remove some of the barriers to such emphasis upon the national scene.

The American tradition of minimal government has been cited as one barrier to a national family policy; it seems clear that this tradition has been changing. There is no longer debate about whether the government has any responsibility or none, but whether its responsibility is larger or smaller. The view of the proper role of government has shifted in the United States; moreover, it has become plain that government has an impact on the structure and function of families, whether or not it intends an effect. Government expenditure for social welfare is equivalent to more than 10 per cent of the gross national product.[37] The tax structure, the influencing of wages, and the deployment of the defense establishment are other major forces that act upon families. Government choice to calculate the effect of these forces upon families might be novel. That it must have an effect of one sort or another, however, would hardly be debatable any longer. To be sure, there would be debate about the decisions that need to be made.

The pursuit of a national family policy has a price tag and, therefore, the comparatively recent American sense of affluence becomes a consideration. Implementation of the "National Housing Policy" would cost far more than the government has so far spent on housing. Federal policies that would be best for families might turn out to be less economical or less productive. The mathematics of affluence may be difficult to define. From a world point of view, the United States has been affluent for some time; from the point of view of several million of its poorest citizens, affluence has still to be attained. Yet, within the past decade, many Americans have come to regard their country's wealth as adequate, or able to be made adequate, to almost any task. This is an attitudinal definition of affluence, and perhaps an important one. It should mean, to a greater degree than ever before, that if a human end is sufficiently desirable, the economic cost may be borne.

It is fairly well accepted that industrialization provided the funds to support welfare services;[38] the stage of industrialization that we regard as affluence may support the conceivably larger cost that would be involved in public policy decisions motivated by family needs. Proposals for such policies are, indeed, occasionally advanced. For example, Margaret Mead has pointed to twin dangers of college marriages. On the one hand, the husband may set his occupational goals too low in order to be able to support his family quickly, unwittingly mortgaging the couple's intellectual future. On the other hand, the wife may support her husband while he completes his optimum level of education, sacrificing her own development to his. The proposal is advanced that in "mature" undergraduate marriages, where both members are doing a high level of academic work, "complete economic independence should be provided." [39] David Riesman advances a proposal that is not entirely unrelated. He points to the need for a psychological moratorium in early adulthood, that is, the need for a period of limited expectations during which there may be an unconscious personal assessment and reorganization. Riesman proposes a work program for young men to meet this need.* [40] Neither Mead nor Riesman was advancing a finished proposal, but stimulating a type of discussion that starts with what needs to be accomplished for the couple's or for the individual's maturation, and moves to public policy. This is the quality of policy development that affluence makes possible.

The increasingly intimate relationship of the United States

---

* The Peace Corps and the Job Corps may be regarded as responsive to this proposal although their motivations were described as economic and social rather than primarily maturational.

with other countries of the world may become another factor in the development we are considering. The powerful movement to achieve racial equality in the United States, though it stems in the first place from the desire to achieve or to provide justice, is supported by America's awareness of its appearance abroad. It is interesting to observe that young Negro leaders are keenly aware of the long-term effect of their activity in enhancing the international status of the United States. Similarly, it is borne in upon Americans how greatly the citizens of underdeveloped countries would wish to achieve comparable wealth to ours, but how they are worried or repelled by the social concomitants that seem to attend industrialization. As other countries struggle with these problems, and have their own experience with the reciprocal effects of economic development and family structure, the United States is likely to find itself instructed and influenced.

These changes—the increasing authority of government, affluence, and international influences—smooth the path to the development of a national family policy. None of them provides the motive for such a policy however. The change that may be making the need for a family policy convincing lies in the central position that the American family appears increasingly to hold for its members. There has been a good deal of concern that the family in the United States is becoming a less vital institution. It was giving up certain functions, children were more and more being emancipated from parental control, and a variety of indices (birth rate, divorce rate) seemed to bespeak disorganization. However, the birth rate has reversed and the divorce rate is no longer rising. The state of being married, as was noted earlier, continues to be undeniably popular. And it is pointed out that two "root" functions of the family, socializing children and serving the personality needs of adults, remain unimpaired.[41] These two functions are becoming more prominent, if not indeed more significant.

A number of observers have pointed to a new family preoccupation with children. For example, Oscar Handlin writes:

> Increasingly, in the past two decades, the activities of the urban population have been concentrated on the coherence and unity of the family. To a considerable and growing degree, organized

communal life, particularly in the suburbs, is child-centered and revolves about the institutions which will preserve the nest within which offspring are reared.[42]

This may be an observation about middle-class families. Of the working-class wife it has been said that "her children and husband occupy her energies and emotions, her inner life and her routine behaviors, much more extensively than is true for the middle-class woman. . . ."[43] Though the United States has historically been oriented to children, there has been some fluctuation of the degree of interest in children as well as of child-rearing patterns. However, the present deepening of interest occurs at the same time as adults appear to be looking to the family to serve an increasingly important function for themselves.

Several relatively independent developments, spanning different periods of time, are now converging. Their effect is to diminish the opportunities for a sense of personal identity and recognition that were once afforded to an adult in the ordinary course of his life. The occupational structure has become increasingly bureaucratic, with every employee "at least potentially replaceable."[44] Thus one's job is less likely to offer personal recognition. Ethnic neighborhoods are being wiped out by urban redevelopment and, if only because of sheer size, the cities are managed more and more impersonally. Fewer Americans than ever before come from the "old country"; ties of ethnic and national origin offer less opportunity for a sense of personal identity. "We have paid for our higher standard of living," writes Otto Pollak in somewhat Kaffkaesque tones, "with an 'open stock' way of life, where nothing is our own . . . because we are likely to find it in the home of a friend, on the back of a stranger, and in the showcase of a store. . . ."[45] In the face of such developments the family is seen today to have "crucial importance . . . as a buffer against the impersonal, competitive, occupational world."[46] "The family," said the Advisers to the Commissioner of Social Security, "is, and will increasingly be, the one place a person is valued for himself [and feels] irreplaceable."[47]

In brief, we have reviewed a number of deep-rooted traditions of the United States which have influenced the development of policies affecting families. Three propositions ("coherence," "pickaback," and "direct response") have been offered to sum up the development of these policies. At least one tradition—that government should intervene as little as possible in social and economic affairs—has undergone change. Affluence and the experience of other countries are also likely to alter the types of policies that we see in the future. At present, the family is taking on new significance in terms of its two root functions. Individuals find themselves valued in their families in a way that is becoming increasingly rare in other institutions. As this trend continues we may, more than ever before, have a situation in which individual and family goals are fully consistent. We may, therefore, anticipate increasing evidence in national policy of the importance of the family in the United States. There should emerge, on a level of parity with other social and economic goals, recognizable goals for families that are primary determinants of national policies— that is to say, a national family policy.

NOTES

1. *Population Bulletin*, XVII, No. 4 (Washington, D.C.: Population Reference Bureau, Inc., June 1961).
2. Arthur W. Calhoun, *A Social History of the American Family* (Cleveland: A. H. Clark), Vol. II, 334.
3. Alexis de Tocqueville, *Democracy in America* (1899), Vol. II, "Social and Domestic Relations": *see also,* Seymour M. Lipset, "Constant Values in American Society," *Children,* VI, No. 6 (November–December 1959).
4. *The Report of the President's Commission on National Goals,* The American Assembly (New York: Columbia University, November 1960).
5. *Integration and Conflict in Family Behavior,* Group for the Advancement of Psychiatry, Report No. 27 (August 1954); Nathan Ackerman, *The Psychodynamics of Family Life* (New York: Basic Books, 1958).
6. Otto Pollak, "Design of a Model of Healthy Family Relationships as a Basis for Evaluative Research," *Social Service Review* (December 1957); Otto Pollak, "A Family Diagnosis Model," *Social Service Review,* XXIV (March 1960).

7. Celia Brody Mitchell, "The Use of Family Sessions in the Diagnosis and Treatment of Disturbances in Children," *Social Casework,* XLI, No. 6 (June 1960).
8. Hope J. Leichter, "Kinship and Casework" (Groves Conference, Chapel Hill, N.C.: April 6, 1959), mimeographed; Hope J. Leichter, "Kinship and Casework," National Conferences on Social Welfare (May 15, 1961), mimeographed.
9. Sanford N. Sherman, "The Concept of the Family in Casework Theory," in *Exploring the Base for Family Therapy,* Nathan W. Ackerman, ed. (Family Service Association of America, 1961).
10. Gerald R. Leslie, "Implications and Recurrent Themes," *Marriage and Family Living,* XIX, No. 1 (February 1957), proceedings of the Family Research Conference.
11. *Social Scientists' Advisory Meeting, Working Paper: Summary of Deliberations, June 20–21, 1960* (United States Department of Health, Education, and Welfare, Social Security Administration), mimeographed.
12. Harold L. Wilensky and Charles N. Lebeaux, *Industrial Society and Social Welfare* (New York: Russell Sage Foundation, 1958); William F. Ogburn with Clark Tibbits, "The Family and Its Functions," in *Recent Social Trends,* President's Research Committee on Social Trends (1933), Vol. 1.
13. Speech at Washington International Center, Washington, D.C.: May 31, 1961, unpublished.
14. Gunnar Myrdal, *Beyond the Welfare State* (New Haven: Yale University Press, 1960).
15. Walter B. Miller, "Implications of Urban Lower-Class Culture for Social Work," *Social Service Review,* XXXIII, No. 3 (September 1959), 219–236.
16. Housing Act of 1949, Public Law 171, 81st Congress, 1st session.
17. Jay Rumney, "The Social Costs of Slums," Hanan C. Selvin, "The Interplay of Social Research and Social Policy in Housing," "Social Policy and Social Research in Housing," *Journal of Social Issues,* VIII, No. 1, 2.
18. Paul F. Wendt, *The Role of the Federal Government in Housing* (American Enterprise Association, Inc., 1956), p. 2.
19. Leo Grebler, *The Role of Federal Credit Aids in Residential Construction,* Occasional Paper 39 (National Bureau of Economic Research, 1953), 55–56.
20. Svend Riemer, "Sociological Theory of Home Adjustment," *American Sociological Review,* VIII, No. 3; "Maladjustment to the Family

Home," *American Sociological Review*, No. 5 (October 1945); Raymond F. Sletto, *Housing Standards and Mental Health* (National Housing Agency, September 1945), mimeographed; Robert K. Merton, "The Social Psychology of Housing," *Current Trends in Social Psychology*, Wayne Dennis *et al.* (Pittsburgh: University of Pittsburgh Press, 1951).

21. Personal Communication, Marc Fried, Center for Community Studies, Harvard University Medical School.

22. Marc Fried, "Developments in the West End Research," paper presented at the 25th Anniversary of the Department of Psychiatry (Massachusetts General Hospital, October 15, 1960), processed; Irving Rosow, "The Social Effects of the Physical Environment," *Journal of the American Institute of Planners*, XXVII, No. 3 (May 1961); Daniel M. Wilner and Rosabelle Price Walkley, "Housing Environment and Mental Health," in Benjamin Pasamanick, ed. *Epidemiology of Mental Disorder*, No. 60 (American Association for the Advancement of Science, 1959).

23. Wendt, *op. cit.;* Grebler, *op. cit.;* Catherine Bauer, "Redevelopment: A Misfit in the Fifties," in Coleman Woodbury, ed., *The Future of Cities and Urban Development* (Chicago: University of Chicago Press, 1953).

24. C. Hartley Grattan, "Senator Flanders: Intelligent Conservative," *Harper's Magazine,* CC, No. 1196 (January 1950).

25. For an annotated bibliography of studies prior to 1951, see Peter H. Rossi, *Why Families Move* (New York: The Free Press, 1955).

26. Early projects in Philadelphia, Chicago, Cleveland, and Milwaukee are described in Woodbury, *op. cit.* Regarding Washington, D.C., see Charles Henry Lewis, *Redevelopment of Marshall Heights,* M.A. dissertation (Washington, D.C.: American University, 1954); Edward J. Mack, Jr., *Survey of a Proposed Redevelopment Area* (Washington, D.C.: Housing and Home Finance Agency, 1953). For more recent studies see Kurt W. Back, *Slums, Projects and People: Social Psychological Problems of Relocation in Puerto Rico* (University of Puerto Rico, August 1959), mimeographed; Martin Millspaugh and Gurney Breckenfeld, Miles L. Colean, ed., *The Human Side of Urban Renewal* (Baltimore: Fight-Blight, Inc., 1958); Herbert J. Gans, "The Human Implications of Current Redevelopment and Relocation Planning," *Journal of the American Institute of Planners*, XXV, No. 1 (February 1959); Marc Fried and Erich Lindemann, "Sociocultural Factors in Mental Health and Illness," *American Journal of Orthopsychiatry,* XXXI, No. 1 (January 1961).

27. Elizabeth Wood, "Public Housing and Mrs. McGee," *Journal of Housing*, No. 11 (December 1956).

28. Resolution of the Executive Council of the American Federation of Labor-Congress of Industrial Organizations, February 1956, cited in James C. Vadakin, *Family Allowances* (Coral Gables, Fla.: University of Miami Press, 1958). See also James C. Vadakin, *Children, Poverty, and Family Allowances* (New York: Basic Books, Inc., 1968).

29. Bureau of the Census, United States Department of Commerce, *Current Population Reports*, Series P-60, No. 35 (January 5, 1961).

30. In the study cited, low income was defined as "equivalent" to an income of not more than $2,500 in 1957 dollars for a four-person family. Robert J. Lampman, "The Low Income Population and Economic Growth," Study Paper No. 12 for the Joint Economic Committee, Congress of the United States (December 16, 1959).

31. Secretary Arthur S. Flemming, address to the Governor's Conference (San Juan, Puerto Rico: August 4, 1959); Secretary Abraham Ribicoff, statement to the House Ways and Means Committee (February 15, 1961).

32. Maurine McKeany, *The Absent Father and Public Policy in the Program of Aid to Dependent Children* (Berkeley: University of California Press, 1960).

33. Alexander Leighton, *Human Relations in a Changing World* (New York: E. P. Dutton, 1949).

34. Alvin L. Schorr, *Filial Responsibility in the Modern American Family*, United States Department of Health, Education, and Welfare, Social Security Administration (1960), pp. 19–20 and 33–37 (reprinted here as Chapter 7, "Social Security and Filial Responsibility").

35. Leichter, *op. cit.;* Eugene Litwak, "Occupational Mobility and Extended Family Cohesion," *American Sociological Review*, XXV, No. 1 (February 1960); "Geographic Mobility and Extended Family Cohesion," *American Sociological Review*, XXV, No. 3 (June 1960); Ethel Shanas, "Some Sociological Research Findings About Older People Pertinent to Social Work," *Toward Better Understanding of the Aged* (New York: Council on Social Work Education, 1958).

36. Reuben Hill, "The American Family Today," in Eli Ginzberg, ed., *The Nation's Children* (New York: Columbia University Press, 1960), Vol. I; David Mace, "Family Life—Blueprint for the Future," *Conference Proceedings* (Golden Anniversary White House Conference on Children and Youth, Inc., 1960); *Social Scientists' Advisory Meeting, op. cit.; Some Planks in a Political Platform for Social*

Welfare (National Association of Social Workers, 1960); *Social Work's 1961 Priorities for Federal Legislation* (National Association of Social Workers, 1961); Nelson N. Foote and Leonard S. Cottrell, *Identity and Interpersonal Competence* (Chicago: University of Chicago Press, (1955); Clark W. Blackburn, "The Family Is Basic to Mental Health—A Proposal for an Official Family Charter," *Highlights*, XXII, No. 2 (February 1961).

37. Ida C. Merriam, "Social Welfare Expenditures, 1958–59," *Social Security Bulletin*, XXIII, No. 11 (November 1960).

38. Wilensky and Lebeaux, *op. cit.*

39. Margaret Mead, "Is College Compatible with Marriage?" *Washington University Magazine* (St. Louis, Missouri; June 1960).

40. David Riesman, "The Search for Challenge," *Kenyon Alumni Bulletin* (January–March 1959). Regarding psychological moratorium, see Erik Erikson, *Childhood and Society* (New York: W. W. Norton & Co. 1950); *Young Man Luther* (New York: W. W. Norton & Co., 1958).

41. Talcott Parsons and Robert F. Bales, *Family, Socialization and Interaction Process* (New York: The Free Press, 1955), chap. 1.

42. Oscar Handlin, "The Social System," *Daedalus*, XC, No. 1 (Winter 1961).

43. Lee Rainwater, Richard P. Coleman, Gerald Handel, *Workingman's Wife* (New York: Oceana Publications, 1959).

44. Otto Pollak, "Interrelationships Between Economic Institutions and the Family," *Social Security Bulletin*, XXIII, No. 10 (October 1960).

45. *Ibid.*

46. John Cassell, Ralph Patrick, and David Jenkins, "Epidemiological Analysis of the Health Implications of Culture Change: A Conceptual Model," *Annals of the New York Academy of Sciences*, LXXXIV (December 8, 1960).

47. *Social Scientists' Advisory Meeting, op. cit.*

PART III

The Air We Breathe

AUTHOR'S NOTE

Disparate essays make up this part and the next. They are plucked from other contexts where they had other primary meanings. Placed together, they make a point that required years, especially a Fulbright year abroad, for me to learn. We tend to see the circumstances in which we live as inevitable, pre-ordained. While we rail at the deficiencies of our society, or mourn them, or deny them, each according to his nature, we all treat our society as much less malleable than in fact it is. Experiences of England and France are introduced to emphasize how different are the choices that are open to us. We three nations are profoundly alike in real and spiritual resources—richer and poorer but as the world goes, rich, democracies, allies, industrialized, bureaucratized—and yet profoundly different in our management of ourselves.

Parts III and IV deal with distinguishable aspects of the malleability of our society. In Part III we are concerned with the relationship of people to their physical and social environment. We seem able to grasp this relationship as a stream flowing in one direction or the other, people impinging on environment or vice versa. But the relationship is not a stream in either direction; it is a continuous series of interactions of which the viewer sees only each moment's equilibrium. So deeply are we immersed in interaction with our environment that we may be quite unconscious of it, much as we are unconscious of the air we breathe. Because we are unconscious of it, we may take its effects as part of the natural order—that is, fated. Yet we change the air and, in the end, vitally affect our lives.

Chapter 10 is pitched at a personal level: the ways in which a man's feeling or behavior depend upon his food or shelter. The following three essays are pitched at a social level: the responsiveness of our cities (and the men in them) to social and economic influences of which we seem to be ignorant and of which, indeed, the origins and usefulness may have become obscure. To change our cities, and man's fate, it may be necessary to take hold of these patterns themselves. Chapters 11, 12, and 13 trace the influence of various administrative, taxing, and planning policies in undermining our most strenuous efforts to improve our cities.

10

The Nonculture of Poverty

This chapter picks no quarrel with the term "culture of poverty" when it is used in a dynamic sense to express the interplay of circumstance and attitude. Rather, it is concerned with the corrupt use of the term that is gaining currency—among some whose prejudices it supports and among some who are clinicians and social scientists and ought to know better. In the corrupt usage, the culture of poverty is a thing in itself—a world outlook with obscure origins and only an accidental relation to reality.

The main purpose of this chapter is to say something about the material determinants of attitude and behavior. To pretend that things or artifacts were all would, it must be conceded, be as simple-minded as to declare that attitudes and rituals are all. It is difficult to describe the flowing interplay of thing and feeling. It is even more difficult to keep it in mind. Therefore, I shall be offering you one vulgarization to correct another.

Two brief, introductory observations may be useful. First, the attitudes that are associated with the culture of poverty—orientation to the present, passivity, cynicism—are a realistic response to the *facts* of poverty. It is true that such attitudes undermine "higher horizons" programs and other promising demonstration

Reprinted from the *American Journal of Orthopsychiatry*, XXXIV, No. 5 (October 1964).

programs. Many poor people are not persuaded that they can gain the carrot at the end of the stick: the price of admission and the attendant furs, perfumes, escorts, and manners to take them to more Beethoven concerts, or anything but child neglect and acute weariness if a woman is successful at leaving public assistance for a job of her own. The husbanding of psychic energy that accrues from passivity and scepticism must be important to psychic survival. I find myself often unsure whether a poor person does well to yield these attitudes. Is anyone sure?

Second, we may readily dismiss those who take a static view of poor people's attitudes in order to remain unaroused or to feel superior. There are more subtle seductions than these, however. For if poverty rests preeminently upon a system of values, how important becomes the sociologist who alone investigates and understands these values! How important become the teacher, the social worker, and the psychiatrist who are the powerful agents of value change! If, on the other hand, ordinary facts like money and housing are important, they are the domain of clerks and laborers or, at any rate, other technicians. Not many professionals are prey to such seduction. But in a speech every now and then one hears the patronizing phrases and the circular reasoning that betray the siren call of self-importance.

Having considered these unsupported observations, we turn to the main business: to say a little about the effects of food and housing on attitude and behavior. It seems reasonable to start with food. In one of the Hoovervilles that are scattered around Paris, my wife and I became acquainted with a young Antioch student, working as a volunteer welfare aide. The people with whom she worked lived in the same type of huts and ate about the same food as those whom they were helping. Christine will not mind my observing how much she looked and acted like her clients. She showed dry, cracked skin, gray color, nondescript appearance, and from early morning to night a great weariness. She showed unbelievable responsibility in her work, but not liveliness, not optimism, not the venturesomeness that brought her to Paris.

Christine is not scientific evidence, but knowing her sent me to the clinical literature on nutrition. Following prolonged malnutrition, says one author,

> . . . various functional changes occur. These functional changes are manifested clinically by symptoms usually placed in the neurasthenic syndrome. They include such common complaints as excessive fatigability, disturbances in sleep, inability to concentrate, "gas," heart consciousness, and various queer bodily sensations. . . . Occurrence [of these symptoms] as a manifestation of tissue depletion of certain nutrients is undoubted.[1]

Who, having worked with poor people, has not wondered about their aches and complaints? Do we wonder about drive and ambition? These are the symptoms that turn up with prolonged malnutrition: "depression, loss of ambition, impotence, and a sensation of being old." Again, "depression, apathy, and lethargy." [2] A more circumstantial account of depression appears in a study of a number of pregnant women. Their diet had been low in thiamine, calcium, and iron, and was improved to a recommended standard.

> Previously [says the report] they worried about everything; housework bothered them; they were unhappy and slovenly in appearance. After three weeks on the improved diet they were much tidier, their faces were washed, and their hair brushed. They were obviously interested in their appearance. They were also much more cheerful.[3]

Finally—translating here from sociology to psychology—what of the observed tendency of poor people to project blame on others? *

---

* A sociological classification of values distinguished between those who feel subjugated by nature, those who feel in harmony with it, and those who feel mastery over it [Committee on the Family of the Group for the Advancement of Psychiatry, *Integration and Conflict in Human Behavior* (New York, Group for the Advancement of Psychiatry, 1954)]. An element of the culture of poverty would be to feel subjugated or, at most, in harmony with nature. [Frank Riessman, *The Culturally Deprived Child* (New York: Harper, 1962). Leonard Schneiderman, *The Culture of Poverty: An Effort at Definition,* based on a doctoral dissertation at the University of Minnesota (Minneapolis: July 1963).] That is, if a poor person had difficulty, he would tend to project responsibility on other forces.

A study of Canadian service personnel, who were being inadequately fed, arrived at this conclusion.

> They blamed their poor performance not on themselves but on their officers. . . . Their reaction was that the other men had cheated. Everything was wrong except themselves.[4]

It is probably not necessary to labor this point. In any case, I am not a nutritionist and cannot add anything to what the authors explicitly report. It is only important to observe that many symptoms that we take to be psychological or cultural may quite possibly be a consequence of malnutrition.

One fact ought, perhaps, to be added. Despite all our talk about poverty in the United States, it comes hard to us to believe that many people do not eat adequately. However, we estimate that at least one in five families with children chooses between an adequate diet and some other neccessity. At least five million of our families with children probably lack some element of a minimally adequate diet.[5] We can speak a little more exactly of our public assistance programs. In no more than two or three states in the country do public assistance agencies budget an amount for food that would be judged adequate by Department of Agriculture standards.[6]

A discussion of the impact of nutrition on attitudes, then, does not deal with a rare phenomenon.

Let us turn now to housing. The following effects appear to spring from poor housing:

> . . . a perception of one's self that leads to pessimism and passivity, stress to which the individual cannot adapt, poor health, and a state of dissatisfaction; pleasure in company but not in solitude, cynicism about people and organizations, a high degree of sexual stimulation without legitimate outlet, and difficulty in household management and child rearing; . . . relationships that tend to spread out in the neighborhood rather than deeply into the family.[7]

On the whole, effects such as those on health (safety, respiratory and skin diseases, and so forth) must be fairly evident. Let us look at the consequences for child rearing, as these are somewhat more complex.

It is common in the slum areas of our cities to observe how extensively family life is conducted out of doors. The pattern may be attributed to habit brought along from Puerto Rico, Europe, or rural areas, depending on which slums one is considering. On the other hand, in a Chicago settlement house, I once questioned the soundness of a daily program for young teenagers. They were kept away from home every night until curfew at 10 P.M. It did not seem entirely a good thing. This is the response that was made. These thirteen- and fourteen-year-olds live in apartments so small that there is no room for them. When they have eaten, sitting on stools and a couch around the table, they drift outside. They will be either at the settlement house or on the streets, but not at home. A study of poor families in the District of Columbia makes this point quite simply.

> In these so-called apartments [it says], there is no place for children . . . The close quarters, the drabness, the lack of something to do drives these children into the street.[8]

Elsewhere, the same group of researchers observe that these children escape parental control at quite early ages, some as early as the age of six.[9] One can hardly overlook the relevance of such a pattern to the fact that children cannot reasonably be kept inside. One must ask the simple questions first. If young children are to be disciplined they must be within reach.

The children are, of course, sometimes inside the house. They come home to sleep, for example. A study of working-class Negroes at the close of World War II found that the majority slept less than five hours a night. The reason: there simply was not enough space for beds.[10] Lack of sleep has its effect on children's growth and behavior. Implications spring to the mind, too, about sexual relations between adults and about sexual stimulation of children. Nor can one discuss child-rearing with a mother who has slept only three or four hours and then leap to a cultural explanation of her lethargy.

When children play inside the house they are, of course, underfoot. No studies seem to be available of the tension that arises between parents and children in very crowded quarters, perhaps because the result is obvious. There *has* been a study of families with two children living in two-bedroom apartments. *They* experience tension—because there is not room for the activities of parents and children.[11] One more study must be cited, because it touches on a matter of interest. The University of Sheffield has looked into the manner in which young people make career choices. Where do they get guidance? What advice from their parents? For children in decent housing there are other answers, but youths in crowded housing get virtually no help from their parents. Whatever their activity, they are together in one room. A youngster is having dinner, a cowboy show is on television, a neighbor drops in to see the mother. Guidance takes place in passing and is conducted in shouts. "You can't hang about this summer, boy! Not like last year." And the boy's irritated answer is swallowed up in the neighbor's story, or in a television gun-battle.[12]

The observations being made must be self-evident. They *ought* to be self-evident. If a reasonable counseling interview requires separation and freedom from interruption, then many of the normal transactions of families must also. If these simple physical requirements are not met, family relationships must develop in other ways. They may develop in such patterns as children freed or freeing themselves early from parental control; a good deal of disorganization in everyday routines; little studying, poor work habits and poor self-discipline; and little communication between parents and children. When these characteristics have been seen among the same people year after year, one may come to think there is some binding relationship. Then one talks about a culture of poverty. But perhaps the link, simpler and less esoteric, lies in the stark facts of the way they live.

An excuse has already been offered for oversimplifying matters. In conclusion, however, two points should be made about the interrelationship of thing and attitude. For this purpose, it is necessary to say a few words about the Negro sit-in movement. Sociologists have now confessed that, according to all that they knew of it, the sit-in movement should never have happened.[13] Their problem—a common professional problem—lies in being captured by smooth trend curves. Moreover, psychiatrists and sociologists had achieved an oh-so-thorough understanding of the

Negro matriarchal family. The boy, indulged but never treated as fully masculine, grows into a cavalier but withal insecure and undependable man. And he learns, for his survival, to turn aggression in or off. How, indeed, could such youths organize demonstrations with semimilitary care and precision? How, indeed, can they walk picket lines with a discipline that does not yield to the most humiliating provocations?

There are several answers. Two of them are relevant here. First, Negro parents have for many years taught their children the principles of equality and opportunity. As studies reported with care, these precepts were surrounded with cautions, stated and merely cued, that Negroes nevertheless may not assert their rights. ("We are equal but some are more equal than others.") Professionals have been attentive, have they not, to the denial rather more than to the affirmation? Yet, when the time came when it was not too dangerous, clearly the affirmation was present to be acted upon. Second, it must be suspected that Negro youngsters are using for rather a different purpose a discipline which they learned from segregation. Because they had to, they learned to block out white people from perception and to seem not to observe their behavior, whether provocative, humiliating, or only private. This discipline is not greatly altered, merely converted to a different purpose, in picketing and sitting-in.* Thus, it may be important that professionals attend to the affirmative attitudes of poor people. Further, habits and attitudes are like bits of furniture. They may persist in the clutter of one's accumulations, but in new circumstances they readily serve new objectives.

In Central America, where iodine deficiency has long been common, dolls and religious statues are modeled with typical goiters. So much do the Indians accept goiters as normal! [14] The current image of the attitudes of poor people may contain its goiters.

---

* Ralph Ellison put the point poignantly (*The Reporter,* March 25, 1965): "The American Negro has a dual identity, just as most Americans have, and it seems to me ironic that the discipline out of which this present [civil rights] action is being exerted comes from no simple agony—or simple despair—but out of long years of learning how to live under pressure, of learning how to deal with provocation and with violence. It issues out of the Negro's necessity of establishing his own value system and his own conception of Negro experience and Negro personality, conceptions which seldom get into the sociology and psychology textbooks."

If poor nutrition and poor housing go unrelieved, they may produce many of the attitudes associated with poverty. Because the
attitudes persist, one should not suppose that they are an independent phenomenon. They depend on material circumstances
and probably are functional in relation to them. One asks too
lightly that the attitudes be yielded if it is not also assured that
they are no longer needed. Finally, it is not necessary to envision
a thoroughgoing change of attitudes. If material circumstances
are changed, attitudes that seemed wholly negative may be
turned to constructive purposes.

NOTES

1. N. Jolliffe, "The Pathogenesis of Deficiency Disease," in N. Jolliffe,
   F. F. Risdall, and P. R. Cannon, eds., *Clinical Nutrition* (New York:
   Harper & Brothers, 1950), p. 33.
2. A. Keys, "Caloric Deficiency and Starvation," in Jolliffe *et al., op.
   cit.,* pp. 241–324.
3. F. F. Tisdall, "The Relation of Nutrition to Health," in Jolliffe
   et al., op. cit., p. 748.
4. *Ibid.*
5. Mollie Orshansky, "Children of the Poor," *Social Security Bulletin,*
   XXVI, No. 7 (July 1963), 3–13.
6. Ellen J. Perkins, "How Much Is Enough?," presented at the Biennial
   Round Table Conference of the American Public Welfare Association, Washington, D.C. (December 6, 1963). *Report of the Advisory
   Council on Public Assistance* (Washington, D.C.: United States Government Printing Office, 1960).
7. Alvin L. Schorr, *Slums and Social Insecurity* (Washington, D.C.:
   United States Government Printing Office, 1963), pp. 31–32.
8. Roscoe Lewis, report quoted by Eve Edstrom, *Washington Post*
   (January 12, 1964), p. E 5.
9. Hylan Lewis, "Child-Rearing among Low Income Families," presented at the Washington Center for Metropolitan Studies (Washington, D.C., June 8, 1961).
10. Allison Davis, "Motivation of the Underprivileged Worker," in
    W. F. Whyte, ed., *Industry and Society* (New York: McGraw-Hill
    Book Co., 1946).
11. Robert O. Blood, Jr., "Development and Traditional Child-Rearing
    Philosophies and Their Family Situational Consequences." Unpub-

lished doctoral dissertation, University of North Carolina (Chapel Hill, N.C.: 1952).

12. M. P. Carter, *Home, School, and Work* (London: Pergamon Press, 1963).

13. Kurt W. Back, "Sociology Encounters the Southern Protest Movement for Desegregation," presented at the International Sociological Association (Washington, D.C., September 1962). Everett C. Hughes, "Race Relations and the Sociological Imagination," presented at the American Sociological Association (Los Angeles, August 28, 1963).

14. W. J. Darby, "International Cooperation in Nutrition Research and Planning," *Science, Technology and Development* (12 vols.), Vol. III, *Agriculture* (Washington, D.C.: United States Government Printing Office, 1962).

11

The Population Recipe

Deterioration of our central cities, congestion, and urban sprawl are generally discussed in economic terms—tax rates, costs of urban land, accessibility to markets, and so forth. The forces that people our cities are more often discussed in family and psychological terms. The desires that people have of their living quarters vary over a wide range even in wealthy countries, including the spacious and highly industrialized ideal of the United States, the compact dwellings served by commissaries and other central services that are the Swedish ideal, and the much more modest demands of Englishmen and Frenchmen. Yet we may take these desires as given, for, where one lives, they seem universal.

Here we shall set out the desires that appear to determine where Americans want to live. The matter has been carefully studied; in accord with the evidence, we shall assume that the most powerful determinant of neighborhood choice is the family's life stage and composition. We shall turn then to the limiting external force that is now widely recognized—segregation. Finally, we shall look to British experience for hints of other forces that determine the manner in which we people our cities.

An excerpt from *Slums and Social Insecurity* (London: Thomas Nelson and Sons, 1964). Reprinted by permission.

THE DESIRE

A young couple, newly married, willingly rents an apartment within the city.[1] The housing needs that the couple recognize are readily met though their income is modest. Within the next decade, they will have young children and feel the need for more space. Income has risen, but not more rapidly than their need for housing. They move in search of room and a more desirable neighborhood for raising children—that is, away from the center of the city and toward good schools and desirable neighbors. They may continue to rent and, as need presses or income permits, they may move more than once. (A substantial percentage of moves, to be sure, are primarily to secure a better job.)

The decade that follows—the husband is now between thirty-five and forty-five—is the most difficult in the sense that resources seem to fall shortest of the need for housing. Family income is approaching its maximum, but the family is at its largest and each of the children requires more space. Moreover, grandparents who have been living separately may now need to be given shelter. The family is likely, if it can, to purchase a house in a suburban area, containing the maximum amount of space possible. In the final half-dozen years in which any child remains in the home, the family may purchase a second, more adequate house. Afterward, when the children have left, there is for the first time enough—even more than enough—room. The parents may remain in the house until illness or widowhood makes another arrangement preferable.

Obviously factors other than the stage of family life cycle play a part in the housing that families desire. Families may wish to move upward socially or simply to live better—"consumership." [2] The relation of family cycle, ambition, and consumership to housing need, as they exist today, are only practices. Some care must be taken to avoid promoting practices into laws. No one knows that families will continue to behave this way a few years from now. For example, Raymond Vernon[3] predicts that because of a trend to decentralized work, the low-income population in New York City will increasingly be moving into what are now regarded as the suburban areas. Middle-income families will move farther out, the high-income families into apartments in the center of the city. Who will venture to predict what sort of housing will be regarded as most desirable for children when this shift takes place?

The middle-class wish is not everyone's wish. Some poor families say that "above all, they want better housing and neighborhoods." [4] Others do not want to make the suburban pilgrimage; like suburbanites, they prefer to live among their own. More important, the middle-class wish is not everyone's attainment. A family's wish may be interfered with in many ways. It may not have enough money or credit to find the kind of housing that would be desired. If the family is Negro, its choices of housing will be severely restricted. If the family is large, it may turn out that suitable housing is not available. If the family is uneducated, or uneducated in city ways, it may not be acceptable in the house of its choice. If there is not a tidy family relationship, that is, if the father is missing, a family may find its choice of housing restricted.

One perceives that these handicaps overlap and reinforce each other: The family headed by a mother is very likely also poor and uneducated. The Negro family is very likely also large and poor. These, then, are the families who are likely to be found in substandard housing. Others frequently found in substandard housing are the old people, who stay on where they have lived for some time, and rural immigrants, foreign and domestic. In terms of values and purposes, slum dwellers include a wide range of kinds of people. One study names fourteen different types, ranging from the "sporting crowd" who seek a good time to the "models" who seek to improve others. [5]

We can now develop the recipe for populating a city. Start with the family cycle and mix in ambition and certain ideas about the good life. Fold in a desire to be accessible to work. (In New York City, the location of perhaps half the residents has been influenced by such a desire.) Flavor with the image of the image,* for example, the idea that children should live in the suburbs *because*

---

* The term is Boulding's. [Kenneth E. Boulding, *The Image* (Ann Arbor: University of Michigan Press, 1956).] He is "prepared to argue that at least in the social sciences a great deal of the empirical research that goes on today is . . . directed toward the image of the image."

certain kinds of families with children live in the suburbs. For spice, see that some people have not enough money, some have not the right skin color, and others are just not right. The yeast in the mixture is general population increase and movement from country to city. The yeast provides mystery, as all demographic totals tend to be inflated over former years, regardless of other population trends.

The recipe produces a fairly uniform product from one large city to another, particularly in the Northeast.[6] Residences in the city proper, or core city, tend to be smaller and smaller. These may be expensive apartments, built for the unmarried, the young couples, and the older families whose children are gone. Or they may be deteriorating houses, once more adequate in space, now converted to multifamily use. Except for high-status, high-rise, and high-cost enclaves, the core city shows a concentration of low-income and Negro or other ethnic groups. With or without children, the low-income and nonwhite families are barred from moving very far outward. They are highly crowded and they press toward the areas that were formerly middle class—the so-called gray areas. Children grow up and leave, however, and old people stay behind. The most central areas of the city are cleared for renewal; if not, they show high rates of vacancy. Therefore, overall figures on the number of people per acre in the central areas nevertheless show a decline.

Some areas of the core city concentrate social problems as hospitals concentrate illness. Disabled in one or another of the fashions that have been noted, families go there not for cure but because it is their only haven. Nearly one-fourth of New York City's neighborhoods are such infirmaries, according to one estimate.[7] In addition to poor income, education, and housing, their residents show a concentration of individual and family tension and social conflicts.

The areas around the city contain the families who are not inside the city—the families with children who are not Negro or poor. The suburbs are not quite homogeneous, of course. The outward movement of the city may engulf smaller cities and rural slums with the families they contain. The decentralization of jobs to the suburbs exerts a pull on low-income as well as higher-income families. Speculation is beginning to appear, tinged with trust that retribution may yet be done, that the present situation may reverse. The outward pressure of jobs and people may produce blight in the nearer suburbs, while public activity is reducing density and blight in the city's center.[8]

SEGREGATION

Segregation provides a visible and well-understood limitation on the housing desires of Negro families. It makes low-income and many middle-income Negroes particularly exploitable. It makes deteriorated housing continuously and highly profitable, even though the housing market may ease. The problem of Negroes is a problem of the city's center; it is not apparent how one problem can be solved without working out the other. As Ashmore writes: "The agrarian past is finished; the heart of our Nation is in the great cities now, and they are afflicted with a grave disease." [9]

It appears that the number of Negroes living in segregated areas in the cities has been increasing in the past two decades. Negroes have been moving from South to North and from country to city. As segregation by neighborhood has been more typically a northern than a southern pattern, Negroes have in effect been moving to areas where neighborhood segregation would be practiced. The "black belts" in nine large cities that were studied "concentrated within their expanding districts in 1940–1960 most of [the cities'] increase in nonwhite population. . . ." [10] The suburbs, in which so much of the overall population increase was taking place, were highly successful in excluding Negroes. For example, a committee reported to the board of county supervisors in a suburban area of Washington, D.C.: "There is almost no adequate housing to be obtained for Negroes in Fairfax County at any price. . . ." [11]

Because birth rates for Negroes tend to be higher than average and because migrants tend to be young, Negro births would continue to create pressure for housing for some time even if migration dropped off.[12] Large-scale building and financing, a comparatively recent development, lend themselves to race restriction. House-by-house turnover depends on individuals and the immediate economic situation. A large developer, on the other hand, may consider that he risks the entire development or being unable to build elsewhere in the county if he sells to a Negro family. By 1950, from 56 per cent (Philadelphia) to 81 per cent (Chicago) of the nonwhite population of the country's major cities were concentrated in nonwhite areas. With increased building in the last decade, the changes that were appearing in 1950 appear to have accelerated. Results for cities may be summarized as follows:

> . . . extension of the boundaries of minority residence areas, the replacement of white by nonwhite population, the creation of new minority colonies, and a limited amount of dispersion. . . . The housing made available by departing whites has evidently been sufficient in many cities to permit considerable decongestion of the minority group residence areas and probably an improvement in the quality of housing available to these groups, as well.[13]

It has been pointed out that federal policies have, in some measure, been responsible for these developments. Abrams[14] classifies the possible positions open to the federal government, once it entered the housing field, as "moral," "parrying," and "discriminatory." On the whole, he observes, the policy has been parrying and sometimes discriminatory. Initially, the Federal Housing Administration, taking what it regarded as a conservative business point of view, encouraged "homogeneous" neighborhoods. By 1949 this policy was beginning to be modified. From that time until comparatively recently, federal policies followed state policies, permitting discrimination when the state permitted it. Apart from deliberate policy, federal insurance and urban renewal programs provided the mechanisms that could produce segregation. These programs are largely responsible for mass building. In urban renewal, mixed slum neighborhoods have been leveled and replaced by all-white neighborhoods—all-white by policy or because the new dwellings were too expensive for Negroes. The displaced Negroes moved to public or to private housing, either of which might be segregated.

Private business practices—permitted or supported by community attitudes—lie at the heart of the problem. It is widely thought that the entry of Negroes into a neighborhood causes a decline in housing values. However, study of the matter by the Commission on Race and Housing produces the conclusion that there are a "diversity of price outcomes according to circumstances. . . ." Indeed, price improvement or stability occurred more often than price declines.[15] Whatever the fact, because of the belief as well as for other reasons, Negroes found themselves unable to buy through real estate agents or to borrow from lenders in order to live in white neighborhoods. "Mortgage credit," concluded the United States Commission on Civil Rights, ". . . is often denied to members of minority groups for reasons unrelated to their individual characters or credit worthiness, but turning solely on race or color." [16] As a result, the Commission estimated that less than 2 per cent of the new homes insured by FHA since 1946 have been available to nonwhites.[17] Local government may also play a role in maintaining segregation, using zoning and condemnation powers for deliberate, if unexpressed, racial purposes. A well-publicized illustration is Deerfield, Illinois, which elected to establish a park on the site of a housing development that was to be available for Negro purchase. However, much less open policies may accomplish the same purposes—for example, minimum lot sizes that limit building to the relatively well-to-do.

These problems have been documented and analyzed with considerable care in the last few years. Their relevance here is to note the impact on residential patterns in a city. Dealing broadly with national income figures, it appears that Negro families pay less on the average for housing than do white families,[18] reflecting their lower-income status. As might therefore be expected, Negro families live in poorer housing. In 1960, one in five of all dwellings in the United States was deteriorating or dilapidated, but almost half the dwellings occupied by Negroes were in such conditions.[19] Where it is possible to evaluate the housing that is secured in relation to payment, however, it becomes clear that more than low income is involved in the poor housing of Negroes; indeed, Negroes pay more for poorer housing. For example, in the "pilot" area of Baltimore, investigators found Negroes paying an average of ten dollars a month more for quarters that were (on a

rating scale) 19 per cent worse than those of their white neighbors.[20] Even in areas of high Negro concentration in Newark,
New Jersey, Negroes were paying higher rents than whites.[21] In
Chicago, "nonwhites pay signficantly more than whites for housing of roughly equivalent quality and spaciousness." [22] White
families receiving aid to families with dependent children in Chicago in 1960 were paying an average rent of $65 a month com-
pared with $83 for nonwhite families. (The additional rent paid
by nonwhites in Cook County was costing taxpayers 3.4 million
dollars a year.) The nonwhite families had poorer housing.[23] In
New Orleans, a neighborhood rehabilitation program sent rents
up "more than was reasonable." Perhaps, the reporter says, this is
"the inevitable price of doing rehabilitation . . . for an ethnic
group which does not have access to the entire supply of housing." [24]

The difficulties that higher rentals or payments create must be
self-evident.* Obviously, it is harder for low-income families to
adjust to overpayment for shelter than it would be for those who
have more income. For low-income families, the choice is frequently between payment for shelter or for food or clothing. Payment for school, or books, or anything else that may bring future
gain is quite a sacrifice. These difficulties create others to rein-

---

* It is implicit in the difficulties poor housing creates and should, perhaps, be
made explicit that people are in pain. The statement of Rudolph Reed may
serve to make this point.

> . . . I am not hungry for berries.
> I am not hungry for bread.
> But hungry hungry for a house
> Where at night a man in bed
> May never hear the plaster
> Stir as if in pain.
> May never hear the roaches
> Falling like fat rain.
> Where never wife and children need
> Go blinking through the gloom.
> Where every room of many rooms
> Will be full of room. . . .

Rudolph Reed was, in the end, denied a house "in a street of bitter white"
because he was "oakener than others in the nation."
From "The Ballad of Rudolph Reed," in *The Bean Eaters* by Gwendolyn
Brooks. Copyright © 1960 by Gwendolyn Brooks Blakely. (Reprinted by permission of Harper & Row, publishers.)

force them. In an effort to meet the cost, Negro families share quarters and live crowded together. Consequently, in our major cities the percentage of families that are crowded (living more than one to a room) is two to four times as high for Negroes as for whites.[25] As Negro families tend to be confined to the gray areas of cities, they reuse housing which is, therefore, ill-adapted to their numbers and patterns. Housing deteriorates further under this onslaught, and landlords and city officials take the position that the situation is impossible to correct. (Indeed, if the surrounding circumstances are accepted as given, they may be right.) In the effort of the Negro family to improve its circumstances (or because it cannot meet a payment and is evicted), it moves from house to house—thus piling a new expense on the others.* If the family manages to buy, it may pay a higher interest rate in order to get credit. For Negroes particularly, it is costly to be poor.

We perceive that segregation has two simultaneous and interacting effects. On one hand, it places on the neighborhoods in which Negroes may live a burden that must destroy the neighborhoods. On the other hand, by adding to the cost of housing, segregation takes from poor people money that might otherwise be devoted to self-improvement. Thus, segregation locks in both sides of an equation that has come to seem a fact of American life: Poor Negroes equal slums. Therefore, they dominate the sections of the city that they dominate and families who feel themselves different seek to live anywhere else.

BRITISH EXPERIENCE

The population recipe produces results in the United States such as this:

> . . . Manhattan proves . . . to be a borough of the very poor and very rich. In the core counties surrounding Manhattan, though pockets of low-rent housing are important and growing

---

* Though Negroes move across county and state lines at a lower rate than whites (4 per cent of Negro families in a year compared with 7 per cent for whites), they move more often within the same county (18 per cent of Negro families in a year compared with 12 per cent for whites). ["Mobility of the Population of the United States, March 1959 to 1960," *Current Population Reports*, Series P–20, No. 113 (Washington, D.C.: United States Department of Commerce, Bureau of the Census, January 22, 1962).]

more so, the general pattern is of a heavy commitment to the middle-income groups. Beyond these counties, in the inner ring, the high-income professionals and managers place their dominant stamp on the income distribution.[26]

The description is not alien to British cities. Suburban areas have far higher proportions of the upper social classes than any other grouping of British towns. Inside the city of London, the East End has been widely known as poor, and professional and white-collar workers begin to dominate the St. Marylebone section. The core of Liverpool is predominantly working class and England is beginning to know streets that are largely West Indian. Still, a contrary process takes place. In the regeneration of old areas, middle-class families live side by side with poorer families.[27] To an American onlooker, British cities tend less than American cities to separate their residents by economic level, like so many cultures of bacteria in a dish of agar. The process of stratification does not appear to be so far advanced.

For example, the town of Dagenham in Great Britain is widely regarded as a one-class district. It has the lowest "social class index" of 157 towns in its population class.[28] A study of Dagenham compares its population with that of the country as shown in Table 11–1.

Table 11–1

OCCUPATIONAL CLASS OF MEN IN DAGENHAM AND ENGLAND AND WALES

	Dagenham 1958 (per cent)	England and Wales 1951 (per cent)
Professional and managerial (Social Classes I and II)	4	18
Clerical and shop workers (Portion of Social Class III)	7	8
Skilled manual (Remainder of Class III)	49	44
Semiskilled manual (Class IV)	22	16
Unskilled manual (Class V)	18	14
Total	100	100

Source: Peter Wilmott, *The Evolution of a Community: A Study of Dagenham after Forty Years* (London: Routledge and Kegan Paul, 1963).

Apparently a good many potential residents in the highest social classes (I and II) have elected not to live in Dagenham. The 14 per cent of the population they represent are evenly distributed among the other three social classes. As the author observes, the residents of Dagenham are "by no means all semi-skilled or unskilled workers." [29] This epitome of a working-class district in England is a full-scale rainbow compared to the single-income, single-class, single-color districts that may be found in the United States.

It is difficult to compare stratification or dispersion of the population in the United States and Great Britain except on the basis of impression, for relevant comparative data are not available. Whatever one takes the fact to be, an appraisal of British governmental processes must suggest powerful forces acting for dispersion that are not present in the United States. Two particular elements of governmental process are significant—the power of government in relation to housing and city planning, and general revenue policies.

The national interest of the United States in housing is mainly expressed in two mechanisms, mortgage insurance and urban renewal, which operate through private enterprise. To be sure, the government supports a program of public housing, but it represents only about 1 per cent of the total housing supply. Government loan guarantees, by contrast, account for almost half the mortgages on owner-occupied property.[30] Thus, the main weight of the federal investment in housing is felt in private enterprise as, indeed, Congress intends.

In Great Britain, on the other hand, the central mechanism of housing policy appears to be public housing—whatever the party in power. The tradition of public housing under national legislation goes back unbroken to 1919. After 1951, when materials were still scarce and building licensed, local authorities were forbidden to allocate more than half the licenses to private builders. In the decade from 1951 to 1960, local authorities built 1.5 million houses and private enterprise 1 million.[31] After determined efforts by a Conservative government, by 1958 private enterprise was building more houses annually than the government. From then on, however, the shortage of privately rented housing mounted to a first-class political issue. Under voter pressure and without any effective alternative in sight, public housing began to move ahead again.

Relatively greater British reliance on government is expressed in other ways. New towns are administered by development corporations and the New Towns Commission—financed from the Exchequer and appointed by the government. Experimentation with home loans takes the form of municipal lending rather than encouragement of commercial lending. Incentives to private enterprise, when the government seeks them, are neither so grand nor so imaginative as in the United States. The chief incentives are mainly negative, that is, the removal of rent controls and diminishing the competitive advantage of public housing. Rehabilitation grants offer an affirmative subsidy to private owners. When even these are clearly lagging the remedy sought is governmental. "The Minister," it was announced, "will be prepared to consider the use of compulsory powers" in relation to owners who are unwilling to proceed voluntarily.[32]

It is not only the use of government as a vehicle which distinguishes British from American housing policy, but also the authority lodged in *central* government. As authority must sometimes be tracked to its den through the minutiae of day-to-day administrative procedures, it may be difficult to define. The point has been put for Great Britain as follows:

> Although the responsibility for initiating and carrying out the various services rests by statute with the local authorities, all the statutes dealing with the more important services are freely sprinkled with provisions which show that in effect the approval of some department of the central government is necessary for the exercise of many of the functions. The general requirement that all applications for loans must be approved and the district audit of accounts are other powerful weapons of control. Local direction is often further controlled by Government departments as a result of decisions taken by the Government on grounds of national policy as to the scale of capital expenditures and the purpose to which it should be directed, e.g., the changes in the years since 1945 as to the number of new houses which it was the objective of government policy to secure. Where particular services are grant-aided, further controls may become applicable. . . .[33]

One can discern at least two qualitative differences from the authority of the federal government in the United States. First, United States government authority in the field of housing is essentially negative, resting in the power to withhold grants-in-aid. The British government also exercises control via its subsidy program; one does not underestimate the effectiveness of such a device. But the British government has, besides, explicit authority in the field of housing. In controlling standards of space and equipment in public housing, it controls a large proportion of the housing market. It approves local building regulations, and may withhold permission for local government borrowing. The central government has broad powers to plan land use; its approval is required for municipal development plans. Second, in the United States, the general overlooking of municipal functioning lodges in the separate states. In their relations with municipalities, states do not necessarily further federal ends; they may at times appear to interfere with federal ends.

These differences do not mean that the British government is all-powerful or in every respect more powerful. For example, land values were fixed in 1947, permitting subsequent condemnation for public purposes at the 1947 value. Legislation in 1954 and 1959 established the right of the owner to receive current values on the private market, returning to a concept much closer to that which is current in the United States. Another example is provided by comparing the enforcement of housing codes. Despite the problems of enforcement in the United States, there are enforcement campaigns—from city to city, from time to time. Violations must be at least as common in Great Britain, but enforcement action appears to be even less frequent. The city of Birmingham, England, has demonstrated that condemnation and rehabilitation may be an effective route to improving the supply of housing, but there has been little attempt to assess penalties when the housing code is violated.*

Despite counter-trends and conflicting evidence, the results of

* Local authorities may be inhibited because some of the housing they own is in as poor condition as the private dwellings against which they would act. For example, when Sheffield, England, embarked on a rehabilitation grant campaign, public-housing tenants suggested that the city improve its own housing as well. ["Municipal Notes," *The Sheffield Star* (November 9, 1962).]

the two qualitative differences—explicit and undiffused central government authority in Great Britain—is that the government's policies, more than those of the United States, are likely to be felt emphatically and across a broad range of housing issues. Some of the effects are as follows.

Building at the peripheries of their towns and, more recently, beyond their borders, municipal authorities have distributed their tenants across the countryside. For example, the London County Council built over half its pre-World War II dwellings outside the County of London,[34] a process that accelerated after 1946. As we shall see, public-housing tenants are a fairly diversified cross section of the population. New town policy, though aimed at decentralization, has consistently held diversification in its sights. The Town Development Act of 1952, as Mr. Harold Macmillan explained, sought "a balanced and healthy creation capable of varied life and employment." [35] Partly because they bind houses to employment, New Towns tend to select young families with moderate or middle incomes. Special provisions have, therefore, been made to correct the concentration of a single age and family type. Allocating housing to the aged and newly married inevitably introduces some low-income families to New Towns, but they are few and the effect is not deliberate. At least, the New Towns relocate moderate and middle-income families beyond the metropolitan suburbs where they would otherwise congregate.

Stratification rests on more than such choices as city center versus suburb. Developments separated by a single city street may house quite different income groups. Public housing developments in the United States may suffer from being isolated within their own neighborhoods. As a matter of legal requirement, their households fall within a fairly narrow income range. The situation in the United Kingdom is different. In every income bracket except the very highest, upward of a fifth of all households are found in public housing.[36] Of those with more than £40 a week, 12 per cent are in public housing.* In a sector of the

---

* Because a direct conversion of pounds sterling into dollars can be misleading, income is given in British currency. In 1961, the time these figures represent, the exchange rate was $2.80 to the £. In an attempt to take into account differences between the two countries in cost of living, a number of students

housing market representing almost a quarter of the dwellings in Great Britain, a sector conspicuously stratified in the United States, all incomes are substantially represented.

Along with government housing policy, general revenue policies affect the population recipe. The financing of local government appears to mask and diffuse the net cost of low-income families to the authorities that plan to house them. The percentage of its costs which local government must meet out of its own taxation is lower in the United Kingdom than in the United States. In 1960 central (or state) government grants provided 42 per cent of local government revenue in England and Wales (not counting support of the nationalized services) and 27 per cent in the United States.[37] More pointedly, the central government subsidy is heavily weighted in favor of localities with the largest number of dependent children.[38] Therefore, the concern of a locality about the tax-paying ability of the children's parents would be somewhat muted. When a locality clears an area, it makes a special annual payment to other localities to which its families move. Such payments add to the impact of central government policies, although negotiated by local authorities.

Further, there is an important difference between the two countries in the relation of housing to education. (In both countries, education is the single largest local government cost.) In Great Britain, the locality that plans to house a family is generally different from and smaller than the education authority. Therefore the decisions to house and to educate are made separately. Furthermore, the cost of education is spread around a larger local unit. In the United States, though there may be two independent authorities, they are likely to cover the same geographic area. The cost of education will be much in the minds of the planning or housing authority. For these reasons, local governments in Great Britain may see poor families as less onerous financially. Consequently, they may be more receptive to proposals for housing them.

Factors that have less to do with government policy are also involved in determining residential patterns in the two countries.

---

have assumed that $5 equal £1. Thus, £40 was a very respectable income indeed.

The rate at which families move is more than twice as high in the United States as in England. Consequently, any wish to fit into a general sorting out of population finds faster expression. Traditional attitudes toward others are important; for example, racial segregation is not nearly so significant in Great Britain.

We perceive, in sum, that government taxing practices and the relationship of central to local government tend to promote mixed residential patterns. As a partial result, Great Britain probably does not suffer to the same degree as the United States from a tendency to limit the residents of each neighborhood to a fairly narrow income range. Although the United States may profitably emulate some British practices, obviously others are deeply rooted in different circumstances and traditions. Emulation is not the point. Most of the practices described were developed for reasons having little or nothing to do with desirable residential patterns. The public administrator seeking to encourage or assure healthy neighborhood patterns may give no thought at all to obscure issues of tax subsidy and central and local government relationship. If he thinks of these issues at all, they may seem well beyond his reach to alter. Yet these issues determine residential patterns.

NOTES

1. This description relies on "Consumer Strategies," by Janet Abu-Lughod and Mary Mix Foley, in Nelson N. Foote, Janet Abu-Lughod, Mary Mix Foley, and Louis Winnick, *Housing Choices and Constraints* (New York: McGraw-Hill Book Company, 1960). Basic data that helped shape or confirm the description are contained in Peter H. Rossi, *Why Families Move* (Glencoe, Ill.: The Free Press, 1955); Kurt W. Back, *Slums, Projects, and People: Social Psychological Problems of Relocation in Puerto Rico* (Durham, N.C.; Duke University Press, 1962); Beverly Duncan and Philip M. Hauser, *Housing a Metropolis—Chicago* (Glencoe, Ill.: The Free Press, 1960); John Mogey and Raymond Morris, "An Analysis of Satisfaction" (1960), typescript; Chester Rapkin and William G. Grigsby, *Residential Renewal in the Urban Core* (Philadelphia: University of Pennsylvania Press, 1960); Edgar M. Hoover and Raymond Vernon, *Anatomy of a Metropolis* (Cambridge: Harvard University

Press, 1959). A description for farm families consistent with this one is May L. Cowles, "Changes in Family, Personnel, Occupational Status, and Housing Occurring over the Farm Family's Life Cycle," *Rural Sociology,* XVIII, No. 1 (March 1953).

2. Gerald R. Leslie and Arthur H. Richardson, "Life-Cycle, Career Pattern, and the Decision to Move," *American Sociological Review,* XXVI, No. 6 (December 1961).

3. Hoover and Vernon, *op. cit.*

4. Hylan Lewis, "Child Rearing Among Low Income Families," address to the Washington Center for Metropolitan Studies (June 8, 1961).

5. Donald M. Salzman, "Redevelopment Effectiveness Contingent on Understanding Slum Occupants," *Journal of Housing,* XIII, No. 8 (August-September 1956).

6. Duncan and Hauser, *op. cit.;* Rapkin and Grigsby, *op. cit.;* Hoover and Vernon, *op. cit.; A Strategy for Improving Housing in Greater Cincinnati* (New York: Action, Inc., 1960), mimeographed; Advisory Commission on Intergovernmental Relations, *Metropolitan Population Disparities: Their Implications for Intergovernmental Relations* (Washington, D.C., 1965).

7. *New Dimensions-New Directions, 1959–1960 Annual Report,* Community Service Society of New York (March 1961).

8. Hoover and Vernon, *op. cit.;* and Philip Stoddard Brown, "How Economic is the Washington Community?", address to the Washington Center for Metropolitan Studies (February 9, 1961).

9. Harry S. Ashmore, *Other Side of Jordan* (New York: W. W. Norton, 1960), pp. 154–155.

10. Alfred McClung Lee, "The Impact of Segregated Housing on Public Schools," in William W. Brickman and Stanley Lehrer, eds., *The Countdown on Segregated Education* (New York: Society for the Advancement of Education, 1960), p. 77.

11. "Report of the Fairfax County Minimum Housing Standards Committee on a Proposed Housing Hygiene Ordinance" (Fairfax, Va., November 1960), mimeographed.

12. Eunice and George Grier, "The Impact of Race on Neighborhood in the Metropolitan Setting," address to the Washington Center for Metropolitan Studies (April 27, 1961).

13. Davis McEntire, *Residence and Race* (Berkeley: University of California Press, 1960), pp. 50–51, p. 164.

14. Charles Abrams, *Forbidden Neighbors* (New York: Harper and Brothers, 1955).

15. McEntire, *op. cit.,* p. 164.

16. *Civil Rights,* excerpts from the 1961 United States Commission on Civil Rights Report (Washington, D.C.: United States Government Printing Office, 1961), p. 65.

17. *Report of the United States Commission on Civil Rights, 1959* (Washington, D.C.: United States Government Printing Office, 1959).

18. Louis Winnick, "Economic Constraints," *Housing Choices and Housing Constraints, op. cit.,* Chapters 1 and 2.

19. *1960 Census of Housing, Advance Reports—Housing Characteristics,* HC(A1)-52 (United States Department of Commerce, Bureau of the Census: April 1961).

20. Martin Millspaugh and Gurney Breckenfeld, Miles Colean, ed., *The Human Side of Urban Renewal* (Baltimore, Md.: Fight-Blight Inc., 1958).

21. Jean Gottman, *Megalopolis* (New York: The Twentieth Century Fund, 1961), p. 709.

22. Duncan and Hauser, *op. cit.*

23. *Facts, Fallacies and Future* and *Addenda to Facts, Fallacies and Future* (New York City: Greenleigh Associates, 1960).

24. Millspaugh and Breckenfeld, *op. cit.*

25. McEntire, *op. cit.;* Duncan and Hauser, *op. cit.*

26. Raymond Vernon, *Metropolis 1985* (Cambridge, Mass.: Harvard University Press, 1960).

27. Edward Carter, *The Future of London* (Baltimore: Penguin Books, 1962).

28. C. A. Moser and Wolf Scott, *British Towns,* Centre for Urban Studies, Report No. 2 (Edinburgh: Oliver and Boyd, 1961).

29. Peter Willmott, *The Evolution of a Community: A Study of Dagenham after Forty Years* (London: Routledge and Kegan Paul, 1963).

30. United States Department of Commerce, *Statistical Abstract of the United States* (United States Government Printing Office, 1962), tables 554 and 107A.

31. Ministry of Housing and Local Government, *Housing Return for England and Wales, 30th September 1962,* Command 1853, H.M.S.O. (October 1962).

32. Ministry of Housing and Local Government, *Improvement of Houses,* Circular No. 42/62 (August 1962).

33. Royal Institute of Public Administration, *New Sources of Local Revenue* (London: George Allen and Unwin Ltd., 1956), p. 20.

34. T. W. Freeman, *The Conurbations of Great Britain* (Manchester: Manchester University Press, 1959).

35. Harold Macmillan, in *Hansard, Parliamentary Reports* (February 25, 1952), pp. 723–727.

36. Unpublished data for 1961 from the Family Expenditure Survey furnished by the Ministry of Labour.

37. Ministry of Housing and Local Government, *Local Government Financial Statistics,* England and Wales, 1960–1961, Table IX, H.M.S.O. (1962); also, *Local Government Finance,* England and Wales, The General Grant Order, 1962, H.M.S.O. (1962). (For the United States, see note 30.)

38. Ministry of Housing and Local Government, *Local Government Financial Statistics, op. cit.*

12

Housing Codes and Financial Incentive

New building alone will not provide suitable housing for all or most of our poor families. We produce housing units each year equivalent to less than 3 per cent of the total supply. A quarter of our housing units are deteriorating, dilapidated, or lack a sanitary facility.[1] Because it is unreasonable, not to say uneconomical, to think of replacing all these buildings, there has been growing attention to techniques and incentives that will rehabilitate housing.* The Housing Act of 1961 made special provision for loans for home improvement and rehabilitation. Many of the newer programs are aimed at neighborhood rehabilitation.

Widespread failure to attempt to enforce housing codes is one of the reasons that so much housing is now substandard. Housing codes are a key element of successful rehabilitation programs. Yet, in current circumstances, it is not at all certain that they can be or will be broadly enforced. When violations become a public scandal, the laws may be enforced with some effect. (In the past decade, slum fires in Baltimore, Brooklyn, Chicago, and Cleve-

An excerpt from *Slums and Social Insecurity* (London: Thomas Nelson and Sons, 1964).

* A deteriorating house, according to the Census Bureau, has one or more defects "that must be corrected if the unit is to continue to provide safe and adequate shelter." A dilapidated house "does not provide safe and adequate shelter."

land, killing fifteen, touched off, respectively, a new ordinance, a grand jury investigation, an angry article in a national magazine, and an enforcement campaign.) But where public attention is not engaged, violations are endemic.

It is when a rehabilitation effort or an investigating body spotlights a neighborhood that it becomes clear how widespread violations are. In the course of the Mack-Concord rehabilitation project in Detroit, it developed that 10 per cent of the houses had to be demolished and 60 per cent of the remainder remodeled.[2] Following upon one of the fires mentioned above, the Kings County, N.Y., grand jury instigated a test survey in fifteen blocks. Before the survey 567 violations had been filed; the survey showed 3,122. The violations found were: rodent and vermin infestation, a wide range of fire hazards, no toilet facilities, no running water, unclean public areas, and overcrowding.[3] Major studies of housing codes in Philadelphia and in fifty of the smaller towns of New York State indicate that, although even the smallest communities control new building, the regulation of existing housing receives little attention.[4] Said the President's Advisory Committee on Housing as long ago as 1953:

> There is a direct and important relationship between the ownership of housing for low-income families and the creation of slums. Irresponsible and unconscionable people are persistently taking advantage of the cities' failure to enforce their occupancy controls and their health, sanitation, and safety codes.[5]

There is no doubt that codes have been more seriously enforced in some cities than in others. In selected neighborhoods, there have been highly successful demonstrations of the effectiveness of code enforcement accompanied by other rehabilitative techniques. In the Hyde Park-Kenwood section of Chicago, for example, with the power of the University of Chicago backing a community conference, community deterioration that appeared inevitable was halted. Baltimore's "pilot project" has been referred to as another example of successful rehabilitation.[6] Nevertheless, the accounts of these efforts read like accounts of guerilla warfare. The enemy is never vanquished but only pressed back. Eternal vigilance is required and, in most places, it is lacking.

Some cities embark on programs of code enforcement without even immediate success—Miami and New Orleans, for example.[7] In any case, the excitement that is generated around a handful of successful demonstration projects is a significant indication of the level at which codes are enforced—or failing to be enforced— generally.

Why is it so difficult to enforce codes? Why do they not work effectively? These questions have many overlapping answers. Codes are antiquated and unclear. Penalties embodied in the law are slight. Owners find it cheaper to pay occasional fines than to make repairs. Municipal enforcement staff is likely to be under-manned. Political interests may not support or may actively sab-otage enforcement efforts. Those who must move because of crowding or because buildings are condemned cannot find even equivalent housing. Absentee owners cannot, without a good deal of trouble, be put under sufficient pressure to produce results. Resident owners may not have the resources to make improve-ments. Tenants may resist enforcement because it means rent rises or that some must move. Even with momentarily successful enforcement, in the long run industry, highways, and other blighting influences take their toll.

Some of the remedies of these difficulties are obvious; some that are less obvious are being developed. A sustained, effective en-forcement program requires a clear law, an adequately manned enforcement body with defined responsibility and support from city hall. In addition, Baltimore has pioneered the use of a hous-ing court, a court thoroughly familiar with housing practices that has special counseling services at its disposal.[8] It has been sug-gested that there should be special organizations to take over and rehabilitate properties that a city forces onto the market.[9] Atten-tion has focused on methods for dealing with recalcitrant land-lords. It has been suggested that any building should be con-demned and torn down if the cost of repairs is equivalent to 50 per cent of its "true" value.[10] New York City has the power to seize buildings, make repairs that are necessary to meet minimum requirements, and recapture the cost out of rent collections.[11]

One cannot review the problems of code enforcement and the solutions that are proposed without concluding that they are superficial, if grave, symptoms of a deeper maladjustment. The hard fact is that profitmaking incentives run counter—so far as the maintenance of housing is concerned—to the best interests of the poor. Tax laws and condemnation procedures combine with the peculiarly vulnerable situation of those who are poor to pay the most profit for the worst housing. Where enforcement is pitted day by day against the businessman's incentive to make profit, enforcement is bound to be in trouble.

Factors that operate in this fashion are the municipal property tax, the capital gains tax, the basis for calculating value in condemnation, and the depreciation allowance. The property tax, as it is based upon valuation, increases as property is improved. Any number of observers and some studies testify that such a basis for a tax leads to neglect of property.[12] A more touching bit of testimony is an information bulletin offered to homeowners by the government of Dayton, Ohio. "Protect your home!" it reads. "Home maintenance does not increase your taxes." [13] Obviously, the possibility of a tax rise deters not only those who are interested in profit, but some who might be improving their own homes as well.

The capital gains tax may have a somewhat similar effect. If the owner's income tax bracket is high, his interest centers on ultimate resale value. Though resale value in other property may depend on maintenance, in low-income neighborhoods it is likely to depend on the value of the land and on the net income that is being produced. Thus, the profit lies in holding on while the land becomes valuable and, secondarily, in current income. Neither of these incentives needs involve maintenance of a building. Condemnation procedures provide one of the reasons that income production determines resale value. Even though income is not a consideration in setting the property tax, it is recognized as a factor in negotiating payment upon condemnation. Thus, for this reason, too, money spent on maintenance brings little cash benefit. The most deteriorated property may eventually be disposed of to the city at a profit.*

---

* Summarizing the opinions of "outstanding authorities" in the investment field, Arthur M. Weimer writes: "Most investors . . . recognize that renewal programs . . . have the effect of bailing out the owners of various properties

The depreciation allowance provides a further element that influences the maintenance of housing. In federal income tax the depreciation allowance treats real estate like machinery and equipment. A high percentage may be written off in early years and declining percentages subsequently. Though a single owner may not receive credit for more than his own cost, upon resale the property may be depreciated all over again. The point of largest profit, therefore, is in the early years. After six or eight years, if tax cost is a consideration for the owner, it becomes profitable to sell and purchase a new property.* This effect may seem to operate in the opposite direction from the effect just cited of the capital gains tax, which leads to holding on to property for increase in value. What the two provisions have in common, however, is that they return no profit for the cost of maintaining or improving center-city property. Maximum profit lies in manipulating tax and financial matters quite unrelated to building maintenance. It lies also in securing high short-term profit: this translates into securing the most tenants that are feasible in the space available, with the lowest possible expenditure.

---

and of shoring up the expectations of the owners of many near-in properties."
[Arthur M. Weimer, *Investors and Down Town Real Estate—Opinion and Comment*, Technical Bulletin No. 39 (Washington, D.C.: Urban Land Institute, November 1960), p. 19.]

* That rapid turnover of real estate is one result of the depreciation allowance was, in effect, agreed upon in hearings before the House Ways and Means Committee. The administration had proposed that profit on the sale of real estate be treated as ordinary (not capital gains) income to the extent of past depreciation. Speaking for the proposal, Dan Throop Smith, professor of finance at Harvard University, asked that it apply especially to real estate. "The opportunities for manipulation," he said, "are particularly great in buildings, where properties can be and are bought, depreciated and sold by a succession of owners in a way that is not feasible for most machinery and equipment." [Hearings before the Committee on Ways and Means, House of Representatives, 87th Congress, 1st session, May 12, 15, 16, 17, 18, and 19, 1961, (Washington, D.C.: United States Government Printing Office), Vol. 2, pp. 955, 1044.] Speaking against the administration proposal, Richard H. Swesnick, of the National Association of Real Estate Boards, said: ". . . Owners would be unwilling to sell real estate except in distress or other highly unusual circumstances, and purchasers would be unwilling to acquire new real property which, as a practical matter, they would have to treat as a permanent investment." (*Ibid.*) Obviously other issues are involved, but the point here is that there is agreement from diverse sources that the depreciation allowance produces rapid turnover.

In practice, the effect of these financial incentives turns out approximately as follows:

> One of the great problems of slum ownership is the fact that slum properties have changed hands many times during their life and each person has expected to make a profit from the sale. The tendency therefore is to raise the price of the building and to seek ever-increasing rents at the same time the physical value of the building is deteriorating. As a building gets older and the price the latest owner pays for it represents more and more profit taking in successive sales, the latest owner must crowd more and more tenants in a dying building to meet his costs, thus hastening its dilapidation. . . . The latest owner may possess what is little more than a pile of bricks and kindling wood, but he presumes the building has a high residual value. If he is lucky, the local government will come along and buy him out at an inflated price for some public work or a slum clearance project.[14]

As buildings are subdivided, crowded, and more deteriorated, they become well-nigh impossible to maintain. Moreover, it becomes impractical to try to maintain neighboring houses. They too become a profitable investment and slum development spirals. If the city steps in and tries to enforce codes strictly, some owners will be able to make no profit at all. They paid too high a price and counted on overcrowding. If it is suggested that the municipality take the houses over, paying for their reasonable value, it develops that this is less than the current owner paid for it. Why pick on him? Once begun, the cycle is not readily interrupted.

The operation of these incentives may be illustrated in connection with two of the slum fires mentioned earlier. Chicago: A six-apartment structure was bought for $25,000. These were converted to twenty-four apartments, in which seventy-two people lived. Collecting more than $1,800 a month in rentals, the landlord recovered his equity in less than eighteen months. Before the building burned down, inspectors found ninety-eight violations of the building code and the owner paid $305 in fines and court costs.[15] Cleveland: A single-family frame house erected in 1885 was bought in 1954 and converted for use by five families. A total investment of $5,000 produced a return of $271 a month. With expenses kept to a minimum, until the fire the owner received an annual return on his investment of over 50 per cent.[16] These examples, though they could be multiplied, are extreme. However, a 30 per cent return for substandard dwellings is not unusual.[17]

Why would families permit themselves to be so exploited? Because they cannot find dwellings elsewhere. Racial restriction is a primary way that families are caught. Offering instruction on "How to Build a Slum," Timothy J. Cooney writes:

> The importance of renting to minority families cannot be over-emphasized . . . they are the key. . . . The all-white sections are essential to successful slum development. They must be maintained (until we decide to turn *them* into slums). The reason is obvious. With a "white only" barricade (or other slums) surrounding our developing slum, there will be no escape for our selected tenants.[18]

Housing shortages also play a role. Paradoxically, inability to pay for adequate housing may play a role. Though space in slums is expensive, no one cares if the people are crowded. In adequate housing, uncrowded, low-income families may find the per-person cost more than they can afford. In sum, low-income families inhabit a company town. They cannot break out. And the company's incentive, in nineteenth-century fashion, is to take the most and give the least.

The significance of these forces cannot be overestimated. The maintenance of existing housing is far more important to poor families than the building of new housing. Programs to rehabilitate existing housing will be token remedies unless the underlying processes can be made healthy. There are not enough, and there cannot be enough, housing inspectors in the country to assure code enforcement against the tidal forces that present public policies establish.

Proposals made from time to time attempt to deal with these problems at two levels. At a somewhat superficial level, a city may offer special tax benefits to developers in return for agreement about rental levels and maintenance.[19] Similarly, cities might exempt improvements from taxation or tax them at a lower rate.[20] Though cities may be using these devices increasingly, they establish a special benefit within a tax structure that is basically unchanged.

Other proposals attempt to reach the profit motive at a deeper level. It is suggested that the price of land upon condemnation should, in some fashion, avoid reflecting undue profits based on slum operation. In addition to saving the municipality money, the effect would be to lower land values—and rents—substantially unless improvements were made.[21] It is proposed that total depreciation permitted on real estate be limited to 100 per cent. Owners who depreciate their property for tax purposes should be required to establish reserves for maintenance.[22] In 1935, Peter Grimm, a New York real estate broker, suggested that municipal taxes should be based in part on "earnings or imputed earnings." [23] Somewhat similar are proposals to base municipal taxes on land value.[24] Taxing land or earnings would provide an incentive to divert funds into building maintenance, for maintenance would no longer increase the tax but might presumably increase the value of the property or its earnings.

Complex fiscal questions are involved in many of these proposals. Cities face the considerable problem of maintaining sufficient tax revenue, and the property tax is so far their primary source. Any reduction in tax levels or encouragement to businesses to locate outside the city would exacerbate a problem that is already serious. The proposals are not listed here for the kind of careful discussion they would require. They are listed to indicate that there are probably ways to redirect economic forces to maintain rather than to destroy the housing that poor families require. The tide of these forces would be of greater overall effect than anything that individual slum families themselves might do.

NOTES

1. United States Department of Commerce, Bureau of the Census, *1960 Census of Housing, Advance Reports—Housing Characteristics,* HC(A1)—52 (Washington, D.C.: April 1961).
2. Mark K. Herley, "Rehabilitation," speech to Potomac Chapter of the National Association of Housing and Redevelopment Officials (Washington, D.C.: March 9, 1961).

3. New York Academy of Medicine, "Report of the Subcommittee on Housing of the Committee on Public Health Relations," *Bulletin of the New York Academy of Medicine*, XXX, No. 6 (June 1954).
4. "Housing Codes are Subject of Two Major Studies," *Journal of Housing*, XIV, No. 6 (June 1957).
5. President's Advisory Committee on Government Housing Policies and Programs, *Recommendations on Government Housing Policies and Programs, a Report* (Washington, D.C.: United States Government Printing Office, December 1953).
6. Martin Millspaugh and Gurney Breckenfeld, *The Human Side of Urban Renewal*, Miles Colean, ed. (Baltimore, Md.: Fight-Blight, 1958).
7. "Home Builders' Slum Cures Failing," *Journal of Housing*, XIII, No. 5 (May 1956).
8. Richard W. Bateman and Herbert J. Stern, "Baltimore's Housing Court Clinic," *Social Work*, VI, No. 4 (October 1961).
9. *Partnership for Renewal, a Working Program*, report of a demonstration project by the Office of Development Coordinator, City of Philadelphia, in cooperation with the Housing and Home Finance Agency (September 1960).
10. Frank P. Zeidler, *Making Urban Renewal More Effective*, 12 reports to the American Institute for Municipal Research, Education, Training, Inc. (Washington, D.C.: August 1960–July 1961), p. 32.
11. "City to Get Power of Slum Seizure," *New York Times* (March 19, 1962).
12. George W. Mitchell, "The Financial and Fiscal Implications of Urban Growth," *Urban Land*, XVIII, No. 7 (July–August 1959); Mable Walker, "Tax Responsibility for the Slum," *Tax Policy*, XXVI, No. 10 (October 1959); Boyd T. Barnard, "Impact and Accomplishments of ULI Panel Studies," *Urban Land*, XX, No. 6 (June 1961); Mary Rawson, *Property Taxation and Urban Development* (Washington, D.C.: Urban Land Institute, 1961), Millspaugh and Breckenfeld, *op. cit.*
13. Department of Urban Renewal, "Normal Home Maintenance Does Not Increase Your Taxes!" *Information Bulletin* (Dayton, Ohio: undated).
14. Zeidler, *op. cit.*
15. Arthur Rubloff, "Let's Tax Our Slums to Death," *Look*, XXIV, No. 26 (December 20, 1960).
16. Daniel Seligman, "The Enduring Slums," *Fortune* (December 1957).
17. Zeidler, *op. cit.*

18. Timothy J. Cooney, "How to Build a Slum," *The Nation,* CLXXVIII, No. 7 (February 14, 1959), 141.
19. Nash, *op. cit.;* Westchester Council of Social Agencies, Inc., Committee on Housing, *Report of the Committee on Housing* (White Plains, New York: July 1957).
20. Walker, *op. cit.*
21. Zeidler, *op. cit.;* Ernest M. Fisher, "A Study of Housing Programs and Policies," prepared for the United States Housing Administrator (January 1960). Included as a working paper in *Interim Report on Housing the Economically and Socially Disadvantaged Groups in the Population.* Conference sponsored by the Metropolitan Housing and Planning Council of Chicago in cooperation with ACTION, Inc. (February 26–27, 1960).
22. Rubloff, *op. cit.*
23. Walker, *op. cit.*
24. Zeidler, *op. cit.;* Rawson, *op. cit.;* Thomas F. Johnson, James R. Morris, and Joseph G. Butts, *Renewing America's Cities* (Washington, D.C.: The Institute for Social Science Research, 1962).

13

Planned Development: Vision or Fancy?

The United States Committee of the 1966 International Conference of Social Work prepared an analysis of urban development
in the United States and its implications for social welfare[1] that
was comprehensive and scholarly. One might add a footnote here
and quibble about a detail there. On the other hand, the report
suffers from a set of mind which is interesting precisely because it is subtle and natural and leads to serious misinterpreta-
tions. This disposition, which may be characteristically American,
is to look at the future with totally unwarranted optimism, even
while the past may be judged more realistically. In truth, contrary to the United States Committee's conclusion, the prospects
for planned urban development must be adjudged dim.

It is widely agreed that the present state of our cities is chaotic,
both in the physical terms of structures and traffic and in the
functional terms of civic relationships. For example, Washington,
D.C., a city meant to be a republican symbol, is dominated by
borrowed aristocratic and baroque forms: Broad avenues that
had been invented for rich men's carriages and easy control of

Adapted with permission of the National Association of Social Workers from
the article by the same title in L. K. Northwood and William Key, eds., *Social
Welfare and Urban Development* (New York: National Association of Social
Workers, 1966).

street demonstrations; great squares used in England and France for the homes of the wealthy few; and monumental buildings.[2] It is debatable that these forms are well suited to a people's city or even that they were well suited before automobile traffic captured the broad avenues for its own. Yet so hungry are we for urban order that a legible street pattern, whether functional or not, helps to make Washington one of our most satisfying cities. Our civic relationships are in a similar state. Archaic and indeed conflicting forms melt together into poorly fitting and overlapping patterns. Most cities lack systematic administration and a sense of integrated purpose. The few that for a time project a sense of effective leadership—New Haven, Detroit, and Atlanta are the current examples—are heralded throughout the land.

The United States report offers as an explanation the "basic proposition" that planning has been hampered by a laissez-faire tradition. The proposition is put as follows:

> Acceptance of the developmental and social planning approaches to the management of urban affairs has been deterred in the United States by the persistence of attitudes and social structures based on *laissez faire*.[3]

Such an observation sinks into the American mind without resistance. It seems a soft impeachment. If that is the problem and everyone so exercised, we may readily expect to see improvement. And we are easily misled by a plausible historical sequence. First we had laissez faire, and now we have the absence of planning. One must plainly have led to the other.

Yet the antagonists today are not private entrepreneurs and an imperial state. That battle has been settled, even if the old slogans are occasionally summoned up. Today's antagonists are rather the old bureaucracies and vested interests against the new bureaucracies. Quite often the structure that needs changing is not some corporation or system of private businessmen but an old and well-established government program—hardly the client that Adam Smith had in mind. In the struggle of established against incipient bureaucracies, the national position has been to avoid frontal attacks and to attempt to accomplish the gigantic tasks we face by establishing new interests—metropolitan planning agencies, urban renewal authorities, community action agencies, regional education laboratories, and economic development authorities—that may operate around the established interests and even obliquely influence them without too much threatening them. Thus, it is not entirely wrong but it is not entirely right to say that the principle being asserted is laissez faire; a more exact term is évitez faire (avoid action).

We have implicitly agreed not to change any existing structure very much, to deal with new problems only by providing increments of money or new programs. As we are nevertheless powerfully moved to bring coherence into our society and to establish human control over economic and technological forces that threaten to overwhelm us, we have turned to paper planning. (Paper planning is the collection of a comprehensive set of ideas and facts about a service or a community without concurrent power to affect events.) The spread of paper planning is not an accident. On one hand, it threatens no one. On the other hand, it offers at least some hope to those who do not understand its fatal defect and at least some activity to the others who, expecting rather little of it, can see no other course and are simply unable to remain passive.

We have more plans, though possibly less planning, than most advanced nations. We have workable programs, community renewal plans, state plans for public assistance, mental health, and education, regional plans for economic development, and all the rest. Is it rash to suggest that turning out these plans has become an exercise much like student themes—cribbed more or less from the teacher or other respectable sources in order to get a grade (or grant), whereupon they are promptly forgotten? Of course the plans, with the requirements for consultation and collaboration that are frequently built into them, are the very stuff out of which red tape and delay are constructed. Thus the paper plans themselves became an instrument of an unspoken and no doubt unrecognized policy of évitez faire.

In the last two decades we have had a remarkable series of laws relating to the city and to planning. Yet none of this legislation undertook to restructure existing interests. In particular, none of the legislation faced two problems that in themselves will defeat the development of a planned urban environment.

The first issue that has never been faced is the creation of a national housing supply that will meet the need of all the antici- pated .population, rich and poor, urban and shortly-to-be-urban. The great housing programs have been impeded and distorted by the pressure on them of the enormous need of poor people to which they were a partial and, except for public housing, a trivial response. Therefore, the poorest and most objectionable have been compressed into urban neighborhoods that forthwith be- come undesirable. The management of these developments are likely to be torn between admitting all desperate comers (and watching the housing deteriorate) and trying to maintain mixed tenancy and respectability (in which case housing becomes over- regulated and offensive to their residents). Our newest devices, demonstration cities and rent supplements, will face the very same problems and may well also go down before them.

It has widely been assumed that a program that would house all our population in standard, uncrowded housing within a few years would be more expensive than we could bear. In fact, it is debatable whether it would be a very great strain. In any case, the more revealing fact is that the costs and programs that are re- quired have not, until very recently at any rate, even been ex- plored.

The second crucial issue that has not been faced is whether the national government, which alone has the necessary scope and power, will take on the exclusionary interests—real estate boards, suburban governments—that establish and maintain vast sanctu- aries from Negroes and poor people. As it happens, they have incidentally established sanctuaries from integrated planning. To try to settle issues for the core city without settling them simulta- neously for the suburbs is hopeless. To try to settle them by agree- ments on planning documents or metropolitan accords is only slightly less hopeless. The difficulty is not a failure of intelligence or a reluctance to negotiate. The difficulty is that, given current values, it is against the interests of those who can avoid it to in- clude minority groups and poor people in their calculations.

We may be forced to face this particular issue soon. After voting rights, segregation of housing is the major visible symbol of civil wrongs and is likely not to be tolerated indefinitely. We have so far approached this problem in the style we prefer, assuring equal access to new housing in which the government has an interest and in various other ways encouraging desegregation. In this particular field more than any other, however, we are being pressed to face the vested interests, the exclusionary interests, head on.

The practice of social work, community by community, clearly reflects the national policy of évitez faire. Ten conclusions of the United States Committee report rotate about words like these: weak coordination, little continuity, relative isolation, imbalance in distribution, and inadequate mobilization. Social work practice is a symbol that the United States is determined to deal with people individually and humanly. In the face of forces that move us toward a mass and impersonal society, the symbol is not unimportant. Nevertheless, social work practice is a symbol only. The homely practice of humanity does not reach many people and does not reach into the major policies that affect them because social work is no more willing than other institutions to yield up its established forms and the benefits that go with them. And despite recent expressions of anger at the profession, the nation does not seem willing to single out social work for restructuring.

In short, it is misleading to suppose that planned urban development has been impeded by remnants of a policy of laissez faire. That view implies freely contending forces that tend, for internal reasons, to eliminate ineffective forms and nourish the best. When the system fails to work, the government may intervene; there is ample precedent for that. While we worry about the present, only rationality is required to improve the future. All that is rather a more cheerful prospect than is justified. Unfortunately, planned urban development has really been impeded by an unwillingness to see private or governmental vested interests eliminated or even much disturbed. Given this tacit agreement, two strategies occur to us. First, we support oblique inducements to change, strategies that will move vested interests in directions that are barely perceived and therefore difficult to oppose. This produces change, to be sure, but it can hardly be called planned change. Second, we encourage paper planning, with the unintended net effect of supporting the status quo. With évitez faire as our policy, the prospect for planned urban development is not so cheerful, after all.

It would no doubt be interesting to look into the reasons that we select a policy of évitez faire. Obviously, an acceptance of self-interest is one. But another reason is that a government as powerful as ours might, if it undertook systematically-planned change, truly manipulate and dominate its citizens. We shall do well to move thoughtfully into such a course. On the other hand, findings of animal studies suggest how late the hour may be. For example, small mammals that are crowded together begin to show pathological symptoms. Their eating becomes disordered and they cannot sleep. In time, they turn vicious and attack one another. When they quarrel about the significance of more space, these mice and guinea pigs in their expensive pens, are they conscious that they are already pathological?

NOTES

1. L. K. Northwood, *Urban Development—Implications for Social Welfare* (New York: International Conference of Social Work, 1966).
2. Lewis Mumford, *The City in History* (New York: Harcourt, Brace, and World, 1961).
3. Northwood, *op. cit.*, Chapter 3.

Community Services: Penalties of Pragmatism

AUTHOR'S NOTE

The chapters in Part IV continue the theme of malleability, dealing explicitly with the organization of community services. Chapter 14 describes the problems in rendering community services in cities just before community action agencies were to enter the picture. Chapter 15 describes the markedly different French pattern of providing social services and its different reaction to a problem that was, in some respects, similar to ours—fractionalization of existing services which, taken together, were miniscule in relation to the need. Chapter 16 attempts to indicate some directions in which the United States might move.

In attempting to make progress in the United States, we have been dominated by what might be called the "grant-in-aid approach" to social reorganization. (A grant-in-aid compels nothing directly but supports specified services or programs—usually, regardless of their context.) We have not anywhere attempted to design and build a modern program of community services suited to modern needs. Rather, we have limited ourselves to setting new services next to old ones or trying to pull old services in new directions by clever offers of money. In the conception of some people at least, the "model neighborhoods" or "demonstration cities" program is intended to achieve genuine restructuring. Realizing that objective depends entirely on whether federal, state, and local governments support or permit restructuring and whether funding levels pass the threshold of providing merely one more increment.

The "grant-in-aid approach" is a major technical device that supports a policy of évitez faire (Chapter 13). In addition to the reasons already offered, évitez faire may appeal to us because, in a nation with considerable conflict and diversity, we seek movement on sufficiently narrow grounds so a majority can be assembled. (See the discussion in Chapter 9 of the principle of direct response.) Whatever the chain of reasoning, the result is that the community services we use are obsolete and confused in their basic structure. The principal explanation for their survival in this form is national acquiescence.

14

Urban Services

Community services are in crisis in the city's center. Many social agencies see the dimensions of the problem; few find themselves in a position to meet the crisis squarely, with economy of effort and breadth of vision at once.

Material on the socially orphaned and the population recipe (Chapters 4 and 11) give hints of the trends that create the need for services; they may be cast a little differently in this connection. As the average income level in the country rises steadily, those with less than the poverty level seem further and further from the average. On the part of the poor, the consequence may be feelings of futility or bitterness which in themselves interfere with self-advancement. On the part of those who are not poor, the gap creates a feeling that something must be done. Sometimes also it creates a feeling of anger and a conviction that the poor themselves must be at fault. (Anger is particularly likely if one can believe that poverty is more or less synonymous with crime and immorality.) In addition to the low-income families who have lived in the city, others enter from rural areas unprepared for city life. Many of the families lack the stable family background which (as we see more easily in retrospect) assured earlier

An excerpt from *Slums and Social Insecurity* (London: Thomas Nelson and Sons, 1964).

immigrant groups a chance for success. These families lack also the open market for unskilled labor which was, at least for the long run, once characteristic of the cities. Urban renewal and highway programs lift the lid on the neighborhoods in which poor families live. Americans could once be unaware; now awareness makes the problem more distressing.

A wide variety of remedies are indicated; among them are certainly community services. The trends that may be described in the general terms above frequently turn out to mean—in personal terms—sickness, passivity, women who work (for very little), children without fathers, fear of moving very far, and self-indulgence (as possible). The recurring combination of these problems has led to the use of the term "problem family." * [1] The term is very far from precise. It may mean that the family suffers from two or three distinct kinds of problems and includes a child who is in some form of danger. Or, it may mean only that the family is chronically late in paying rent. The term and its variants may well have outlived their usefulness. They lump together too many different kinds of families and suggest too easily that their problems rest on personal will and adjustment alone. At any rate, awareness that poverty is a syndrome leads naturally to a search for appropriate services.

The same trends that increase the problem unfortunately diminish the services that are available. Physicians and dentists tend to follow their paying patients to the suburbs.[2] The cities have substantial revenue problems. Public schools in the core city tend to be underfinanced; moreover, they cannot secure sufficient competent personnel. Voluntary welfare agencies also experience difficulty in raising funds. Their income may keep pace with cost of living but not with growing need,[3] and extended waiting periods to receive service are common in certain kinds of agencies

* And its variants: multiproblem, multiple problems, hard core, hard to reach, resistive, chronically dependent, antisocial. The origin of the concept is ascribed to Bradley Buell. He referred to finding that 6 per cent of the families in St. Paul suffered from such a compounding of problems that they absorbed over half the community's services. His word was "multiproblem." "Problem family" was used a decade earlier in England "to characterise a group of families living in squalor and unable or unwilling to make constructive use of the social services." [A. F. Philp and Noel Timms, *The Problem of the "Problem Family"* (London: Family Service Units, 1957), p. vii.]

(mental health clinics, family service agencies). The solutions for diminished services—increased funds and special incentives for professional personnel—may be hard to achieve but are at least easy to state. The organization of services in the central city poses more difficult problems to which there are so far no agreed-upon solutions.

Fundamentally, the city is changing more rapidly than the professions and agencies that cope with its problems. Welfare departments, counseling agencies, health departments, and even schools have centralized their activities in the interests of efficiency and coordination, only to find that the poorest people do not regard "downtown" as accessible. (Settlement houses would have had most difficulty in centralizing their activities. Consequently, they find themselves still dealing with neighborhood needs—better perhaps than any other community agency.) Recognition of the difficulty produces an impulse to station staff members in neighborhoods or at least have them spend more time out of the office. However, other changes have accompanied centralization of services: Agencies have become more professional and more bureaucratic.

Staff time now includes heavy elements of reporting, accountability, conferences, and consultation. It is not only his bodily presence in the neighborhood that is required of a health educator or social worker. His continued presence is required; he needs to subordinate the calls on his time that the central office makes (filling out reports, attending staff meetings). Not all the agencies that press staff members to spend time in the field have faced the implication for their own processes. It is not unusual for a professional to spend as much time in auxiliary activities as in providing direct service. With professionalization also has come specialization; that is, greater efficiency in meeting special needs accompanied by an inability to meet varied needs. With professionalization, finally, has come social as well as physical distance from poor people. Professionals are now very widely concerned because there is not genuine communication between the service worker and the low-income patient or client. It is suggested, for example, that the slum dweller tends "to use agencies and professional personnel as if they were legitimate extensions of the kinship unit."[4] However, an attempt to be informal—to offer gifts for help that has been received, for example—is precisely the sort of advance that professionals have been trained to resist.

The choices that community services face are far from simple. They are asked to decentralize, which appears to be less efficient and economical, though additional funds are not in evidence. They are asked to be less specialized, though families are presenting more difficult problems. They are asked to coordinate, though this in itself requires staff time. All these demands are being met to some degree—substantially in some cases and experimentally or half-heartedly in others. A "site service" office was provided in an urban renewal area in New York City.[5] All-purpose professional social workers were provided in a renewal area in Dayton.[6] In Atlanta, the Community Council established a coordinating committee in renewal areas.[7]

New types of services are also developing in relation to the particular needs of families in urban renewal areas and deteriorated housing. Because finding housing for poor families and helping them use it properly requires competences in counseling, home economics, and real estate, some services combine these specializations.[8] Because of resistance to urban renewal and because federal regulations now require it, citizens in renewal areas are being involved in the decisions made about their neighborhoods. Obviously, citizen participation rests in some cases on firm conviction about individual rights. But it is probably fair to say that the attempt to involve the affected citizens in making decisions is more often perfunctory. Organization of neighborhood residents by blocks for their own recreational and rehabilitative purposes is, broadly speaking, a type of citizen participation. "Block organization" has, of course, been practiced by neighborhood workers for some time; it is receiving renewed attention as a device for neighborhood rehabilitation.[9] Although it is an attractive concept, its rehabilitative potential should not be overestimated. Some areas require rebuilding and others require at least code enforcement before people can be expected to hope that their own efforts are worth while.

Even these efforts move outward from established disciplines or agencies. Dissatisfaction with the results of coordinating devices and expansion of existing services have led to interest in the development of new disciplines, frequently referred to as "urban generalists." The term conveys a general dissatisfaction with specialization and, in addition, with the fund of knowledge that any professional has about city problems as such. One aspect of this movement has been an attempt to define and develop urban extension agents, "urban counterparts of traditional agricultural research, education, and extension programs." [10] The work of the urban extension agent has been described as follows:

> The agent would serve as a communications link. The results of urban research findings with respect to community-wide activities and problems would be translated into terms meaningful to the various components of the urban population. While thus serving as "implementor," the agent might simultaneously bring the needs of this urban population into focus for the researcher. . . .
>
> The function of the urban extension agent is to clarify and to enable, to assist people to function more adequately in a complex, specialized, technically oriented society, of which their community and their neighborhood are parts. With this aid citizens may regain some awareness and understanding of the forces impinging upon them. Fundamental to the work of the urban agent is the assumption that public and private services available will be drawn upon more meaningfully. . . .[11]

Unfortunately the analogy has serious defects. The agricultural extension agent teaches farmers how to earn more money, on the basis of decades of research findings. The urban extension agent will be teaching people how to live as others want them to live, on the basis of intuition and convention rather more than research. At any rate, the search is symptomatic of a need for professional flexibility and perhaps of a need for new professions.

There may be a need as well for forms of organizing services in the center of the city that achieve organizational unity and provide accessibility to block dwellers. At least one such proposal has been made. Noting that the problem of organizing urban services may be markedly different from the rural problem, Bertram M. Beck proposes that a structure be developed that would bring together all the services appropriate to a city neighborhood. "Urban redevelopment boards" would receive funds now labeled as public assistance, child welfare, urban renewal, and health and education grants. A visible feature of this organization would be neighborhood units. Beck writes:

> Physically, the neighborhood units might well be expanded settlement houses or neighborhood centers built to offer combined health, welfare, and community service. Adjacent to school facilities and sharing many services in common, these centers would be designed for pleasure and comfort—the heart of a force for reinvigorating city life. People would come to the center to seek help and also to seek pleasure. Public assistance, social insurance, and child placement services would be a part of the center. Probation officers would also have quarters there.[12]

Findings that would support such a proposal developed out of a Pittsburgh urban renewal study.[13] The conclusion that a new design of providing service is required is based on two deficiencies in conventional designs: (1) the absence of some kind of rallying point for the neighborhood by which it can presumably derive more value out of existing services; and (2) problems which have defied solution through conventional methods. These two deficiencies go to the heart of the problems for which no solutions had been found or, indeed, offered by the early 1960's. Not only do people move away from the city; services move away—in space and in attitude—from the people who live in the city. A structure was not available that reconciled specialization and professionalization with meeting people's patent needs for service and a sense of trust for the people serving them.

NOTES

1. Bradley Buell and Associates, *Community Planning for Human Services* (New York: Columbia University Press, 1952).
2. Frank F. A. Rawling, "Doctors Moving Out," *Urban Sprawl and Health,* Report of the 1958 National Health Forum (National Health Council, Philadelphia: March 17–19, 1958). Rudolph H. Friedrich, "Dentists Follow the Highways," *Urban Sprawl and Health, op. cit.;* Luther Terry, "The City in National Health," *Public Health Reports,* LXXVII, No. 5 (Public Health Service, Washington, D.C.: May 1962).

3. Robert H. Hamlin, *Voluntary Health and Welfare Agencies in the United States* (New York: The Schoolmasters' Press, 1961).

4. Marc Fried, "Developments in the West End Research," presented at the 25th Anniversary of the Department of Psychiatry, Massachusetts General Hospital (October 15, 1960), p. 11.

5. Community Service Society of New York, Committee on Housing, *Not Without Hope* (March 1958).

6. Albert G. Rosenberg, "Principles of Community Organization in an Urban Renewal Program," presented at the Conference on Citizen Participation in Neighborhood Conservation and Rehabilitation (Pittsburgh, Pa.: September 12, 1958).

7. Fulton County Department of Public Welfare, *Slow but Sure,* Annual Report (Atlanta, Ga.: 1960).

8. John G. Vaughan and Jane Herron, "The Urban Counseling Service of the Better Housing League of Greater Cincinnati" (October 1961), typescript.

9. Martin Millspaugh and Gurney Breckenfeld, in Miles Colean, ed., *The Human Side of Urban Renewal* (Baltimore: Fight-Blight, 1958).

10. The Ford Foundation Annual Report (New York: October 1, 1960–September 30, 1961).

11. Martin L. Cohnstaedt and Thomas K. Philipson, "The Urban Extension Agent," *Adult Leadership*, X, No. 8 (February 1962), 225.

12. Bertram M. Beck, "Children on the New Frontier," *Child Welfare,* XL, No. 4 (April 1961), 4.

13. Health and Welfare Association of Allegheny County, *An Analysis of the Impact of Social Factors in the Urban Renewal Program* (March 9, 1962), 12.

15

Social Services in France

French social services and social security rest on an ideology that is compounded of myth and principle, in varying mixtures. Facts are not indispensable to central beliefs. They are rationalized with beliefs if possible; otherwise they are ignored. French ideology is not characterized invidiously. In itself, it becomes a fact of considerable social and psychological importance. One might speak of American ideology, in the same sense, as being built around the insurance principle.*

French ideology is compounded of such concepts as solidarity, social justice, family policy, categorical programming, benefits as a right, mutuality, decentralization, and flexibility. They overlap one another and American principles, but most of the words used are out of tune for us. For the student who begins to perceive an

An excerpt from *Social Security and Social Services in France*, United States Social Security Administration (Washington, D.C.: United States Government Printing Office, 1965).

* For example, "One discovers amidst multiple services the classic opposition between insurance and assistance. This opposition is without doubt technically false because from the time that capitalization is abandoned, as is more and more generally the case, in favor of redistribution, it is always the active workers who, at a given moment, assure the maintenance of the inactive, in bearing the cost of their benefits. But psychologically the distinction retains great importance." [Pierre Laroque, "Service social et sécurité sociale," *Revue Belge de Sécurité Sociale*, IV, No. 2 (February 1962), 197, 198.]

organic French ideology, all these terms take on new overtones. For our purposes, in understanding French social services, we must simply bear in mind that not only the organization of services but their intention are a disquieting mixture of the familiar and the alien.

Social service is used here to mean the variety of organized services provided to people, excluding those that are thought to be fundamental or universal: general education, medical care, housing. Social security is used to include all the social insurances. A glossary is provided at the end of the chapter because literal translations of French terms may lead one astray. For example, *service social* and *travail social* have quite the reverse connotations from their English translations. (Terms defined in the glossary are italicized the first time they appear.)

Three aspects of the organization of French social services will repay exploration. First, social security initiates and maintains a wide variety of social services, through programs called *health and social action*. Second, social security *caisses* employ on their own staffs one-quarter of all social workers in France. Third, the French use a variety of devices to coordinate the social services at national, departmental, and local levels. Each of these aspects is based on principles that are different from our own. As we take them up in turn, we shall be moving from the general to the specific—that is, from social services to social work and then to the special function of coordination.

HEALTH AND SOCIAL ACTION

Social security programs support social services in two fashions. In paying for services received by beneficiaries, inevitably social security becomes a major source of fees for social services—convalescent homes, retraining centers, special schools for children. In this relationship, social security is only a customer, but provides an assured demand and source of payment. The relationship is not unfamiliar to us: In the United States, public assistance vendors have been paid directly for some time; social insurance moved into large-scale payment for services with the initiation of health insurance. Closely related is a second, more alien fashion of supporting social services—*action sanitaire et sociale*. Social security programs devote a portion of their resources to providing selected social services often, but not exclusively, designed to meet the needs of beneficiaries.

The rationale for health and social action is twofold. First, for reasons implied by the concepts of solidarity and social justice— that every French citizen is responsible for all others and that national income should be redistributed in favor of the most needy—the provision of defined benefits is in itself insufficient. For people who are not average—whose needs are not met by legal benefits—measures must be provided that meet the specific need. The point has been put as follows:

> Social action, precisely because it does not benefit all families, provides an attempt at solidarity inside the system of family allowances. While legal allowances are divided among all families in relation to their responsibilities but not to their resources, social funds go specially to help those who face particular difficulties.
>
> . . . Social action permits at one and the same time an effort to adapt the aid of caisses to diverse individual needs . . . and to do research, experimentation, with new forms of allowances which may and must inspire the legislator.[1]

Second, it is good business for social security to engage in prevention and to stimulate community services. Accidents cost more than safety programs. Hospital care costs more than the convalescent home for which a patient may be ready.

The funds for health and social action are provided by dedicating a percentage of social security contributions—4 per cent of the contributions for family allowances, 3 per cent of those for workmen's compensation, and 1.10 per cent of *social insurance* contributions. Local, regional, and national caisses have separate health and social action funds and receive their share of contributions directly. In 1960, the total amount of money involved was about 650 million francs or 132 million dollars. By way of perspective, this was well over half as much as the French government spent for *aide sociale* in the same year.

A number of principles have been defined by regulation or practice as the program proceeded. Though there were antecedents, health and social action first took legal form in 1945 and reflects an impulse to organizational unity that was strong at the time. An arrangement was made to redistribute funds between localities or regions when this seemed warranted. Further, a national *Comité Technique d'Action Sanitaire et Sociale* broadly prescribes the way funds may be spent. Nevertheless, because the intention of health and social action is to achieve flexibility, regions may vary in their support of certain activities. There is variation as well between the interests of local, regional, and national caisses.

Funds may be given in the form of grants to other agencies or used for direct administration of social services. In practice, there has been a recent sharp rise in directly administered social action, from 35 per cent of the cost in 1957 to 48 per cent in 1961. Social action funds are seen as complementary to other sources of support. Therefore, subsidy is given to voluntary agencies only if they have independent sources of support as well. To be sure, once a voluntary agency (rehabilitation center, children's holiday camp) is organized, its income may be chiefly payment for service by social security agencies. A final common policy: When money is given regularly, or when much is given, the caisse is likely to expect to be represented on the council of administration of the voluntary agency. A growing tendency to use subsidies for capital grants rather than administration probably reflects in part the caisses' wish to be free of continuing responsibility.

The simplest indication of the services that are supported is the recommendations for 1963 of the *Comité Technique*. The figures given in Tables 15-1 to 15-3 are percentages of total available funds that may be spent for each purpose.

Table 15-1

PRIMARY CAISSES OF SOCIAL INSURANCE

	Per cent
Supplementary allowances to beneficiaries	50
Maternal and infant care program	12
Health equipment	25
Social work	8
Miscellaneous	5

Source: *Les Institutions sociales de la France,* Documentation Française (Paris: 1963), p. 184.

Table 15–2

REGIONAL CAISSES OF SOCIAL INSURANCE

	Per cent
Hospital equipment	40
Campaign against mental illness and alcoholism	24
Campaign against tuberculosis	8
Campaign against cancer	8
Reeducation and rehabilitation	10
Maternal and infant care program	3
Miscellaneous	7

Source: *Les Institutions sociales de la France,* Documentation Française (Paris: 1963), p. 185.

Table 15–3

FAMILY ALLOWANCE CAISSES

	1963 Recommended average	Recommended range*	Actually spent by all caisses during 1961 *
	Per cent	Per cent *	Per cent *
Supplementary aid for housing	20	10–35	31
Supplementary aid for vacations	20	10–35	21
Household training and homemaker service	12	5–20	14
Child and maternity placement	11	7–22	7
Social work	9	5–18	8
Supplementary allowances, experimental and extending legal provision	10	0–20	7
Other financial assistance	3	2–6 ⎫	
Educational activities	3	1–5 ⎪	13
Social service centers	4	2–6 ⎬	
Training and social research	3	1–5 ⎭	

Source: Union Nationale des Caisses d'Allocations Familiales, *L'Action Sociale des caisses d'allocations familiales* (Paris: UNCAF, 1963); *Statistiques concernant l'action sociale des caisses d'allocations familiales en 1960 et 1961* (Paris: UNCAF, 1962).

* The Comité Technique provides a recommendation within which variation is permitted. Actual expenditures in 1961 are also listed to show roughly how the recommendations are followed.

We observe that the social insurance caisses deal largely with health-related action; the family allowance caisses deal with social action. The needs of the aged are not included in the listing

—these are the responsibility of regional caisses and the national caisses.

The first test of health and social action must be the test of effectiveness. Among the social service programs that were instituted after the war, Maternal and Infant Care (*PMI*) was perhaps the most significant. Spreading an extensive network of consultation and surveillance, medical and social, PMI is given credit for steady improvement in the infant mortality rate. Although PMI is far from reaching its objectives of a consultation with every pregnant woman and the lowest infant mortality rate in the West, its scope is nevertheless remarkable. In 1961, over four million home visits* were made in connection with the program. Although public services provided half of the *assistantes sociales* who made these visits, social security agencies—legally regarded as voluntary agencies—provided a much-needed one-third.[2]

Programs of household help, household training and homemaker service loom large in the priorities given to the caisses. Household training, somewhat like home economics in the United States but located in social service agencies as well as in schools, has substantially improved preparation of young girls for adulthood. Twenty years ago, a few young women were trained in nutrition and child care, but today nearly all receive this training. As for homemaker service, about 5,000 *travailleuses familiales* are now licensed by the French government. The number is thought to be inadequate, particularly in rural areas. Still, of a random sample of families receiving family allowances, 7 per cent said they had used homemaker service at some time. Over half of those had received help from the caisse to pay for it.[3]

One cannot speak of social services in France without mentioning vacations, an institution that has assumed preeminent importance. In the representative sample just mentioned, one-quarter of beneficiaries said they had received aid at some time for a vacation. About a million children a year receive aid to take a vacation.[4]

---

* In comparing the two countries, we bear in mind that the population of France (48 million) is about one-fourth that of the United States, the number of births in 1962 (835,000) about one-fifth.

It is not difficult to count the money that caisses spend for social services. By any yardstick, as per capita expenditure (13 francs) or as a percentage of contributions or benefits, health and social action does not loom large. Yet it is also clear that the services to which the caisses have given priority have matured in a comparatively short time. Could the same goals have been achieved in other ways? The same objectives could presumably not have been achieved by voluntary agencies unassisted. Though well established in such traditional fields as child care, few voluntary agencies operate in other significant areas. Moreover, existing voluntary agencies emerged from the war with resources greatly depleted by inflation. Social action provides voluntary agencies with the money they need; government money would have had to be funneled to them somehow. However, the government could have chosen to organize public services instead of the ambiguous system that was worked out. So far as effectiveness goes, the same end could have been achieved. Consequently other tests of this system must be considered—what have been its effects on voluntary social service; has social security been made flexible; and has flexibility led to overlapping and confusion?

The voluntary social services were at first fearful of the effect of the social action programs, as organized. Their anxiety has been expressed as follows:

> In the face of caisses having very large financial means, with an integral, unified structure, recognized in the law, these [voluntary] agencies appear numerous but poor and isolated and often ill prepared for the transformation of techniques that is required in most sectors of health and social action. . . . They had to call on the financial help of the family allowance caisses at the very moment when they most feared seeing the caisses succumb to the temptation of monopoly.[5]

The caisse requirement that it be represented on the council of administration when a subsidy is given would seem to provide a direct means for dominating voluntary agencies. In fact, the matter appears not to have worked out this way. Voluntary agency management appears to welcome caisse representatives. Representatives seem to see themselves as observers and, on some matters, expert advisers, rather than as actually involved in administration. When representatives become deeply interested, voluntary agencies feel they have a friend in court for further subsidies. In the first ten or twelve years of the new system, upward of 60 per cent of social action funds was granted by caisses to outside agencies. The absolute amount of money increased continually and can only have aided the growth of voluntary agencies. Since 1957 the percentage of the subsidy given externally has declined sharply. In 1960 and 1961 even the absolute amount of the subsidy declined. If these trends continue, the voluntary agencies may change their outlook. Meanwhile, however, they have expanded their work in a way they cannot have anticipated. The observation of a European Study Group appears to be a fair summary: "Far from hindering public or private initiative, the welfare action of the family allowance agencies has favored its development." [6]

Has social security been made flexible by programs of health and social action? The answer would have to be "somewhat." Health and social action is the single significant area in which local and regional caisses have managed to maintain a measure of autonomy in the face of increasing governmental control of their operation. Caisses show a tendency to allocate such funds according to local inclination. For example, in 1961 the family allowance caisses varied as follows in the percentage of social action funds spent for social work. [7]

> 29 caisses spent less than 5 per cent
> 63 caisses spent between 5 and 8 per cent
> 21 caisses spent between 9 and 14 per cent
> 1 caisse spent 22 per cent

The caisses vary not only in the objectives to which they devote funds, but in their choices about direct administration vs. subsidy. They tend also to use funds to experiment around the edges of *legal benefits*. Some examples: A family allowance for a daughter whose help is required at home; allowances beyond the legal age for apprentices and students; and an allowance to borderline cases of invalidity. [8] Some of these experiments are picked up and incorporated into the legal system.

It seems clear so far that, beside providing external resources for beneficiaries, health and social action funds encourage variation between one caisse and another. However, a more sensitive system is intended, adjusting to the social circumstances of families as well as of regions. *Supplementary benefits* are provided to meet those needs that legal benefits do not. Supplementary benefits are, in general, based on an income test and given for specified purposes—housing, vacations, household help, and replacing legal benefits for which there is technical ineligibility. It is puzzling that there is not more call on these funds. Apparently very large proportions (50 to 80 per cent) of those who apply for supplementary benefits receive them. Yet the total amount involved in supplementary allowances is small—roughly 100 to 150 million francs a year. Viewed from within the social security system, one might gain the impression that there is not much stark need among the populace.

To be sure, supplementary allowances are not regarded as the basic method for dealing with residual need. Is *aide sociale,* then, so generous that there is only small occasion to call upon supplementary allowances? One form of aide sociale is available to meet the cost of medical care for those in need. In 1961, *aide médicale* cost a total of 463 million francs—94 million dollars. (About half of the people involved received aid as a supplement to social insurance.) Another form of aide sociale, aid for the aged, cost a total of 336 million francs—69 million dollars, almost entirely to supplement the cost of care of aged people in institutions. Sums of the same magnitude were devoted to the mentally ill and the disabled. Comparatively insignificant amounts were spent for other purposes. One limitation of aide sociale becomes apparent. It is limited to a few fairly narrow categories of need. Moreover, it does not support income at a level that, many Frenchmen will agree, makes decent living possible. For example, the income ceiling for aide sociale for the aged is 3,100 francs a year for a single person—$50 a month.

As France has virtually full employment, there may be some feeling that there is not real need—apart from the categories of people to whom aide sociale is available. One can test such an impression only by examining family income, although it cannot of course be evaluated by United States prices or standards. It may be estimated that median family income is 700 to 900 francs a month,[9] but the question at this point is how many families have considerably less than median income. Unfortunately, the distribution of family income is not known. However, a dependable distribution of income from salaries and wages is available. In 1961, 27.5 per cent of salaries in industry, commerce, and the services fell below 417 francs ($85) a month.[10] For the single people represented in this quarter of the population, this probably accounts for their total income. For the others, income may be supplemented by another wage or by a family allowance. Piecing together the two bits of information (median family income and the distribution of wages) it seems clear that the income of many families is moderate—by French prices and standards. The income of a not inconsiderable proportion must be very low indeed. Who would they be? Single people. Families with only one wage earner. Families with one or two children. Families with an allowance for several children and a *salaire unique,* but with only one low wage.*

Unmet need is not negligible, but several reasons are offered why there is not more call for supplementary allowances. French families are proud and do not like to ask for help (even though assistance is a right). They spend very little for housing (by our standards quite true). They manage by borrowing. Beyond these explanations, one may speculate that beneficiary and *assistante sociale* know how limited funds are. Therefore applications are made and encouraged in only the most desperate situations. Although there is flexibility, it is limited. Moreover, it has been advanced as an advantage of supplementary allowances that they tend to demonstrate the spots at which legal allowances are weak-

---

* There may be a tendency to overlook the problem of a large family with a low wage, because family allowances amount to a substantial sum. For example, in Paris in 1964, a family with four children and the mother at home received between 380 and 545 francs a month in benefits, depending on the ages of the children. If the wage earner received the legal minimum wage, he brought home 372 francs. Thus total monthly income may be 900 francs ($184)—for a family of six in Paris!

est. On the other hand, because they are officially an open avenue to help, supplementary allowances may tend to cover up the less serious weaknesses of legal allowances.

In sum, the organization of health and social action provides a measure of flexibility—because of the autonomy of the caisses, because they are able to stimulate the organization of services that beneficiaries need, and because they are able to meet certain kinds of special need. We shall return to flexibility in the section specifically devoted to social work.

We now explore whether health and social action leads to overlapping and confusion. The question contains two significant facets—the integration of social services with one another and the integration of social services with social security.

A variety of mechanisms provide integration at both national and local levels. At the heart of the coordination process is the Comité Technique d'Action Sanitaire et Sociale. Its membership tells its story: The Ministers of Health, Labor, and Education, representatives of the various functional elements and levels of social security, physicians, and members representing family organizations. We have already indicated the type of prescription that the Comité Technique regularly issues. These priorities are related to national priorities and to other services. The Ministry of Public Health and Population has governmental responsibility for coordinating social services. The Ministry regularly prepares the basic material from which the government planning body (*Commissariat au Plan*) projects four- or five-year plans for *équipement sanitaire et social*—the physical plant for health and social action. As a result, the internal planning of the Ministry is itself being strengthened. Since the Ministry of Public Health and Population shares the cost of équipement sanitaire et social with social security, the caisses and the Ministry of Labor are consulted in the course of preparing plan material, as are a number of other interested parties. Once presented to the Commissariat au Plan, varying points of view are considered in planning for équipement. The views of the Ministry of Finance are of paramount importance. In the end, a national plan is adopted by the legislature and becomes a crucial reference document in the deliberations of the Comité Technique. One perceives that at the end of a long, complex, confusing, and sometimes perhaps confused voyage of negotiation and collaboration, lies a year-to-year consensus on the manner in which health and social action funds should be spent.

The Comité Technique has counterpart committees in each region where, within limits, national recommendations are adjusted to meet local situations. A counterpart series of relationships—simpler, because fewer choices are possible, but involving similar interests—appears to achieve the objective of regional consensus. Several special observations should be made about the consensus that evolves. First, national priorities are rapidly reflected in health and social action. For instance, enactment by the legislature of a requirement that all large housing developments include a social service center was accompanied by an allocation of social action funds for the purpose. One might also be concerned about the degree to which coordination focuses on planning for capital needs. The national plan shows awareness of this danger—awareness that physical facilities are useless unless staffed and that some significant programs do not rely upon physical facilities at all. It is possible that the danger is not serious at this moment, when the need for capital outlay is vast, but it may become serious when more discriminating choices must be made. For example, the danger may yet arise that so many institutions for the aged will be built that communities will rely primarily on institutional care.

A final point on the consensus about social services: We observe that social security control of health and social action funds is, in turn, subject to other pressures. Social action funds are one of the major sources of support of social services and therefore of vital interest to the community. Still, a result is achieved somewhat closer to the objectives that social security agencies seek—that is, meeting the needs of their beneficiaries. For example, within the broad priorities that are given, caisses may establish convalescent homes and retraining centers. The situation has two closely related advantages for social security beneficiaries. First, the social service is provided. Second, it is provided in a manner which leads to an intimate working relationship between the social service and the social security caisse. An injured worker may move through hospital care, convalescence, and retraining without encountering a difficult referral or a gap in community responsibility for his rehabilitation.

SOCIAL WORK

The assistante sociale has a somewhat different function, differently situated in society from an American social worker. The profession has developed recently; the social service diploma dates only from 1932. Thus, social work has developed concurrently with social security and family policy and has devoted itself, in part, to their ends. Further, social work has developed out of nursing and out of medical care.* The first year of social work training is essentially medical; 5,000 of France's 18,000 assistantes sociales are in some fashion involved in the PMI program. Because, possibly, of these ties to the tasks at hand and to medical care, social work is an eminently practical profession. Some observers believe that the emphasis on medical care, particularly among older social workers, leads also to a rather brisk, authoritative attitude. It has been suggested, finally, that the newness of the profession leads to an emphasis on the whole family. Where professional history is much longer, in England for example, it is said that social workers develop and defend bureaucratic interests for particular family members or specialized family functions.[11]

All French social workers are licensed by the government, and a high proportion are employed in public or quasi-public agencies, facts that may have important professional consequences. First, each social worker feels a derivative responsibility for all national objectives assigned to his profession. For example, the situation of a neglected child who failed to receive adequate public protection became the occasion for a debate in the National Assembly. It appeared that the social worker who had failed to take the situation to court might be liable to prosecution. Second and on the other hand, the obligation of a social worker to his client and especially to respect the client's confidence has been

---

* Although an American might attribute the origin of modern American social work to Jane Addams or Mary Richmond, the French tend to name Dr. Richard Cabot of Massachusetts General Hospital, a small illustration of the power of one's mental set over history. [P. F. Armand Delille, "Répercussion du service social et des lois sociales," *Travail Social*, No. 4 (1960), 28.]

spelled out in law. (This was the essential dilemma in the situation of the neglected child.[12]) Consequently, in perhaps a greater degree than in the United States, the social worker feels a responsibility and status independent of the agency by which she happens to be employed. Third, French social work appears to be a comparatively unified profession. Because the preparation required of social workers has been rising, there are differences in the background of those who are licensed. Nevertheless, they are all eligible for membership in the professional association and, above all, appear unanimously to share the ethics of the profession.

With these brief observations, we may turn to the use that is made of the assistantes sociales in social security. All the caisses employ a total of more than 4,000 assistantes sociales.[13] They constitute slightly more than 3 per cent of the administrative personnel of the general régime of *Sécurité Sociale* and about 15 per cent of the administrative personnel of the family allowance caisses.[14]

Assistantes sociales function primarily in three ways. First, they provide an information service for those with special problems or who find normal administrative channels insufficient. The service is usually provided through the mechanism of a *permanence,* an established time and place in each community where the assistante sociale may be consulted for any reason. Second, the assistante sociale completes the omnipresent dossier and social history for supplementary allowances and social services and, in special situations, for legal benefits. Third, she may be assigned part or all of her time to a service role in collaboration with other voluntary or public services. For example, she may be responsible for maternal and child care visits. She may do family counseling in a social service center.

We must ask a number of questions about this organizational system. What is the coverage of social security social work? What is its quality? What is its impact on its host agencies? What are its dangers? The French are, on the whole, dissatisfied with the coverage that is achieved because they see needs beyond those that are being met. Nevertheless, any of several studies produces figures that are impressive to Americans. Of families insured under

Sécurité Sociale, almost one in four say they have at some time approached a social worker for help.[15] Of family allowance beneficiaries, well over half have seen a social worker at least once. Only small percentages in various cities—9, 24, 14, 11 per cent—do not know how to reach a social worker if they wish.[16] Other social work programs in which social security only collaborates also show impressive coverage. In the new housing areas, approximately 20 per cent of the populations use the social service centers.[17] In some measure, these percentages are interrelated. We have indicated the central importance of the PMI program; many of the contacts are made in connection with PMI, whether in a social service center or at home, by a social worker belonging to one agency or another.

When one examines the basic groups being reached, the French intention to humanize the programs, to make them flexible, takes on new meaning. Because of the nature of social security, obviously the old, the sick, and the large families are disproportionately in touch with the programs.[18] There is some evidence, however, that those who are poorest do not fully benefit from the array of services and benefits to which they may be entitled.[19] They may not know their entitlement; often they do not have the education to establish their rights or needs. It is the poorest families, however, that are likely to benefit more from the work of the assistante sociale. The point has been summed up as follows:

> . . . For reasons at once material and psychological, independent of the wish of caisses, social aid does not always go to those who need it most, but more often to those who have attained a certain social and financial level. . . . Only social work escapes this rule . . . because it is less administrative and more human.[20]

One study observes that the middle class views the social worker as a technician. The workers and peasants view her as more personally responsible for dealing with their problems.[21] We must suspect that the poor are reached disproportionately not only because they wish it, but because a program like PMI tries especially to reach them. Wherever the initiative lies, it must result in benefits that are more nearly if still not entirely equitable.

In suggesting that the use of social workers leads to greater equity or, as the French would say, social justice, we have suggested one effect of extensive contacts with social workers on the program for which they work. Another effect lies in the public attitude toward social security, which is generally popular.[22] The survey findings that demonstrate this surprised a number of public officials, who had heard a good many complaints about bureaucracy and complexity. It is possible that the surveys turn up public reactions to the institution of social security, rather than to the way it is being administered. At any rate, social work, although obviously a minor factor among a number, appears to contribute something to the popularity of social security. Asked for the most useful of the social actions of the family allowance caisses, 10 per cent of families name social work. Asked what they have gotten from social workers, families name information, advice, and material aids and only 10 per cent say "fine words, nothing more." Asked what they would do if a mother and sick children needed care, one-fifth would ask for a social worker at the caisse. Those social security recipients who have used social workers at some time are somewhat more satisfied with social security in general.

The meaning of coverage and popularity is doubtful unless something is also known about the quality of service that is rendered. It may be difficult for an American to evaluate service which rests on somewhat different assumptions. However, of the interviews that family allowance agency social workers conduct, two-thirds take less than twenty minutes.[23] There is much variability in what is being asked of the social worker; in some cases only direction to another service. Yet, by American standards, not a great deal can be accomplished. Clearly, social work revolves around practical problems and practical helps—nutrition, vacations, sickness, pregnancy, budget problems, housing, and financial assistance.[24]

On the whole, these practical helps that social workers seek to give appear to leave clients feeling that their problem has been met.[25] This is not the most damaging observation that might be made of a profession. At the same time, the need for work that is deeper and more delicate becomes clear. Perhaps one client out of seven or eight presents a marital or psychological problem. There is much concern about child protection, and more interviewing time is certainly given to such matters.[26] Professional leaders are hoping to meet these needs; the social work curriculum has been revised to include such instruction. Perhaps 100 of the 1,200 social workers in the general régime of Sécurité Sociale are now prepared to do such work.

One might also approach the question of quality by asking whether the larger objectives of social workers are being accomplished. For example, the drop in the infant mortality rate is attributed to the PMI program. And it is said that the establishment of social service centers reduces the malaise that has been evident in new housing developments. Still, social work is only one factor among many. At least a negative conclusion about quality seems justified—there is no evidence that French objectives are failing to be met by the quality of French social work.

Two dangers of rather different significance may strike an observer. First, it may appear that a system is growing up that offers new possibilities for state control of individuals. The role of the social worker is ambiguous, to begin with, and could readily rationalize a managerial function. The ambiguity is put as follows:

> The assistante sociale presents herself at the same time as a counsellor of families and a counsellor of organizations, at the service of the people and at the service of the community. This double role . . . is not without difficulty. . . .[27]

Her practical and medical orientation might incline her temperamentally to a controlling role. And now, under a series of new laws, she occupies a powerful strategic position.

She operates under a law which intends, though it may not be fully implemented, to provide socio-medical supervision of every pregnant woman. She is the entrée to supplementary allowances, even if legally she does not decide the matter.[28] She is increasingly the entrée to other social services. Another law requires that a family deal with only one social worker, increasing the effectiveness of the assistante sociale who has the family *in charge*. Middle-class families cannot be much intimidated, but the social worker could be powerful in relation to the poor families who are so often her clients. Similar developments have met with resistance in France. The *Code de la Famille* provided that payment of family allowances could be suspended if they were not used for the benefit of the child. The provision was rarely used, if ever, because of public resentment at intrusions on family privacy.[29]

It is puzzling that the steps listed above involving social workers could be taken without provoking a murmur of dissent. Perhaps social workers are very widely trusted. On the other hand, there coexists in France very strong feelings about personal liberty and strong pressures toward central control. One official stated: "We are an anarchy within a monarchy." As a practical matter of day-to-day living, many practices are accepted that might be angrily rejected in principle or if someone made an issue. At any rate, social workers do not appear to act in a managerial role nor do social security administrators press such a role on them. Protections against such activity exist at different levels. Strong public feeling about personal liberty is at least an ultimate protection. At the level of social security administration, social workers occupy a position that frees them of pressure. They are not regarded as a normal link in the chain of administration but as partisan to the beneficiary. Perhaps their professional independence assists in establishing such a position. Administrators seemed satisfied that the social workers' role should be defined in these unique terms. As for the social worker herself, she gives allegiance to a code of ethics that emphasizes the client's right to freedom of choice. Her professional association explicitly requires her to "respect the liberty of the client, his convictions, his responsibilities." [30] This injunction is widely professed and, apparently, practiced.

The second danger of the situation of social workers lies not so much in fundamental issues as in the natural tendencies of administration. Social workers might conceivably be used for general administrative rather more than for professional purposes. There is, in fact, such a tendency and it is particularly troubling in light of a serious shortage of social workers. The director of *FNOSS* has proposed that auxiliaries assist social workers and that social workers be relieved of purely administrative tasks.[31] The Minister of Public Health and Population has written in this vein to departmental officials responsible for social work.[32] But if there are to be auxiliaries, funds must be made available. Moreover, the social worker's task does not lend itself to ready distinction from administrative tasks. The accessibility of the social worker and the generalized nature of her mission are among her strongest assets. Yielding these will save precious time but will also create a problem which social workers and administrators recognize. Therefore, the push to define and to distinguish social work within social security moves—but slowly.

COORDINATION

We have already discussed coordination at the level of high policy. We have seen the ties between the national plan, the Ministry of Public Health and Population, and the Comité Technique d'Action Sanitaire et Sociale. We must now add other groups which play a national role deciding priorities, scale of investment, and so forth, in order to focus upon the coordination actually achieved in dealing with beneficiaries. At that point we shall find the social worker in a crucial role.

Three additional groups must be named which are involved in coordination at the level of high policy. The Economic and Social Council is a forum at the level of the National Assembly for labor and social interests. The High Consultative Committee on Population and the Family advises the Prime Minister on policy issues. For example, it issued a report which has become the basic document in policy for the aged.[33] The *Conseil Superieur de Service Social* advises the Minister of Public Health and Population on matters relating to social work. Its work is of particular importance because in day to day practice the social worker is becoming the coordinator of social services. The membership in all these groups overlaps, the particular balance in each depending on the function that is primary. *FNOSS, UNCAF,* the Ministry of Labor, and other significant interests are, of course, represented. Although the inter-relationship of these councils and committees is the basic fact of coordination, stage center is held by the Ministry of Public Health and Population and the Conseil Superieur de Service Social.

The sponsors of social services are numerous and the sources of funds are varied. Moreover, auspices and support for a particular service may be worked out in different ways from one *départe-*

ment to another. As the Ministry of Public Health and Population is not the only source of funds, it requires other means to carry out its responsibility to coordinate social services. First, it influences the national plan and the recommendations of the Comité Technique, in the manner previously described. Second, it may issue instructions to the central government representative in each département—the Prefect. The Prefect and, in particular, the departmental directors of Health and Population,* take such steps as are open to them to carry out the instructions of the Ministry. The letter that was mentioned earlier, outlining the proper responsibilities of social workers, is such an instruction. Obviously, those most influenced would be the medical social services, under the direct control of the Ministry's representative in each département. Fourth, the Ministry of Public Health and Population accredits training institutions and issues licenses for social workers, homemakers, and instructors in domestic science. Fifth, the Conseil Superieur de Service Social oversees a system for coordinating social work and advises the Minister on steps which he may wish to take.

We now have the background to focus upon the locality and the actual service a social security beneficiary receives. A decree establishes in each département a Committee of Liaison and Coordination to enumerate and plan the coordination of social workers. The Conseil Superieur in turn examines and passes upon the acceptability of the plans. A majority of the départements have so far submitted plans. It is said that government agencies originally did not know to whom to address certain kinds of social inquiries. This problem is now being met successfully. There are conflicting opinions about the success with which coordination is working generally. It is too early to know whether more than paper coordination will be the result. However, the current law is based upon a system of coordination that was developed in the Paris metropolitan region, voluntarily first and later under departmental regulations. The Paris system under the

---

* The structure is not dissimilar to the regional organization of the United States Department of Health, Education, and Welfare. A Prefect in each département represents central government. Representatives of each Ministry are also located in each département, responsible both to Prefect and to their own Ministries.

decree of 1959 has been adopted and appears to be workable in at least a few other areas.

Three simple, but radical, principles determine the operation of the Service of Coordination in Paris. First, no more than one family social worker may work with a family. Second, unless there is special reason, each family social worker is responsible for all families in a compact geographic area. Third, no work is done twice. In practice, all the social workers in a designated area are assigned to specific responsibilities. The family workers operating in a neighborhood may work for the municipality or be assigned to the task by a caisse, the health department, or a voluntary agency. The social workers in the area elect a Supervisor of Coordination, who is responsible for promoting interagency collaboration and is the referee when there is difficulty. The Director of the Service of Coordination is responsible to a committee chaired by the Mayor.

Naturally, there are difficulties. Industrial social workers, a large group in France, are sometimes uncooperative; specialists also raise difficulty. Nevertheless, the plan proceeds. Requests for service come to the Service of Coordination and are dealt with by the family social worker. Specialists such as school social workers keep in touch with the family social worker when they are dealing with the same family. The family's right to choose its social worker is explicit in the law. If the family prefers another social worker, the transfer is duly arranged, but no family may have two family social workers. If the family social worker feels a family is entitled to a supplementary allowance, she may file the required social study with a caisse. The study is forwarded through the Supervisor of Coordination, who is expected to know and avoid duplicate requests. The caisse may then pay the supplementary allowance without any investigation of its own. Upon discovering that this would not be done in the United States, one social worker observed: "But I am a professional. I'd be offended if someone felt it necessary to repeat the investigation."

It seems clear that coordination is being achieved in the Paris region. The saving in the time of professionals and clients that is implicit in the one-time-only performance of tasks must be formidable. Coordination also achieves a result in acceptability of social work. The permanence of the Service of Coordination is a well-established, well-known, thoroughly acceptable place of recourse for all sorts of people. They come for advice or referral about rent control, illegitimate pregnancy, emigration, and so forth. In the département of the Seine in one year, 600,000 families were taken in charge by Service of Coordination social workers; 1,300 social workers made 870,000 visits to homes and held 600,000 interviews in a permanence.

The French are greatly interested in one other method of coordination. We have noted that a law now requires provision of a social service center of stipulated size in new housing areas. Certainly, one objective is to replace social ties—the natural ways of dealing with difficulty—that were taken for granted in the crowded central cities. Beyond this, however, there is calculated interest in bringing as many social services as possible together under one roof. The centers are formally organized under a director, but visiting services are also given space. The use that is made of these centers suggests that they have an advantage in visibility and acceptability over ordinary dispersed housing for social services. It is too early to judge whether an advantage is also being achieved in coordination of the separate services.

CONCLUSION

Does the French system work in the French context? It seems fair to question the consequences of building supplementary allowances into the social insurances. The supplementary allowances, although they doubtless provide flexibility, may make it possible for officials to be content despite extensive deprivation. The other aspects of the relationship of social security to social services that have been described seem effective. The hodgepodge of private and public responsibilities, local, regional, and national, seems quite as complicated and unnecessary to an American as our partially federal, partially state-federal system must seem to a Frenchman. Nevertheless, it functions. It functions perhaps with waste, but in a coordinated fashion, carrying conviction about the ideas that are important to Frenchmen. The tie of social action to social security and the incorporation of a social work function in social security appear to accomplish what they are intended to accomplish. They have produced a rapid buildup of services and a program somewhat more flexible or human than would otherwise have been possible. And the French may be achieving order out of the chaos of social services by the most antique method of all—that is, by proclaiming, "Let there be order!"

NOTES

1. M. Rain, "Réflexions sur dix années d'action sociale," *Réflexions sur les prestations familiales* (Paris: UNCAF, 1958), p. 59.
2. "Rapport sur la protection maternelle et infantile," *Journal Officiel de la République Française*, No. 7 (1963), p. 153.
3. Alain Girard and Henri Bastide, "Enquête de l'INED sur l'action sociale des caisses d'allocations familiales et le salaire unique," *Information Sociales*, XII, No. 3 (March 1958), UNCAF. Also appears summarized in *Population*, XIII, No. 1 (January-March 1958), 145.
4. Mme. G. Girard, "Sécurité sociale et service social dans les pays de la C.E.E. (France)" (May 1962), mimeographed, p. 68.
5. Rain, *op. cit.*
6. European Office of the United Nations, "General Report of the European Study Group on the Contribution of Social Security to the Development of Family Welfare Programmes" (Geneva: May 1963), typescript.
7. *La Clientèle du service social des caisses d'allocations familiales,* Recherche sociale, C.A.F. (Paris: UNCAF, 1961–1962).
8. Jacques Doublet, "Réflexions sur dix années de législation," *Réflexions sur les prestations familiales* (Paris: UNCAF, 1958).
9. French statistics tend to be collected in terms of special occupation classes or sizes of family, and a median family income is difficult to establish. At one extreme, market surveys found the 1961 median family income to be 600 francs [Institut pour l'Étude des Marchés en France et à l'Étranger (Paris, 1963), data in private communication]. At the other extreme, one may divide total distributed national income in 1961 by the estimated number of French families. This gives average monthly income of 1,257 francs. However, an arithmetic average is too high unless income happens to be evenly distributed, and, of course, it is not. The range cited is based in part on a consumption study of 1956 [Centre de Recherches et de Documentation sur la Consommation, *Consommation*, No. 2 (1960), 70],

augmented at the rate of 10 per cent a year (the rate of increase in distributed income minus the rate of population growth) to produce a 1961 figure—853 francs. Data on wages and salaries are, of course, different from family income, but seem consistent with the range suggested.

10. *Études Statistiques,* nouvelle série, No. 2 (April-June 1963). These figures do not include the highest incomes (employers) or the lowest (small shopkeepers and agricultural workers). They include only those who worked a full year for the same employer, presumably receiving high wages compared with those who changed jobs or worked sporadically.

11. Pierre Laroque and Sir Allen Daley, *Health and Social Workers in England and France* (Geneva: Regional Office for Europe: World Health Organization, 1956), p. 156.

12. The basic dilemma between community protection and the client's right to privacy is a familiar one in the United States and may not be quite resolvable. The issue was dealt with by amending the *Code de la Famille* to make it clear that penalties would not be applicable to a social worker who disclosed a confidence to her administrator or to a proper judicial authority. However, the issue was not really that the social worker wished to disclose a confidence and could not but that she felt that she should not.

13. Mme. G. Girard, *op. cit.*

14. Assistantes sociales employed by the caisses may be assigned to work for other agencies. Conversely, caisses frequently use for their own work assistantes sociales paid and officially employed by other agencies. Other social service personnel employed: 600 teachers of household management, 400 homemakers, 100 teachers, and smaller numbers of child care and paramedical personnel.

15. Jean-Daniel Reynaud and Antoinette Catrice-Lorey, *Les Assurés et la sécurité sociale* (Paris: Institut des Sciences Sociales du Travail, Université de Paris, June 1959).

16. Girard and Bastide, *op. cit.*

17. Jacqueline Herbrich, data from unpublished studies, l'Association pour le Logement Familial (Paris: 1963); Mlle. Pitrou, unpublished studies (Paris: CREDOC, 1963).

18. Reynaud and Catrice-Lorey, *op. cit.;* Recherche Sociale, *op. cit.*

19. Pitrou, *op. cit.;* Girard and Bastide, *op. cit.*

20. Girard and Bastide, *op. cit.*

21. M. Hervert, "La Famille usagère des services sociaux," *Supplément, Action Familiale,* No. 24 (December 1956), 17.

22. Reynaud and Catrice-Lorey, *op. cit.*
23. *La Clientele du service social des caisses d'allocations familiales,* 1961–62, *op. cit.*
24. *La Clientele du service social des caisses d'allocations familiales,* 1961–62, *op. cit.; Girard and Bastide, *op. cit.*
25. Hervert, *op. cit.*
26. Mlle. Postic, "Recherche et premiers résultats d'une méthode d'analyse du travail social spécialisé," *Informations Sociales,* XIV, Nos. 8–9 (August–September 1964).
27. André Philbert, *La Politique social de la France,* Documentation Française (1960), 201.
28. Hervert, *op. cit.*: "Many of our respondents, confusing social work and insurance, do not see that the material aid that may be given to them in a particular case was foreseen by regulation."
29. Ordinances provide as well for *tutelles officielles,* an arrangement resembling protective service in the United States. However, court review is required in *tutelle.* The number of cases is not large. H. Bonnard, "Les Tutelles officieles en Gironde," *Informations Sociales,* XVI, No. 2 (February 1962).
30. La Commission Nationale de Déontologie de l'Association Nationale des Assistantes Sociales et des Assistants Sociaux, *Déontologie en service sociale* (1961), mimeographed.
31. M. Michel, *Compte rendu des journées d'études sociales* (FNOSS, October 1962).
32. Antoine Veil, pour le Ministère de la Santé Publique et de la Population, *Fonctionnement des services sociaux et conditions d'activité des assistantes sociales.* (Paris: January 26, 1962).
33. *Rapport de la Commission d'Étude des problèmes de la Vieillesse* (April 1960).

GLOSSARY

action sanitaire et sociale—health and social action. The concept covers a wide range of direct provision and subsidy of health and social services.

aide médicale—the form of *aide sociale* devoted to meeting the cost of medical care.

aide sociale—public assistance. *Aide sociale* is the residual relief program operated at the level of the commune. It does not include supplementary allowances which are provided by the *social security* agencies. (*Assistance publique* is a discarded term for financial assistance, now applied to some child care and health functions. In some jurisdictions, it applies specifically to the administration of the hospitals.)

assistante sociale—social worker. The feminine pronoun is used throughout because they are almost invariably women.

assurance sociale—social insurance. In this sense, it describes the functions of *Sécurité Sociale* as an organization, that is, omitting family allowances.

caisse—fund or agency. The term is used as in International Monetary Fund, that is, to mean either a repository of money or the agency which receives the money. There are 122 *primary caisses* dealing with *social insurance* and 16 *regional caisses* related to them. Originally there were also 16 *regional caisses* for old-age pensions; many of these have been merged with the *regional caisses* for *social insurance*. As for family allowances, there are 114 local *caisses* and no *regional caisses*. One national *caisse* serves *social insurance* and family allowance purposes.

Code de la Famille—family code. An extensive codification of French law relating to families, adopted in 1939 and amended from time to time.

Comité Technique d'Action Sanitaire et Sociale—Technical Committee of Health and Social Action. See *action sanitaire et sociale*. The Committee is charged with establishing a national scale of priorities in *health and social action* for the guidance of national, regional, and local bodies.

Commissariat au Plan—Planning Commission.

Conseil Superieur de Service Social—High Council on Social Work.

déontologie—ethics.

département—department, local unit of government similar to county.

équipement sanitaire et social—equipment or physical facilities for *action sanitaire et sociale*.

FNOSS—*Fédération Nationale des Organismes de Sécurité Sociale,* National Federation of Social Security Organizations.

health and social action—see *action sanitaire et sociale*.

in charge—(*en charge*)—the family or polyvalent social worker who assumes primary responsibility for servicing a family is said to take the family *in charge*. This may mean intensive contacts over a long period of time or may be limited to a few contacts. Authority over the family is not implied.

legal benefit—social security benefits available as a right. See *supplementary benefit*.

permanence—a regularly established time and place in an office or in a community where people may have recourse for help or referral. Entry to a service is commonly by recourse, in person or by telephone or mail, to the *permanence*.

PMI—Protection Maternelle et Infantile, the national program devoted to the welfare of mothers and children.

primary caisse—the local administrative agency for *social insurance*. See *caisse*.

regional caisse—a supervisory body for *social insurance*. Also the administrative agency for old-age pensions. Metropolitan France contains 16 regions. See *caisse*.

salaire unique—an allowance for families with one or more dependent children and only one source of income or very low income. The allowance is based on regional wage rates and the number of children in a family.

sécurité sociale—literally, social security. May be used generally to include all the *social insurances*. Is used in this sense in Caisse National de Sécurité Sociale. As an official program *Sécurité Sociale* deals only with medical care, illness, invalidity, and death. The term is more commonly used in this limited sense, with family allowances excluded. In this chapter, social security is used in the more general sense. To refer to the more limited program, *assurance sociale* or *social insurance* is used.

service social—social service is a literal translation but is misleading. As it is used, it means social work.

social action—see *action sanitaire et sociale*.

social insurance—see *assurance sociale*.

social security—see *sécurité sociale*.

supplementary benefit (also supplementary allowance)—a social security benefit available at the discretion of the administrative agency.

travail social—social work is a literal translation but is misleading. As it is used, it means social service. *Assistantes sociales* are only one group of travailleurs sociaux (social service workers).

travailleuses familiales—homemakers, one of several groups included in home aid (aide menagère).

tutelle officielle—official guardianship, an arrangement similar to protective service in the United States.

UNCAF—*Union Nationale des Caisses d'Allocations Familiales,* National Union of Family Allowance Agencies.

16

The Future Structure
of Community Services

I am using "community" or "social" services to mean the variety of services provided to people under community auspices, excluding those that are thought to be fundamental or universal. In this meaning, social services include family service, day care, and job training. They do not include general education, medical care, or police protection. A profound alteration in the organization of community services is under way.

We have fallen into the habit of thinking that the financing of social services controls their structure and that the two must be organized along parallel lines. That is, we have visualized voluntary social services as centrally financed and—flowing from that—centrally organized and coordinated. This vision has never been even approximately accurate, but it seemed a reasonable ideal or objective. Events have now made even the objective untenable.

The community chest and united fund movements represent an effort to centralize fund-giving and distribution. In recent years, the movement has provided about a fifth of all contributions to voluntary health and welfare agencies and touched about a fifth of such agencies. Obviously, united funds are not able to

Reprinted from *The Social Welfare Forum, 1965* (New York: Columbia University Press, 1965). Copyright © 1965, National Conference on Social Welfare, Columbus, Ohio.

control the other four-fifths of voluntary health and welfare, but they are a powerful influence. The social planning councils that grew up within community chests or beside them drew their power from the chests. For two decades the voluntary organizations that stayed out or broke out of this pattern and the voluntary givers who wished to extend the pattern have struggled more-or-less privately. Some sort of balance seems to have been struck between the contenders.

If centralized fund-giving has held its own vis-à-vis the independent voluntary agencies, however, both have suffered from a decline in the amount that was being contributed. The decline would by now have made headlines if it were not hidden in fugitive figures that only technicians cherish and understand. In 1945 voluntary donors gave 790 million dollars for a variety of welfare services, including family service and child care, recreation, institutional care of the aged, and maternity home care.[1] By 1962, this total had become 1.6 billion dollars,[2] an increase of 100 per cent in a period during which prices increased more than two-thirds and the population more than one-third. Since all these figures are approximate, let us limit ourselves to observing that voluntary giving buys no more service per person today than it did in 1945. Why have I said that giving has declined? In the same period, the purchasing power of the average family has increased by almost 45 per cent, an improvement reflected in the way everyone lives and in our standards of service. There is no fixed standard for social services any more than there is a fixed definition of poverty. Perhaps standards for social services should rise faster than the American standard of living; one could argue the point. But *in relation to their income,* the American people seem to be giving for voluntary welfare services only two-thirds of what they did in 1945.

One forgets numbers, but the facts that they represent are familiar. It has been extremely difficult to expand community services and to improve their quality. It has seemed that expansion at one point had to be at the expense of contraction elsewhere. Without wanting to undercut federated giving, agencies and boards have examined all other possible sources of income— agency memberships, fees for service, payment from public agencies. In the past four or five years, the Family Service Association of America has undertaken to reevaluate its categorical objection to accepting unrestricted grants from public funds.[3] Other sources of income may be useful to voluntary agencies, but, obviously, public funds present the largest potential resource—and a major philosophical problem. We shall come to this problem a bit further along. For the moment, the point is to illustrate the straitened circumstances of voluntary social service and, in particular, of centralized financing.

The story on the public side has been quite different. Public expenditure on social welfare has increased far more rapidly than population and prices. On the whole, this development has been assimilated in accordance with one of several views. Public services have been regarded as sightless leviathans which feed and roam about a world of their own. Though their presence is unmistakable, they will not intrude and are not to be aroused. Or public services have been viewed as another world power with which coexistence is desirable. A sense of unity is stretched, without too much strain, into a sense of duality. Funds proceed from not one but two primary sources, and there are, if not one, only two main centers of service. Or, finally, public services are viewed as new centers of service which ought to be brought into a single planning relationship with the old ones. In pursuance of this sensible objective, some social planning councils have made sober, sustained efforts to achieve common community planning. General inability to bring this off successfully must be taken as evidence of the degree to which council influence derives from united funds.

The "sightless leviathan" approach to public services may be rejected out of hand. The ideal of one or two centers of organization is viable if government would support it. But government has not supported this concept; it may be time to face the fact that it *will* not. One may remember, for example, debate about whether public welfare departments might serve as the central social service agency in a community. The notion may seem particularly attractive for rural communities where there are, after all, no other candidates for the role. On the other hand, many have thought that welfare departments carry the mark of Cain—

the means test*—and would not be consulted by the self-support-ing. Whichever side one is on, this argument already has a quaint, dusty sound. For, in the last few years, government has moved around the notion of centralized service in half a dozen ways that come readily to mind.

There was some criticism, at least in professional circles, when the government undertook a grant-in-aid program to combat ju-venile delinquency. On one hand, it seemed a way to channel more money into needed services. On the other hand, it seemed clearly to separate one youth service from another and to lead to the establishment of overlapping agencies. Not long afterward, the Social Security Act was amended to encourage and, in some cases, to require services for current and potential public assist-ance recipients. We have added grant programs for retardation and community mental health. About the last program, too, there seems to be a bit of doubt. However, the issue is defined in terms of government vs. voluntary responsibility rather than a general vs. a problem approach. Finally, we have seen the initiation of the war against poverty. Portions of the program flow through existing agencies; portions do not.

All this has taken place since 1961; and the list is not exhaus-tive. Several points are illustrated. First, each program is defined precisely in relation to the problem with which it deals. Such a narrow legislative response is not an accident of the past few years but is implicit in our political system and may be expected to persist. Second, although some of these funds or services are di-rected through existing agencies, many are not. When they are not, they undermine any notion we may have that coordination of services can be brought about by federated financing. Third, coordination has not been overlooked in any of these programs. Most of them require the development of a coordinated plan and evidence that it will be implemented. We shall return to this point.

To sum up so far, in the voluntary field centralized fund-rais-ing has established itself in a strategic though not dominating position. But its ability to support community services barely

* Cain put the proposition from which the means test may be derived: Prove that I am my brother's keeper.

keeps pace with prices and population. In an economy where change and improvement are general, the demand for services increases rapidly. Consequently, agencies look everywhere for funds. Especially, they are tantalized by swelling public purses. Public services have become increasingly important in their own right, quite apart from their influence on voluntary agencies. Therefore, government policy is the key to the possibility of centralized financing and the possibility of coordination via centralized financing. The government is not using that key; a realist must judge that it *will* not.

These conclusions may seem depressing, but perhaps they are liberating. Labor market experts confidently predict that employment of professional and technical workers and others like them is expanding more than twice as fast as overall employment. The need for social services is well known. Obviously all services, and community services among them, are going to expand. Possibly, while we have been clinging to principles that are obsolete we have overlooked rich possibilities for financing social services. At any rate, we have overlooked them as a matter of ideology, for in fact a variety of possibilities press themselves upon us and are already beginning to be exploited. These possibilities arrange themselves under three headings: the potential sources of support of community services; the relationship of voluntary and public agencies; and, if support is not to be unitary, the achievement of coordination.

An alternative to monolithic support of community services is multiple support. Presumably, the voluntary donor will continue to be one of the sources of support. It seems clear, too, that the government will increasingly support social services through the channels for which there is ample precedent—its own well-established agencies, new agencies, and grants-in-aid. But if centralism and "unitarianism" are to be abandoned, then an insistent question presents itself. Why should any institution of our society be excused from making a contribution for the social service needs with which it is intimately concerned?

One thinks of Blue Cross and the other voluntary insurance plans. No doubt, a case can be made that payment for homemaker service would save hospital beds and also provide a net saving in money. One thinks of industry in a new context, not only as a dispenser of philanthropy but as a source of support for more-or-less work-connected services. A few progressive industries regard it as their responsibility to retrain displaced employees. But why just a few? One thinks of social security and its aged, widowed, and disabled beneficiaries. The 1948 Advisory Council on Social Security, impressed by the possibilities for saving money, proposed to pay the costs of rehabilitating disabled beneficiaries. The proposal has been revived.[4] The Social Security Administration and the Vocational Rehabilitation Administration have studied possible measures to finance rehabilitation out of social security funds. In short, we have quite possibly been operating from the wrong question. We have been asking why voluntary donors and the government cannot do more. At this point in history, we should be asking why any major American institution is excused from a share of responsibility.

In the area of the relationship of public and voluntary agencies we may be about to lose the last clarity we have held dear. We have been anxious that a voluntary agency, if it received unrestricted public funds, might yield to natural feelings of possessiveness. The agency might not press government to assume new and appropriate functions. This concern was formulated in a framework made up of at least two elements.

First, experimentation was regarded as the peculiar province of voluntary agencies. They would yield up demonstrated services in order to move on to new ones. But voluntary agencies no longer do more experimentation than public agencies. Nor, if a radical statement is permissible, is the need for experimentation most urgent, but rather the day-to-day work that applies what we already know.

Second, in the rapid expansion of public services until World War II, pockets of service seemed nevertheless reserved to the voluntary agencies. Government's massive entry into community mental health signals the end of one of these private preserves. Government will enter other fields in time, for we cannot, without government participation, support all the services that we shall have. Therefore, speaking relatively, the problem will not be whether the government carries its responsibility but whether voluntary agencies can carry a responsibility they define as uniquely theirs. Thus, the experimental role and the role as agent of certain special services are evaporating as a rationale for voluntary services. Determination of a proper program function will depend very much on the community situation and will vary from community to community.

If these arguments make government sound very powerful indeed, then they highlight a matter that should give us the deepest concern. It is in relation to the power and responsibilities of government that voluntary agencies may be most constructive in the decades ahead. It is difficult for complex programs to be sensitive to individual needs; moreover, their natural tendency is to become defensive. Therefore, we shall increasingly require informed criticism of community service programs. At the same time, because of our complicated society and our complicated responses to it, the issues in program development become increasingly difficult to grasp. Those of us whose idealism has roots in the depression tend to wish for broad citizen movements and to observe that they are not forthcoming.[5] Perhaps such movements to cleanse and reform will come again, but they are not summoned by nostalgia. Nor are we yet clear what sort of citizen movements will result from indigenous participation. An alternative or parallel device is to deal with highly technical, bureaucratic issues in technical, bureaucratic form. This is the crucial service that voluntary agencies can render: to know what is done for people and what fails to be done, to know what is well done and what is done poorly, and to bear witness.

The refusal to take unrestricted public money has been intended to safeguard the voluntary agency's role as critic. Other safeguards may now have to be found. If the voluntary public agencies are going to keep pace at all, they are going to do it with public money. If public funds must sap their resolution, then they will find themselves undermined at every turn. Their safeguard must lie not in abstinence but in a higher conception of public service. There may, from time to time, be voluntary agencies that suffer the wrath of agencies or people they have criticized. That is a fair risk. It should be possible to find safeguards other than a simple refusal to accept funds. With care it may be possible to diversify public support so that no one agency of government is in a controlling position. It may be possible so well to establish citizen understanding of an agency's role as critic that the use of public subsidy for penalty or reward becomes dangerous to the user. It may seem fantastic to speak of independence despite extensive government support of voluntary agencies. In Europe, however, the arts have been publicly subsidized for many years. Attendant problems of control have been manageable; the artists' independence has not been undermined. There is now a strong movement under way to provide public subsidies for our own artists.* Why need community service agencies be more vulnerable than authors, painters, and musicians?

We turn finally to coordination. When those who were concerned visualized single sources of funds for social services, they tended to assume that parallel lines of communication would follow naturally. If funds are to come from everywhere, no one has power to prescribe coordination. In granting money, public programs are now tending to require evidence of coordinated planning and management. Agencies that come to mind are the President's Committee on Juvenile Delinquency, the Area Redevelopment Administration, the Joint Task Force on Housing and Health, Education, and Welfare Services, and the Office of Economic Opportunity. These agencies are asking for a coordinated plan, first, because of a pragmatic recognition that funds are going to be scattered. Second, since no one else is providing coordination, they require at least a sense of planning around the particular problem that is being addressed. It is the quality of problem-centeredness that deserves to be noted. With the failure of other devices, every problem requires its own coordinating mechanism.

Obviously, broader or more effective concepts of overall planning and coordination are required. Despite serious efforts, most social planning councils are now effectively related only to a segment of community services. This constriction of their horizons

* Strong enough to secure enactment of a law in 1965.

follows naturally from the development in community services that has been outlined. We have seen that united funds represent a significant but relatively smaller segment of community services —a trend that may be expected to accelerate. If councils define their functions and leadership parallel to their source of funds, they also deal with a diminishing portion of community services. They may identify the most important other agencies—urban renewal and welfare departments, for example—and try to draw them into the planning orbit. Even where councils have somewhat succeeded, however, the planning relationship is ambiguous. Agencies supported by united funds have a vital interest in the planning; they participate more and are affected more. Much less is at stake for others. In response to this problem, councils that were once organizationally tied to united funds have constituted themselves independently. Even so, common leadership and funds skew the planning focus. If councils are to do the overall job, they must diversify their income and leadership, following the lead of the services for which they plan. If it was ever possible for councils to succeed in doing this overall job, it may now be too late. They may retain a coordinating function for agencies supported by centralized philanthropy, while broader planning bodies are established over their heads.

It appears that the establishment of overall planning bodies is well under way in a number of cities. Considering the nature of the problems the cities face, one inevitably applauds breadth. It is not at all clear, however, that these overall bodies represent a single type of development, even though they appear at the same time and under the stimulus of the same foundation or government grants. Some are much more heavily public bodies than the planning organizations we have known; others are not. A few have made peace with existing planning organizations, but most have not. Some are heavily oriented to physical planning; others not. Most, perhaps all, are dominated by the ideas of planning for poverty and delinquency. While this is satisfactory in terms of problem-centered coordination, it is not promising in terms of all the problems and services that are omitted from these terms. Perhaps the single generalization that is available is that diverse experimentation is under way. We are certainly not ready to select among the experiments. It is possible that we are in transition to another stage in planning that cannot yet be visualized.

We have touched so far on coordination at the community-wide level and in relation to particular problems. Even if well done, neither type of coordination necessarily builds a simple, well-marked path between a citizen and the social services he requires. Having dwelt a good deal on complexity, it is time to say something about simplicity. It is quite possible that we are overly sophisticated and tolerant in the matter of organizing social services. We know so well the power of vested interests and their rights that we avoid far-reaching reorganizations. We prefer to plunk a new social service down next to the rest, hoping that people whose jobs depend upon old methods will learn from contiguity the desirability of new methods. The results are apparent. We have a chaotic condition, understood only by experts. Citizens usually do not know the services available to them. When they know, they do not understand how to get them.

The condition has existed so long that we have become inured to it. We have come to think that such disorganization would not exist if there were any real alternatives. The countries of western Europe use at least four devices to connect citizens with social service that we have not yet tried. They are the Services of Coordination of Paris, the obligatory social service centers of new towns in France, the social counselors of Holland, and the Citizens Advice Bureaus of England.[6] In common, these represent an investment of public funds and legal support. They are postwar devices, adopted partly because of citizen impatience. They represent departures, in one way or another, from principles that some hold immutable. They depart, for example, from these principles:

1. A public agency must assure, by its own investigation, that expenditures are justified. This must be done whether or not it has already been done and no matter how small the expenditure or how expensive the investigation.
2. A person with no training may speak only to a person with some training, and a person with full training speaks only to the Dean.

3. An agency employee must work in a direct line of authority to his agency. Agency employees cannot be pooled, thus clouding their agency's control over them, in order to give one-stop neighborhood service.

None of the European systems may be a perfect model for us. But their success suggests that, with less subtlety and more determination, we might achieve coordination where it counts most—across the street and two houses down from the man who needs help.

We conclude with Schorr's fearless forecast for 1985: Twenty years from now we shall have much more in the way of community services, though we shall think it not enough. We shall have more of the services we know—casework, job training, day care. We shall have services of which we have not yet dreamed. For example, we shall have a way to share the burden that comes to so many families with the chronic illness of a parent. With hospital care not required and institutional placement not acceptable for some, many daughters and daughters-in-law are spending as much as two or three years in unremitting drudgery. We shall not avoid the problem, but we shall find ways to relieve these families.

Services will be financed categorically. Generality will be the ideal, but prudence and political reality will have their way. Voluntary support of social services will continue, but other sources of support will be more important. There will be some feeling that government support has gone too far, but there will be unanimous acceptance of government services that we now think unlikely. There will be support of community services from a variety of new sources: industry, labor, the insurances, and the social insurances. Voluntary agencies will continue to perform service in fields with historical links to the 1960's, but their rationale will be different. The sources of their funds will be mixed and will not seem important. Rather, the agencies will be distinguished by a proud sense of independence and a vexingly critical outlook. We *may* have a better organized system of community services. That, it is difficult to say with assurance. That depends on whether we can be rational.

NOTES

1. Thomas Karter, "Voluntary-Agency Expenditures for Health and Welfare from Philanthropic Contributions, 1930–55," *Social Security Bulletin,* XXI, No. 2 (1958), 14–18.
2. Ida C. Merriam, "Social Welfare Expenditures, 1962–63," *Social Security Bulletin,* XXVI, No. 11 (1963), 3–14. This figure for contributions for welfare services does not include an amount for recreation (approximately $368 million).
3. Memorandum to member agencies, Family Service Association of America (January 25, 1960).
4. Subcommittee on the Administration of the Social Security Laws, Committee on Ways and Means, House of Representatives, *Administration of Social Security Disability Insurance Program* (Washington, D.C.: United States Government Printing Office, 1960), p. 26; *The Status of the Social Security Program and Recommendations for its Improvement,* Report of the Advisory Council on Social Security (Washington, D.C.: United States Government Printing Office, 1965).
5. Nathan Glazer, "The Good Society," *Commentary,* XXXVI, No. 3 (September 1963), 226–234; "A New Look in Social Welfare," *New Society* (London), II, No. 58 (November 7, 1963).
6. Regarding coodination in France, see preceding chapter. Regarding the Citizens Advice Bureaus, see Alfred J. Kahn, Lawrence Grossman, Jean Bandler, Felicia Clark, Florence Galkin, and Kent Greenawalt, *Neighborhood Information Centers* (New York: Columbia University School of Social Work, 1966); Mildred Zucker, "Citizens Advice Bureaus: The British Way," *Social Work,* X, No. 4 (October 1965). The social counselors of Holland have possibly not been described in writing. During World War II, individuals took on neighborhood responsibility for locating sources of food, and so forth. After the war municipal social welfare departments employed them, apparently successfully, to provide neighborhood referral, advice, and community organization services.

PART V

One Nation ... Indivisible

AUTHOR'S NOTE

Following the Detroit riots in July 1967, it seemed to me that most senior government officials I saw went through a period that was akin to clinical depression. In judgment they were unaffected, but they did not show their accustomed energy and seemed, in one way or another, to be adjusting to a sense of loss. The radical fringe and apocalyptists had been warning that our house is on fire; once again, the metaphor turned into reality. In a showplace city of the war against poverty, the insult was double. The loss suffered by those government officials may have been their sense of innocence—their conviction that earnest intentions and exhausting activity would alter or, at least, retard events. If good will and vigorous activity will not suffice, where can a pragmatic people turn?

I had come by a somewhat different route to the same question. "Policy Issues in Fighting Poverty," Chapter 17, observes that our terrible impatience with one another may be felt by poor people most of all. It offers the view that poverty in a wealthy country has less to do with some scientific minimum standard of living than with what people regard as a fair share of the country's goods. And it observes how deeply poverty in the United States plunges into the mind, isolating individuals and walling off groups from one another. In these terms, the question is not simply whether we can do enough but how to do enough in a manner that heals and draws us together.

Answering that question requires a theory; elements of the one with which I work will be evident in the last two chapters. Chapter 18, "National Community and Housing Policy," and Chapter 19, "Alternatives in Income Maintenance," attempt to point out practical possibilities in those two fields. The two chapters incorporate these assumptions: that we must have broad residential integration; that we must direct a larger share—not only a larger sum but a larger proportion—of the nation's income to people who have less; and that in securing such redistribution, we can no longer widely require Americans to answer to the worst four-letter word they know—that they are *poor*.

Housing and income maintenance are not the only fields of social policy that may lead us to national community. They are important policies, obviously, and they are discussed to show that they can be shaped to a variety of human ends. We cannot long dodge the knowledge that we are in charge, if we want to be.

17

Policy Issues in
Fighting Poverty

In our current approach to poor families in this country, the government is substantially embarked upon what might be called a case approach. We are untangling all the threads in the skein of poverty—attitude and environment, individual and family, motivation and opportunity. We muster this understanding in order to turn to the poor, family by family. We are aware that motivation, if it can be stimulated, must find a response in opportunity. But we are working, on the whole, from the family or individual outward. Only the painfully readjusting relationship of Negroes and whites represents a relevant fundamental change. This change, though significant, is not the only one that is required. It is hardly necessary to dwell on the validity and importance of the case approach. Nevertheless, if we hope to make much progress with poor families, we must ask if the case approach is enough. Many kinds of ideas may be relevant in considering changes that would be desirable in the climate that surrounds poor people or in the structure of our society. To illustrate, we shall deal here with two kinds of ideas that seem profoundly important: the climate of social pressure in which we live and our view of equality.

Reprinted from *Children*, XI, No. 4 (July–August 1964), United States Department of Health, Education, and Welfare, Welfare Administration, Children's Bureau.

A TENDENCY TO PRESCRIPTIONS

In preparation for the 1960 White House Conference on Children and Youth, each state submitted a separate report. Curiously, despite some differences in facts reported from state to state, most state reports revealed a marked anxiety in appraising the trends. If an increasing number of women were working or if, on the other hand, women found it difficult to work, the consequence was in either case anxiety. Young people were marrying earlier; the damage that would result was described with alarm. Were the same young people failing to marry and, consequently, producing illegitimate children? States were certainly concerned about that. Moreover, is is not hard to recall when there was a trend toward *late* marriage—a cause for alarm in the 1930's. It was plain in these state reports under how much anxiety and pressure we operate.

Also, we seem increasingly to address ourselves to one another in prescriptive terms. Do not smoke cigarettes! Do, even if you are a woman, be creative! Periodical literature has shifted, in the last couple of decades, from fiction to articles and from longer articles to shorter articles. After reading a short story, one can accept the character's solution if one wishes; or one can judge that the character is different from oneself, or after all, fictional—and ignore him. However, an article leaves a reader neither escape route. If it is short, it is likely not even to have qualifying statements. Thus, even the length and form of magazine writing reflects an inclination to order one another's lives.

These two points apply to all of us. How very natural, then, that the helping professions should bring pressure and prescriptiveness to bear upon the families who are our more-or-less voluntary clientele. Are we in fact exerting such pressure? The problem is recognizable at each of the levels at which we operate.

In face-to-face contact with families there is a growing tendency to tell them what to do. The evidence that social workers are becoming prescriptive is assembled elsewhere.[1] Educators are beginning to complain that the pressure in schools is bringing to college a "prematurely dry, harried, anxious undergraduate." [2] Our hopeful recent invention, Peace Corpsmen, and other volunteers are least of all equipped to know the limitation of direct instruction. Simple instruction is appropriate in a wide range of situations, but inappropriate in others. Today the two kinds of situations are being confused.

At another level, in developing demonstration projects, insufficient thought is given to effects on people at the project's end. For example, we lavish equipment and staff upon kindergarten children, who then proceed into poverty-stricken first grades. We have learned how these children progress in their preschool experimental phase, but what does the transition do—to personality as well as to learning? We have hundreds of counseling and training projects that sweep people up in a hopeful attempt to improve their circumstances. Many of these projects have a life of one year, during which we count up indications of their progress—training courses initiated, work undertaken, housekeeping improved. But what happens to these people when the project evaporates?

These questions do not simply ask whether conscientiously collected results are accurate. They make a more disturbing point. Projects that are brief or that are not fitted with the greatest care into people's lives may reinforce the most handicapping attitudes of poor people: Lucky today—unlucky tomorrow! It's no use trying because the cards are stacked! To the extent that casual projects even begin to succeed, the pressure of hope is added to the pressure from outside.

Finally, there is the level of the public climate. As cut off as they may be, many poor people read newspapers and see television. The national determination to end poverty is reflected on millions of television screens in poor homes. Some families undoubtedly respond with pleasure. Others are fearful; they cannot be certain what is intended, and they feel the force of the determination being asserted. I happened to visit a high school the day after a metropolitan newspaper described its rehabilitative program. A social worker or public official might find the article admirable but the children saw it differently. They were angry at being called blighted and delinquent. They resented an apparent determination to change them. Nor was the faculty pleased. The newspaper's emphasis on the success of new staff members poked clumsily at a fragile sense of unity in staff relationships.

All this was said by William Blake in two lines, and with more spirit.

> He who would do good to another must do it in Minute Particulars.
> General Good is the plea of the scoundrel, hypocrite, and flatterer.

We live, all of us, under pressure. In this circumstance, we may confuse war against poverty with pressure against poor people. These are not the same. On the contrary, it is self-volition that we hope to achieve. Self-volition is a hardier impulse than we sometimes recognize, but it is ironic to suppose that self-volition can be compelled. It would be pleasant to believe that this requires only a tactical change. Obviously, improved techniques and more thoughtfulness with client, project, and public pronouncement would help, but a deeper problem is probably involved. Pressure and prescriptiveness are rooted in our reactions to complexity and change and in our impatience at being thwarted. We may treat the poor worse than we treat one another; we shall hardly treat them better.

Let us leave the question of social pressure, at this point, and turn to our view of equality.

POVERTY AND ALIENATION

We usually talk as if equality and opportunity were indistinguishable. Historically, equality of opportunity has been our major theme. But European travelers detected a separate theme and, in the nineteenth century, commented upon it with delight and awe. "Nothing in American civilization struck me so forcibly and pleasurably," wrote Harriet Martineau, "as the invariable respect paid to man, as man." [3] In this definition of equality, a man is respected and respects himself no matter what his station or opportunity. But now we have a spate of descriptions that show that we are in rather a different situation. Many of us have been oblivious of poor people or viewed them, when necessary, with scorn. Very many of the poor, for their own part, view the rest of us with resentment or themselves with contempt. The technical term that sums up this development is "alienation."

It is an interesting fact that poverty in Europe does not appear to produce the same degree of alienation. In Sheffield, a gang of "teddy-boys" listened to the recorded conversation of one of our teenage gangs. The teddy-boys were appalled by the evidences of violence that they heard. In London, because slum houses may be unnumbered, mental health visitors need a device to locate their patients. They are advised to look down a line of backyards. If one backyard is noticeably littered and dilapidated, that is the home of the mentally-ill patient. In the worst slums of Britain, in Liverpool and Edinburgh, stoops are whitened and crisp lace curtains hang at the windows—flags of self-respect.

It has been observed before this that alienation need not accompany poverty.[4] It seems necessary, therefore, to understand in what circumstances poor people feel and are accepted as integral to society. The explanations must include a closed-class system, which we would reject, and a sense of working-class solidarity, which we have never achieved. The explanations must also include that society will not move very far or fast without attempting, in some degree, to bring the poorest along. Yet we have moved very far and very fast since the war. We have not brought the poor along. And we have the temerity to be surprised at their attitudes and, some of us, to proceed to study them as an alien social system.

LIMITATIONS OF OPPORTUNITY

We are, of course, very seriously embarked on an effort to provide equality of opportunity. It is right to be pleased at this turn of events. But this effort can lead us to the beguiling misconception that equality of opportunity will narrow the gulf between privilege and poverty. The reasons that it will not narrow the gulf are already part of our knowledge.

First, opportunity is related to ability to seize opportunity. Understanding of this fact is the essence of our new sophistication but it presents a thorny problem. In France, for example, aid designed specifically for the poor goes disproportionately to those who need it less than others.[5] In England, an avowed welfare state, housing for those in "housing need" benefits the poor less than others.[6] In the United States, too, the poorest families tend not to get into public housing.[7] They do not receive financial aids given for education.[8] And we are discovering that those most in need of job training tend not to benefit from the program that Congress has enacted. If one steps back from the problem in each particular case, one general point becomes clear. It is precisely characteristic of those who are poor that they cannot meet entrance requirements and cannot manipulate bureaucracies. On the other hand, those who are not poor are resourceful in these matters. We have so far dealt with this problem by devising better rules from time to time. This misses the heart of the problem: the poorest are the least able to use any rules.

PRIVILEGES BEYOND INCOME

Second, in the United States privilege can no longer be audited in dollar income. To know privilege, one must count tax advantages and chargeable business costs, the favors of one's debtors and wooers, and conventions and sabbaticals.

One must count also the distribution of public services. It is generally assumed that public services tend to benefit those who are poor; but it would be useful to perform a balancing-up. Education is the largest expense of local governments. It is a familiar, if uncomfortable, fact that those who are poor get the worst public schools. To take another example, the roads and highways are public but mass transit is largely private. Public roads benefit those who have cars, while the poor pay their way. In short, in the years to come a major share of advancement in standards of living may occur in forms that do not show up in average family income. If we fix our eyes firmly on a dollar standard, we may be congratulating ourselves in the midst of widening inequity.[9]

These first two points test the limits of what we mean by equality of opportunity. If we are talking of nineteenth-century opportunity—that is, formal opportunities for cash income—we shall still be left with serious twentieth-century inequity. In any case, the final point reaches deeper. In the end, opportunity means jobs, but many are poor because they are not able to work. Many are poor because they are old. Are we taking a long view? Some people will be poor fifty years from now because they have not had adequate homes and schooling in the past fifteen years.[10]

Many children are poor because they are socially orphaned. They are born into families in which, although a father has not died, there is no genuine father. For the mothers in many of these families, work cannot be a solution. Work may be an ultimate solution for the children, but are they to be poor meanwhile?

Other people cannot use opportunity because, in one way or another, they are disabled, because they cannot learn a new skill at the time they must, because the effort on which we are embarked will, at its best, fail to reach everyone.

Finally, we must recognize that we are no longer in a situation in which there is likely to be work for *comparatively* unskilled people. We have not yet arranged to provide the number of jobs that will be wanted. On the contrary, in the net we are losing job places every week. Until we see our way clear to rectifying this, we should not have unreal expectations from occupational training. By the most extravagant estimate, perhaps no more than half the poor families could reasonably improve their situations if suitable training were provided and a connection with a job arranged.

A COMMITMENT TO ONENESS

For these reasons, opportunity will not unaided produce respect for man, as man. Drugs, delinquency, and despair, the three Ds of alienation, are all about us. We face the prospect that the gulf between the prosperous and the poor will widen. The statistics of poverty will count fewer of the untrained, but the remainder will be familiar—the aged, the families headed by women, the poorly (though better than now) educated. These will be the new (or still) alienated class—smaller, perhaps, but ever more cut off.

We must pursue the business of being one nation, or we shall be divided. The objective of achieving an integrated society is equivalent in importance to that of wiping out poverty. It requires measures of its own. What might they be?

The present attack on poverty moves in the right direction. It sets out to commit the nation to oneness. But clearly we are required to make this commitment on a new scale. One opportunity for such a commitment lies in our ability to produce goods at a continually increasing rate. We might, then, declare a moratorium on self-aggrandizement among the prosperous. That is, for the next ten years we might undertake to invest the *annual increase* in Gross National Product in our own poor people and, although this is another question, in the poor people of the world.

In the first year this would amount to 20 billion dollars, perhaps more—assuming a net increase of GNP over population. Does the figure seem fanciful? If we provided public assistance for children at the less-than-adequate level at which we now provide it for old people, we should be spending 4.5 billion dollars more on public assistance alone.[11] And we must think of much more than public assistance—education, medical care, housing, job training, social security, and so forth. A moratorium would move us to think in the magnitudes that are required to abolish poverty, and it would do more. All of us would be investing potential goods in the effort rather than only sentiment. More important, a moratorium would give us a symbol for what has not so far been brought into focus—an integrated society.

It does not seem appropriate to attempt to spell out the mechanics of a moratorium. A few observations may be necessary, however, to avoid an appearance of naivete. A moratorium need not interfere with self-advancement. It does not refer to normal profits and salary raises, but to the additional 3 or 4 per cent of goods and services that our economy can produce each year. Nor does it refer to goods that must be allocated to actual population growth. A moratorium would probably require no management devices that we do not already extensively use—that is, control of taxes, money, and credit.

We might, in the end, be giving up very little: It may be a necessary condition of long-range advance that the poorest be given a radical step toward adequacy. This point has been made by Gunnar Myrdal.[12] I am convinced that to those of us who have a decent income the continually rising standard of living brings no satisfaction. We should be relieved and delighted to substitute for a new refrigerator or a second television set a sense of commitment and community.

ORGANIZATION OF THE DISADVANTAGED

Let us turn to a second measure or series of measures that may assist in achieving an integrated society—more aid and encouragement to poor families to organize for their own purposes. Here, at any rate, we have an objective to which we have given lip-service. Some work runs aground on middle-class assumptions and language. Social agencies are now keenly aware of this problem. Some work runs aground because those who attempt it have ulterior motives. They seek citizen participation in an area that is to be cleared for urban renewal. Often poor people suspect—out of prior experience—that they are only to be used for someone else's purposes. The suspicion may preclude communication even when it is mistaken.

But there is the beginning of other work that is more successful. Civil rights groups such as CORE and SNCC started to move forward when, turning their backs on charitable objectives, they began to operate out of self-respect and self-interest. Therefore they have paid rather little attention to public assistance recipients and public housing residents. Now, however, on the East Coast at least, demonstrations for more liberal assistance and better housing have been organized among the poorest Negro groups.

The best of the organized community efforts to deal with juvenile delinquency also attempt to assist poor people in organizing for their own ends. To be sure, Mobilization for Youth has a more difficult problem than CORE. Though conscious that hidden motives can destroy its usefulness to poor people, MFY must nevertheless keep minimal peace with the Establishment. Even the attempt is hopeful, but a sound resolution of this problem has yet to be worked out.[13]

The problem of self-organization among poor white people is, in a way, more acute than among poor Negroes. Poor white people have no comparable movement and they are losing even the advantage that a white skin gave. If they are not reached in some other manner first, they may be candidates for a *White* Muslim movement.

At the core of the problem of stimulating self-organization is the anxiety that it provokes in many of us. Where militant organization takes place, it proves profoundly unsettling to the administrators who are involved. One may wonder where self-organization will end, once it begins. Research in the civil rights movement teaches something about this. It has been observed that the crime rate among Negroes drops sharply where protest action begins.[14] The moral is clear. We do not have a choice between tension and peace. We have a choice between tension that is constructive and tension that is destructive.

SUMMARY

To sum up, while the case approach is sound and necessary, other issues are also involved. As we are all under pressure, we may—under the delusion that we are pressing against poverty—exert pressure against poor people. Our techniques are powerful and may lead us, for a time, to believe people manipulable. But in the end we shall learn the latent lesson of all fables: Seduction works better than force.

Further, equality of opportunity is very far from full equality. It cannot, alone, promise us an integrated society. We cannot any longer expect to come to this by accident—and time runs out. We have permitted segregation to escalate into the situation of the 1960's. We dare not wait to see into what situation alienation will escalate. We require an integrated society and we must seek it for itself.

NOTES

1. Alvin L. Schorr, "The Trend to Rx," *Social Work*, VII, No. 1 (January 1962).
2. William C. DeVane, Address to the Association of American Colleges at Washington, D.C., January 14, 1964.
3. Harriet Martineau, *Society in America* (London: Saunders and Otley, 1837), Vol. 3.
4. Charles Horton Cooley, *Social Organization* (New York: Scribner's, 1912).
5. Alain Girard and Henri Bastide, "Enquête de l'INED sur l'action sociale des caisses d'allocations familiales et le salaire unique," *Information Sociales* (Paris: UNCAF, March 1958).

6. Alvin L. Schorr, *Slums and Social Insecurity* (London: Thomas Nelson & Sons, 1964).

7. *Ibid.*

8. Elmer West, *Financial Aid to the Undergraduate; Issues and Implications* (Washington, D.C.: American Council on Education, 1963).

9. Richard M. Titmuss, *Income Distribution and Social Change: A Critical Study in British Statistics* (London: Allen and Unwin, 1962).

10. Mollie Orshansky, "The Aged Negro and His Income," *Social Security Bulletin*, XXVII, No. 2 (February 1964).

11. *Ibid.*

12. Gunnar Myrdal, *Challenge to Affluence* (New York: Pantheon, 1963).

13. George Brager, "Organizing the Unaffiliated in a Low-income Area," *Social Work*, VIII, No. 2 (April 1963).

14. Fredric Solomon, Walter L. Walker, and Jacob R. Fishman, "Civil Rights Activities and Reduction in Crime among Negroes," presented at the meeting of the American Orthopsychiatric Association (Chicago, March 20, 1964).

18

National Community and Housing Policy

What are the nation's objectives in housing? To see every family housed? Congress said that in 1949 and it is still unexceptionable. To wipe out poverty? The President and Congress have not quite run that banner up the masthead of the housing agency. Still, what they have said is firm enough, and perhaps we may assume that it applies to housing programs. To create and support a sense of community? That explicit objective is the platform for this chapter.

As used here, "community" means that all one hundred and ninety million of us should feel that we have an assured and respectable place in the nation. It means that all the people in one elevated train or one bus or one public park should feel some sense of common bond. We may feel a special tie to other Poles or Presbyterians or Pennsylvanians, but we will not feel set apart from those who belong to other groups. We will not deliberately treat them badly, and we will not be oblivious to their serious problems. The closed-in face, the angry spitting face are our problems. Even more serious are the self-hating, hopeless, or vengeful people who accept the judgments behind such faces. Thus, the sense of national community has two aspects which are

Reprinted from *The Social Service Review*, XXXIX, No. 4 (December 1965). Copyright 1965 by the University of Chicago.

really one—a sense of identity as an American, which naturally concedes to others their sense of American identity.

The evidence that we lack such a sense of community is all about us. It was manifest in our surprise at the announcement that quite a large number of our people are poor. It is manifest in delinquency and addiction rates. It is at work every day in phenomena harder to count but not less terrible—marital or parental cruelty, defeat, and private desperation. The newspapers do not fail to cover this story in their own way, with detailed accounts of assault before onlookers who are horrified and passive. Here and there settlement houses and others have struggled to produce and preserve a sense of community. They have made one point: that such a struggle may conceivably be successful. But have they not also made another point: that it is terribly difficult to maintain an island of community in a sea of seclusiveness, contempt, and hatred?

It is sometimes said that a sense of community is undermined in our country because we are industrial. The argument is familiar—we are detached from a sense of family, a sense of work, and a sense of place. But no European country has paid the same price. Community is eroded, it is said, by bureaucratic organization. Still, France, which is said to be the most bureaucratic country of all, requires citizens to aid one another, and enforces the law. A sense of separation from others may have roots in Puritanism or the open frontier, but these are history. Nothing requires that each of our loyalties should contain an animosity—Forest Park against Hyde Park, poor against less poor, off-white against non-white. Nothing in our current situation bars us from a sense of identity with the main body of our society.

Clearly the problem flows from existing conditions. It is these conditions that we must change. This observation is often made in such a large and general context that it is not really possible to enter a detailed discussion of the changes that are necessary. However, this chapter is limited to the question: What can housing policy do to create a sense of community? It deals with three major concerns: Housing supply, segregation or stratification in residential patterns, and the citizenship role of poor people in relation to housing.

HOUSING SUPPLY

If we are to be one nation, those who have money and power must devote the resources required to produce housing for poor people. Complicated reasons may be advanced to account for our failure to provide adequate housing; it is easy to be drawn off into the more-esoteric realms of sociology or economics. But a simple fact is the core of the problem. We have never spent for housing of the poor a sum of money that begins to offset the disadvantage they suffer. Two pairs of numbers will establish the dimensions of the complaint they might make. In 1962, the federal government spent an estimated 820 million dollars to subsidize housing for poor people. (The sum includes public housing, public assistance, and savings because of income tax deductions.) In the same year, the federal government spent an estimated 2.9 billion dollars to subsidize housing for those with middle incomes or more.* (The sum includes only savings from income tax deductions.) That is, the federal government spent three and one-half times as much for those who were not poor as for those who were. That is very nearly the relative proportion of the poor and non-poor in the population, so one might say that the federal government spends equally per capita for the rich and the poor. What majestically even-handed justice is reflected there!

These are not conventional and some will say not impeccable statistics. Public assistance, public housing, and income tax are not often combined. There is no doubt, however, that they represent the consequential federal subsidies for housing. Only urban renewal is omitted—because it is impossible to divide the federal subsidy between business and residential purposes and to determine what portion of the latter would be for poor people. Loan guaranties are not included in these figures either. As they do not cost the government money, they are not regarded as subsidies. In any event, both omissions weight the estimates on the conservative side. Neither urban renewal nor mortgage guaranties conspicuously serve poor people. Finally, there is no doubt that an

---

* A note at the end of the chapter provides the reasoning on which estimates of the subsidies were based.

income tax deduction is quite as effective a grant of money as a public assistance payment.

However, the pair of figures offered above does suffer from dealing with one hundred and forty-five million people who were not poor as if they benefited uniformly from federal subsidies. Closer examination shows that the subsidy is heaviest for the largest incomes. Therefore, a second, rather more refined pair of figures may be helpful. In 1962, the federal government spent 820 million dollars to subsidize housing for poor people—roughly 20 per cent of the population. For the uppermost 20 per cent (with incomes over $9,000) the federal subsidy was 1.7 billion dollars. A family in the uppermost fifth got about twice as much, on the average, as a poor family.

The composite picture is as follows: The income tax deduction is by far the government's largest direct subsidy for housing. It gives more to those who have more. The two programs that express the national conscience in housing—public assistance and public housing—together manage to raise poor families to per capita equality with the income tax subsidy that goes to all the rest. No more than that! Indeed, in a way less than that, for the poorest fifth got half the subsidy that went to the wealthiest fifth. That will not build a sense of community; and it will not build the housing that is needed.

How is it that we do no more for the poor than for the rich? How is it that we think that we are pouring enormous amounts of money into housing for the poor? To begin with, we are chronically afflicted with an impediment to vision called "slum clearance." Eighty years ago a British Royal Commission for Inquiring into the Housing of the Working Classes[1] observed, with dismay, that poor people rarely benefited when land was cleared and model houses erected. Somehow or other, the issue of providing enough dwellings for *all* people fades from the mind when attention is focused on rebuilding streets and neighborhoods. When the total supply remains inadequate, despite conspicuous new working-class districts, it is naturally the poorest who do without. As Octavia Hill pointed out, the Royal Commission was relearning a lesson that should have been learned thirty years earlier.

Again in the 1930's the British failed to do the job with slum clearance. With the slum clearance drive that took shape in 1955, they solemnly restudied the same text.

The situation in the United States is no better. From the Housing Act of 1937 until now, despite everything that experience might teach us, Americans have looked to slum clearance and its metamorphoses—urban renewal and community renewal—to provide housing for poor people. Urban renewal has a responsibility to the poor people whose lives it alters. Judging from the record, it has not taken this responsibility with sufficient seriousness. But the tools given to urban renewal are suited, if anything, to producing a city beautiful or a city prosperous. Although the tools are or must be made adequate to housing dislocated families, they can do little at best for all the others. Urban renewal deals with land which, even when subsidized, is expensive. Therefore it is likely to be regarded as an achievement when it provides housing for families with incomes of $5,000 or $6,000. Despite the current emphasis upon city-wide planning, the great sums of money are funneled into one project area or another. This purview is too narrow and the process moves too slowly to produce dwellings by the hundreds of thousands.

To turn to the record, from the Housing Act of 1949 to the end of 1963 about one hundred thousand new and rehabilitated units had been completed. If all of them had gone to poor people they would have made a very small contribution indeed to solving our national problem. Here the problem is encountered in a single statistic. One must avoid being hypnotized by the striking buildings we see rising in every city. One must keep in mind their magnitude in relation to the magnitude of the problem. Preoccupation with slum clearance, to the exclusion of all else, is an historically-proven method of failing poor people to the tune of a rousing campaign song.

Another device with which those who are interested delude themselves is research and demonstration. Some issues are researchable, and some are not. For example, President Lyndon Johnson has proposed a direct housing subsidy to poor people. The idea has been tested out on occasion, with some success and some difficulty. But it is necessary to ask whether any project is a genuine test of what would happen if we embarked on a new national program of this sort. The whole housing market would be transformed, and crucial activities, such as construction and code enforcement, might change character. Apart from what can and cannot be studied, there is a time for study and a time to act.

It is not necessary to labor this point. Properly used, study and demonstration may avoid mistakes and lead to action. But demonstration-grantism should not substitute for action when its time has come. For those moments when it may be appropriate, we may turn to one of W. H. Auden's ten commandments for men of action:

> . . . Thou shalt not sit
> With statisticians nor commit
> A social science.[2]

If we are to avoid diversions, what alternatives are open? First, public housing is open. The problems and prospects of public housing are well understood, as well as the new directions in which it should move. If we assume a progressive direction, public housing is a vehicle for substantial increase of dwellings open to poor people. Second, a direct housing subsidy to poor people offers the possibility of dealing directly with large numbers.* Still, a direct housing subsidy might do little to improve the supply of housing. If more homes were not built the subsidy would, in the end, bring poor families little benefit. Therefore, third, the new low-interest-rate program of the Federal Housing Administration might receive the financing necessary for rapid expansion. Although only three years old, the program has already produced as many units as urban renewal. However, this program carries no federal subsidy and is, indeed, not intended to deal with the poorest families. Therefore, fourth, the urban renewal principle of direct cash subsidy for the production of housing might be extended to poor people.

---

* The magnitude of programs is our main point. The housing subsidy proposal presented to Congress in 1965 carried a first-year cost of $50 million—3 per cent of the $1.7 billion subsidy that goes to the uppermost 20 per cent of the population.

These four possibilities may make clear the kinds of concepts that are relevant to producing enough housing for poor people. Obviously, more space and details are required to propose a program. The country is spending 2.1 billion dollars less on the housing of poor people than on the rest of us. If we are to achieve a sense of community, we might begin by spending equally.

RESIDENTIAL PATTERNS

It is probably not necessary to document the observation that Americans tend to live in single-class neighborhoods. Apparently, however, we have been a little too willing to assume a universal tendency to lock into the centers of our cities those who are poor, Negro, poorly educated, and poorly housed. It now appears that this is an accurate profile only of our largest metropolitan areas and those in the Northeast. In many of the metropolitan areas of the South and the West, the classic picture is reversed: poverty and deprivation are characteristics of the suburbs.[3] Thus, our cities do not provide consensus on preferred locations. There is consensus only on classifying and separating people somehow, and inside each town and county we are sorted out into neighborhoods of specified income, or specified color, or specified religion, or specified combination of all of these.

The forces that produce residential separation are all too familiar. The family cycle plays a role. People with children feel the pull of the suburbs; others may not be so charmed. Racial segregation plays a role, historically at least. A city council or housing authority can, of course, assist racial segregation without excess guilt by locating low-cost dwellings in renewal areas or yielding too readily to opposition in higher-cost areas. Local and state tax structures play a role that is often overlooked. Officials become adept at calculating the increase in property tax that is necessary to provide services to a housing development of specified size, income, and family composition. Eventually, they avoid tax increases by zoning actions to prevent developments that would make increases necessary. The Commission on Intergovernmental Relations has called this practice "fiscal zoning." [4] Banks, builders, and real estate brokers, in pursuit of nothing more odious than a secure profit, combine to assure the pure poverty of one neighborhood and the pure wealth of another. Evidently, successful businessmen have misjudged the effect on real estate values when Negroes move into white neighborhoods.[5] It is difficult to know whether they are just as wrong about the outcome if $12,000 houses take their places next to $20,000 houses.

We have constructed a tight myth that feeds from the forces just named and feeds back to strengthen them. The myth is simple: If someone with less money or any other characteristic both exotic and inferior moves next door, then one is not safe in his bed, his children are not safe in school, and his mortgage is endangered. The myth is wrapped around an irony, as myths so often are. We have created poor neighborhoods in all our cities, neighborhoods in which people are afraid to live. Not only the people outside are afraid; those in the neighborhoods are afraid. They are afraid of being assaulted; they are afraid of being shamed; they are afraid of being exploited—by one another and by functionaries of various sorts.[6] From these neighborhoods springs the violence that makes us afraid to walk the streets of our own cities. We created this problem by the myth, and now the problem justifies the myth.

The myth is now possibly the portion of this syndrome that is most resistant to change. Therefore, it may be worth pausing to see how it is dealt with by those who should understand it best. Social scientists have been struggling for some two decades against the conviction that stratification is inevitable. On the whole, academics that they are, their impulses have been toward heterogeneity or democratic mixture. But they had to concede that people try to stratify themselves. Their studies have seemed to show that difference leads to conflict. Conversely, the evidence has seemed clear that people feel satisfaction when they are like one another.[7] Reformers like Paul Goodman and Catherine Bauer have scorned such notions, but their wit was more telling than their bibliographies. The situation has been awkward. At this juncture there appears a solution (also put forward in England in the last few years) that will permit us to have and eat our cake at once.

It is reported that the developers of Columbia, a new town between Washington and Baltimore, have taken counsel with social scientists. One might applaud the determination and vision of those who would plan a new town. But their consultants have not served them as well as they deserve. The town will have room for a variety of economic classes, from those with moderate income upward, but each class in its own section. Slogans for such a town may come to mind: "Integrated but equal!" "Democratic but not extreme!" The proposal is reminiscent of the timid experiments in desegregation that followed World War II. Each building in a development was segregated, some for Negroes and some for whites, and so the total development was regarded as integrated. These strained compromises have vanished.

The problem which all these studies and earnest ideas fail to recognize is that they are conducted inside the myth. The operating principle may be stated in a Gertrude Stein-ism: If like must like like, like likes like. What else! The nub of the problem is to take hold of the myth and call it a lie, loudly enough so that people do not feel bound. The prospects, if that takes place, are not unpromising. Studies have shown that Negroes and whites get along fine as neighbors—a small breach in the like-likes-like principle where once it was thought strongest. Studies have shown that people redefine likeness when they wish to, focusing on common interests rather than on color, on children in school rather than on precise level of income.[8] And city-planning literature brims with the advantages that would develop: Employers and employees would be able to find one another. Commuting would be reduced. Neighborhoods would not empty during the day and fill up at night or vice versa. The greatest advantage of all, of course, and the central point, is that so much xenophobia might be dissolved.

The myth is used to justify all the rest, but more material advantages are also involved. Change requires that several forces be altered. It is hardly necessary to make proposals about racial segregation. Obviously, ending it is part of the problem that must be pursued by citizens, city councils, housing authorities, and all the rest. Neither is it necessary to discuss how schools must be improved. If we take the steps we should, families are less likely to think that they must take their children to the suburbs. The financing structure of local government must be altered. In the first place, officials should be educated to calculate the marginal costs of additional services. That is to say, they should appreciate the situations when average costs will decline with additional families. Beyond this, however, expenses of local governments must be shared so that low-income families will not be seen as a threat. Anything that increases the amount of state or federal aid to localities is likely to have this effect, but it is possible to act directly. For example, a subsidy may be paid for a specified period to a locality in which a dislocated family finds housing. The subsidy would be calculated to cover the cost of public services during an adjustment period—say, five years. Moreover, banks and builders must be educated to the desirability of mixed development. The government can itself set an example by scattering public housing and mixing public housing with moderate-income FHA dwellings.

We shall not, in the end, erase family preferences. That is far from what is intended. We need only to melt down the rigid conduits through which personal preferences now flow. Then we shall have more diversity, more freedom, and more sense of unity.

THE CITIZENSHIP ROLE OF POOR PEOPLE

The terms "citizen participation" or, more recently, "indigenous leadership," are used variously. One meaning of these terms is simple—that poor people who are touched by a public decision (a housing decision, in particular) have techniques and a measure of power which they exercise to influence the decision in what they regard as their own interests. It is peculiarly difficult to discuss the matter at this particular moment. Everyone approves of indigenous leadership, but never has more respect been paid to so little reality. Citizen participation has never been a conspicuous success in housing programs, even though it is a legal requirement. Accounts of genuine, lasting success by indigenous leaders are hard to come by. It goes without saying that this generalization does not "put down" but rather adds luster to the few successful efforts that are known.

It may be useful to begin by uncovering the high cards that are stacked against successful indigenous leadership. First, cynicism about the fruits of one's own activity is taught to poor people by the facts of everyday life. Second, poverty-stricken people who were once better off introduce a distinct ideological strain. In views they are conservative and in mood optimistic and grateful, despite their come-down. These attitudes may serve their conviction that they retain or will regain their earlier status, but, as Harold Wilensky observes, they also "function to reduce working-class solidarity and social criticism from below." [9] Third, analogy of the efforts that the poor might make to trade union or civil rights movements overlooks a difference in sense of identity. Negroes and industrial workers possess a status which, in general, seems permanent and which they may regard as desirable. A poor person whose aspiration is awakened can only wish to become something other than poor. No sense of identity is present around which people can organize.

Fourth, the professional workers who set out to stimulate indigenous leadership inevitably have other motives, which are not necessarily blameworthy. Professional workers are sensitive to secondary consequences of achieving their ends, such as having an important neighborhood program lose favor and funds. They may understand better than the residents of a neighborhood the larger ends that will be served—by clearance, for example.

Finally, when poor people do assert themselves, they are likely to threaten established interests and pay a penalty. Public attacks on Mobilization for Youth in 1964 may have been a case in point. One issue was apparently that Mobilization for Youth gave promise of successfully advancing the independent interests of poor people.[10] Not only did it teach poor people to picket schools, but it also provided them counsel to go to court as plaintiff against municipal agencies. It is hard to know, from the outside at any rate, whether Mobilization for Youth won this point. In any event, professional workers all over the country will have read the message of the savage attacks and learned to interpret with more delicacy the next clarion calls to citizen action.

The obstacles are not listed in order to say that indigenous participation should be abandoned. They are listed because it is important to understand that it is difficult to achieve. It is intolerable to talk as if citizens have only to pack a luncheon and embark on an Independence Day picnic. There are two major reasons why indigenous leadership should be promoted. It is being said of late that the sense of being helpless is the crucial psychological experience of poverty.[11] Each time a man is moved, against his will or without his will, confirms a pattern of living that keeps him poor. If one is attempting to alter some of the elements of a lifetime of poverty (poor education and training, for example), it will be wise to alter as many of the components as he can reach. With a critical combination of elements the human spirit takes off against all odds. The nation seeks to provide the maximum opportunity for take-off.

From the point of view of the professional worker or community agency, indigenous participation must be sought for another reason. Agencies know much less about how to deal with poor people than they need to know. An inevitable bureaucratic process "enfeebles" the response to direct client need or wish.[12] With the increase in what is called "good" government, it becomes harder to get anything at all done, whether good or bad.[13] It may seem glib to suggest that agencies accept the built-in motive force and corrective to their ways of working that indigenous leadership would assert. Boiled down to people and daily activities, such acceptance means that agencies should not fight with all the weapons at their command when the ignorant and ungrateful go over their heads or suggest that they do not know what they are doing. Yet it may be that our professional, technocratic, and political systems must find room for such concepts or grind to a halt.

A reasonable assessment of human capacities and bureaucratic tendencies must raise doubts about whether a housing authority can consistently promote independent citizen activities. Other important and sound considerations govern the authority. Although it may set out with the purest vision of democracy, matters may look different as unattractive personalities emerge and time schedules fall behind. Perhaps, therefore, urban renewal funds should be given in unrestricted block grants, not subject to housing authority control. In particular, the grants might be made to various housing associations and settlement houses and, when they are available, to universities that have been experimenting with urban extension. Much of the money will doubtless be used wastefully, but this is not a field in which anyone knows how to achieve high efficiency.

In summary, there are two major reasons why citizenship participation must be built into housing policy, despite uncertainty of success and all the difficulty. One reason has to do with its function for poor people; the other has to do with avoiding ossification of our system of governing and serving ourselves. Each, in a different dimension, is a method of promoting communication between the haves and the have-nots, between those who are served and those who serve. To the degree that we achieve these objectives, we move toward a sense of community.

CONCLUSION

Three elements of housing policy relate to a sense of national community. First, housing must be supplied in the quantity needed. If we are to be a single nation, we shall make a larger investment and divide it more justly. Second, no one would attempt to tell a family what sort of neighbors it must have. But history and public policy have conspired to produce just that result. It is widely thought that a family must seek to live among so many mirror images of itself. Because the myth exists, it does, in fact, have effect. We are now in a position to set the process going in the opposite direction. Third, we must pursue the tedious, seditious task of nourishing political sense and effectiveness even among the least of our people.

These significant elements of housing policy bear price tags, each in a different coinage. Housing supply costs money; that is perhaps easiest to calculate and dedicate. Mixed residential patterns will cost status. At least until we reorient ourselves, it will be harder to know that one is moving up or has arrived. Indigenous leadership will cost security. Poor people, if they influence decisions, will certainly move them in directions that are uncomfortable for others. Money, status, and security are a high price to pay for community; the high price may explain why we have permitted ourselves to get into difficulty.

Each of the three efforts can be and, indeed, usually is viewed independently. One might think an adequate housing supply important but mixed residential patterns visionary, unrealistic. Or one might think all efforts important but not in the magnitude that has been suggested. However, we must recognize that the hour is late. We must devote all the resources necessary to be one nation, or we shall be two, or several. Whoever considers the consequences of inaction must think a sense of national community well worth its price.

NOTE: The estimates of the federal subsidy for housing were prepared as follows:[14]

The federal subsidy for public housing was $157 million in fiscal 1962. Assistance payments from federal funds for Aid to Families with Dependent Children, Old Age Assistance, Aid to the Blind, and Aid to the Permanently and Totally Disabled in fiscal year 1962 totaled $2.2 billion. It is arbitrarily assumed that 25 per cent of this, or $552 million, was spent for housing.

Non-business real estate tax deductions from income tax totaled $263 million by those with less than $3,000 income and $4.8 billion by those with more income in calendar 1962. Non-business deductions for interest by those with less than $3,000 amounted to $273 million and by those with more to $10 billion in calendar 1962. Interest attributable to home mortgages is calculated at two-thirds of the total, on the basis of a small sample study by the Treasury Department.

In the first pair of figures, actual tax savings are calculated at 25 per cent of the deductions, on the basis of a sample study by the Treasury Department. In the second pair of figures, tax savings for the uppermost 20 per cent of the population (incomes over $9,000) are calculated at 25 per cent of allowable deductions up to income of $15,000, at 30 per cent between $15,000 and $20,000, and so forth, up to 90 per cent at $200,000 income and over. Calculations of actual tax savings in income tax are at 1962 rates. For 1964 or 1965, actual savings would be a smaller percentage, but the total of deductions would be higher.

More than half of the income tax returns took a standard deduction rather than itemizing deductions. Although the standard deduction was, in intent, an average of deductions that might be itemized, it is not in its effect a subsidy for housing or any special item. That is, its advantage accrues to the taxpayer regardless of what he spends on housing. Therefore, no estimate was made of the saving from standard deductions. (The advantage for those who buy homes tends to lie in itemizing deductions; those who buy homes tend to have moderate incomes or more. Therefore, it is likely that inclusion of the savings from standard deductions in the estimates would reduce the imbalance between the uppermost 20 per cent and all the remainder. The poor, who would not be paying tax in any case, would not benefit from standard deductions. Therefore, inclusion of the savings from standard deductions in the estimate would increase the imbalance between the lowest 20 per cent and all the remainder.)

The federal subsidy for urban renewal in fiscal 1962 was about $160 million, but is not included in the calculation of the federal subsidy, for reasons given in the text.

NOTES

1. Great Britain, Royal Commission for Inquiring into the Housing of the Working Classes, *First Report,* London, 1885.
2. W. H. Auden, "Under Which Lyre—A Reactionary Tract for the Times," *Nones* (New York: Random House, 1951).
3. Advisory Commission on Intergovernmental Relations, *Metropolitan Population Disparities: Their Implications for Intergovernmental Relations* (Washington, D.C.: 1965).
4. *Ibid.*
5. Davis McEntire, *Residence and Race* (Berkeley: University of California Press, 1960).
6. Lee Rainwater, "Fear and the House-as-Haven in the Lower Class," Symposium on the Social Psychology of Low-Income Housing, American Psychological Association (Los Angeles, September 6, 1964).
7. Gordon Campleman, "Some Sociological Aspects of Mixed-Class Neighborhood Planning," *Sociological Review,* XLIII, No. 10 (1951); Leon Festinger, Stanley Schachter, and Kurt Back, *Social Pressures in Informal Groups* (New York: Harper and Brothers, 1950); William H. Form, "Stratification in Low and Middle Income Housing Areas," *Journal of Social Issues,* VII, Nos. 1–2 (1951); Herbert J. Gans, "Planning and Social Life: Friendship and Neighbor Relations in Suburban Communities," *Journal of the American Institute of Planners,* XXVII, No. 2 (May 1961).
8. Gans, *op. cit.*
9. Harold L. Wilensky and Hugh Edwards, "The Skidder," *American Sociological Review,* XXIV, No. 2 (April 1959).
10. For a summary of developments before MFY and New York City

arrived at agreement, see Herbert Krosney, "Mobilization for Youth: Feuding over Poverty," *The Nation,* CIC, No. 19 (December 14, 1964).

11. For example, see Dan W. Dodson, "Power as a Dimension of Education," *The City Church,* XIV, No. 1 (January–February 1963).

12. Harold L. Wilensky, "The Professionalization of Everyone?" *American Journal of Sociology,* LXX, No. 2 (September 1964).

13. James Q. Wilson, "An Overview of Theories of Planned Change," in Robert Morris, ed., *Centrally Planned Change* (New York: National Association of Social Workers, 1964).

14. See United States Department of Health, Education, and Welfare, Social Security Administration, Bureau of Family Services, *Trend Report* (December 1962); United States Treasury Department, Internal Revenue Service, *Statistics of Income . . . 1962, Preliminary, Individual Income Tax Returns for 1962* (1963); and unpublished studies in the Treasury Department.

19

Alternatives in Income Maintenance

We Americans should not treat the search for a workable system of income maintenance as if we were shopping for a new automobile—trying to pick the single program with the shiniest look and the best ride to replace the vehicles that now serve us. The likelihood is that nothing will be traded in when we adopt our newest program. We shall have a somewhat more diverse array of programs, providing much better support for people's incomes—if we choose well—and much more nuisance to the orderly-minded among scholars and administrators. This is both a prediction of what is likely to happen and my personal view of what would be best.

The half-dozen distinctive approaches to income maintenance are readily defined and their advantages and disadvantages are not hard to state. Unfortunately, this kind of presentation pits one program against another, as if to force a choice among them. Moreover, even a carefully defined program is shaped in each person's mind by what he thinks a number of other programs will be doing. With assumptions about surrounding programs not fixed, contending arguments fail to meet.

In order to avoid this, I have chosen to name each type of ap-

Reprinted from *Social Work*, XI, No. 3 (July 1966), with permission of the National Association of Social Workers.

proach to income maintenance, identify the assumptions and issues that seem controlling, and either reject that type of program or locate it within the system that will take shape in perhaps the next ten years. Obviously, others might make other choices. Six distinct types of programs will be defined and discussed: public assistance, in-kind, social security, negative income tax, guaranteed income or universal demogrant, and the partial demogrant.

WORK IS NOT REPLACED

We begin with a set of assumptions that is, in a narrow sense, not income maintenance at all. One assumes that work will constitute the major source of income for American families in the foreseeable future. It has, of course, been argued fluently that computers and automatic equipment are rapidly making man's work obsolete. The evidence does not seem compelling; most recently the National Commission on Technology, Automation, and Economic Progress came to the following conclusion:

> There has been some increase in the pace of technological change
> . . . but there has not been and there is no evidence that there
> will be in the decade ahead an acceleration in technological
> change more rapid than the growth of demand can offset, given
> adequate public policies.[1]

Side by side with the economic factor is a psychological one. Americans are greatly devoted to work or, at least, to a belief in its virtue for one's character and for feelings of personal worth. Because such values have force, it is likely that while work diminishes modestly we shall methodically be inventing an outlook that denies the change and that clothes leisure with the semblance of work. One may take a year off to travel but it will be called a reward for outstanding work or a training period for work that is to come. One may dally in the most pleasant cities of the world but it will certainly be to confer with one's peers or otherwise to improve oneself. One may start work older and retire younger, but patently because the demands of modern work require more education and justify earlier retirement.

For these reasons—both economic and psychological—the writer does not visualize a set of income maintenance programs that widely replace work. We recognize the significance of ready availability of work for those for whom it is appropriate, given the attitudes of the time. Any man struggles with resentment and self-doubt against his neighbors' or his own feeling that he should be working. We cannot provide him with a less-than-adequate income, but a job would be better.*

PUBLIC ASSISTANCE

The income maintenance program with which we are most familiar is public assistance. Definitions of this are tricky and slip away as one explores other income maintenance possibilities; it is defined operationally here as the income maintenance program administered by welfare departments. At the moment the program rests universally on a means test, that is, an individual determination of needs and resources, applicant by applicant. The means test has proved to be a degrading experience for many applicants. It has pitted workers against clients and is terribly wasteful both of money and professional time. The profession of social work undertook in 1964 to oppose continued use of the means test.[2] At the least, that implies a radical simplification of the administration of public assistance—a simple scale of family needs instead of budgeting, and affidavits instead of interviews and proofs.

Two other problems with respect to public assistance are the low levels at which assistance is paid and the fact that so many people are not helped. Virtually no recipient receives help at a level that avoids poverty; in general, AFDC children are treated with special penuriousness. Only about one poor person in four receives help at any given time. For these reasons, the profession has from time to time proposed a noncategorical program (or the addition of a miscellaneous category to the existing program, which would achieve the same result) and a mandatory federal standard of minimum payments. Such a program can be achieved only if the federal government is willing to operate public assistance programs—at least in some areas—for some states do not have the resources to contribute even a small percentage of

---

* Here one could discuss the significance of the minimum wage and of publicly provided employment opportunities. They are of course important but for the purposes of the discussion are not regarded as income maintenance.

the cost and others would not be willing to do so. It is worth considering what would result from federal operation of a noncategorical program.

There would be thirty million people or more receiving public assistance at levels not lower than the definition of the poverty line. Among these would be men and women who are, or might be, able to work; no investigations would be made of them, nor would they be asked why they are not working. The problem of incentive—about which we have been so troubled recently—would be compounded. No one who could work full time at the minimum wage or even a little more would gain much in income by leaving public assistance. Incentive scales can be devised that might cope with this problem, but they get caught between opposing pressures. Either the bottom of the scale pushes downward and many people receive inadequate income, or it moves upward and people with comparatively decent incomes—$5,000 or $6,000 a year—receive assistance. Finally, the cost of the program is naturally quite large.

Because people who are now working would stop, the cost of the program would exceed the total poverty deficit in the United States—perhaps costing annually as much as 20 billion dollars.

Such a program would not be constructive for many of the people involved. It is not good for one to feel that no effort he makes can improve his situation. In any event, the nation would probably not tolerate such a program. If Congress gave it serious attention, conditions about employability and training would certainly be attached to it, and an investigative procedure would be added to assure that people were not simply malingering, that children were receiving proper care, and so on. We would shortly be back in the dismal business of the means test. Recipients would feel the keen edge of community displeasure at their slothfulness and many would be deterred from asking for help (that is the purpose, to be sure). We would once again be tutored in the lesson we seem never to learn—that the effects of poor laws are not an accident but deliberate. We are brutal in the giving of money we define as relief; we are sweetly charitable only when we have succeeded in defining the gift as something else—social security, urban renewal, business deduction.

In fact, the public assistance program visualized by the Committee on Economic Security in 1935 was meant to be residual—a safety net for a few who fell through all the other protections. The concept is as right in the 1960's as it was in the 1930's. Public assistance does not make a good mass program.

IN-KIND PROGRAMS

A second type of program that is currently enjoying a renewal of popularity is the provision of services or goods "in kind"—recent examples are Medicare, food stamps, and rent subsidies. Restricted programs have on occasion stirred powerful emotions in social workers, but these recent ones seem to have escaped our wrath. In-kind programs may represent a public conviction that beneficiaries are not to be trusted to manage their own funds, a view that certainly went into the development of the food stamp program, and it is to this paternalistic implication that many social workers react.

Despite their resurgence, in-kind programs are not currently being proposed as the dominant source of income for anyone; therefore, not much space will be devoted to the issues involved. They are probably a sound type of program so long as they remain a subsidiary type. They are acceptable so long as they are not *felt* as controlling. In-kind programs may be especially suitable when the public interest is most deeply engaged (as in the nutrition of children) or when the state is in a better position to organize services than the family would be to buy them (as in medical care or rent subsidies). We might therefore seek a very broad extension of three specific programs—school lunches for children, medical care for those who are not aged, and rent subsidies to broaden the supply of low-cost housing.

SOCIAL SECURITY

The social security system offers a third line of development in income maintenance. In principle, social security provides benefits for stipulated risks in exchange for a regular payment during one's work life. The program is both categorical—that is, limited to the aged, the disabled, the orphaned—and directly tied to work. It has, therefore, succeeded brilliantly exactly where public assistance has failed, in providing a payment to which everyone agrees the beneficiary has a right.

By the federal standard of poverty, almost two out of five people who receive retirement benefits and a larger proportion of those who do not receive benefits are poor.[3] The issue that must be faced is the degree to which social security is an antipoverty program. In the wake of the War on Poverty, a certain amount of sentiment has developed that social security should be *primarily* an antipoverty device. The Commissioner of Social Security observes that limiting the program to antipoverty would have been stirring in 1910, "but we can do much better in the United States in 1966." [4] Social security may prevent poverty, to be sure, but it may also replace income well above poverty for those who have earned it. The point of view has much to recommend it. Quite apart from the effect on others, limitation of social security might do the poor a great deal of damage in the end. There would undoubtedly be a drive to define such a program in poor law terms while parallel programs for the nonpoor were established beside it.

The difficult question is how to apportion benefits within the social security system. It may be that we should move by stages to a minimum benefit that avoids poverty for most people. The minimum benefit for an aged person is now $44; doubling the figure would be a long step toward the desired objective. Wage-related benefits, justified by higher earnings, would also be raised but not so quickly at first. Such a strategy would provide an interesting international reversal. England and Sweden began their systems with a flat-rate payment that was essentially an antipoverty device. Recently they have moved to add a wage-related benefit on top of that. In effect, in establishing an antipoverty minimum we would be moving toward a similar two-decker system from the opposite direction.

Apart from the adequacy of the social security payment, its coverage can readily be broadened. Only something over one million aged people are now uncovered by social security or similar public systems. They may be provided status under the social security system, following the precedent of the amendment in 1965 that "blanketed" people over seventy-two into social security. The net public cost would be comparatively small, as the majority of these people now receive public assistance. In not too many years a special provision to include uncovered aged people would become vestigial, as we rapidly approach the point at which 100 per cent of the population is covered by social security contributions.

More radical ways of broadening social security are also conceivable. No doubt we shall see the day when people who have contributed for fifteen years may receive a benefit while they spend a year in school. The notion would serve society in a variety of ways, but its time has not yet come.

Also reasonable is a program called "fatherless child insurance," which was first proposed by Lord William Beveridge.[5] Under such a plan divorced women would be treated like widows for social security purposes. The special attraction of this program is that it would go precisely to children in broken homes, the very group that is now conspicuously overlooked. Something about the proposal conveys a sense of hedonism—"Leave your husband and get a payment!"—and blocks further consideration. Such consideration is well warranted, but few people are willing to discuss the program seriously.

At any rate, we may expect from social security both a minimum payment that guards against poverty and complete coverage for the categories of the population it serves—the aged, disabled, widowed, and orphaned. In addition we have already noted that medical care should be extended to all age groups. Unemployment insurance should also be mentioned: Benefit levels need to be raised, coverage improved, and the period over which payments may be made lengthened.

NEGATIVE INCOME TAX

A fourth line of development in income maintenance is the negative income tax—a payment related, according to some reasonably simple formula, to the number of persons in a family and their combined income. Although no important principle is involved, it is generally assumed that such a program would be operated by the Internal Revenue Service in connection with the income tax program. A radically reformed program of public assistance might greatly resemble the negative income tax, accounting for our earlier difficulty in defining public assistance.

The negative income tax is an attractive idea. It appeals to the principle of equity in a way that few people find possible to dispute. That is, a family of four with an income of $6,000 undeniably receives a gift of at least $340 (the value of four exemptions at a 14 per cent tax rate) from the government as a credit against their tax. With a $2,000 income such a family receives less and with no income no payment at all. Many are coming to think that poor people should receive at least some payment for the value of their exemptions. The concept is also attractive because it seems simple to administer. It is a program that would, for once, reach all needy people, without categorization. It is an efficient program, for it gives money to poor people without diverting it to others who do not need it.

Despite these advantages, the negative income tax might, if enacted, be fated to play a minor role in income maintenance. It suffers from the difficulty noted in the discussion of public assistance that payments must be scaled carefully to income in order to sustain the feeling that one can improve oneself. Unfortunately, such a scale is most easily constructed when payments are to be small. Although the negative income tax may be supported widely, some of the support comes from those who see it as one element in tax reform. Such a perspective effectively casts the payment per person in the neighborhood of $84 a year (a $600 exemption at a 14 per cent rate), a contribution but obviously far short of what is needed.

More important, even a substantial negative income tax would, like public assistance, provide the money payment in a poor law framework. It would be paid not for past work, not because of childhood or old age, not for any of the dozens of reasons that have been converted into social rights, but for the one reason we have so far failed to make into a right—want. I have the impression that poor people would, if they were consulted, reject the negative income tax. At any rate, civil rights leaders have shown less-than-spontaneous enthusiasm for the notion. It was conspicuously absent from the recommendations laid before the June,

1966, White House Conference "To Fulfill These Rights." [6] Poor people would say that they want to make good as others have— they will be glad to take the fringe benefits that go with making good (including exemptions, pensions, benefits, allowances, and insurance payments), but are willing to be spared a negative income tax. They are probably right. Some may be so far-sighted and so altruistic that they offer poor people what they do not want and deny them only what the nonpoor conspicuously have —income as a matter of undisputed right.

In short, it appears that the negative income tax is in the poor law tradition and would, as a practical matter, turn out to be a small amount of money. On the other hand even $300 or $400 a year is an important amount of money to a poor family and every move toward equity is a move in the right national direction. I do not visualize the negative tax as a substantial development in income maintenance, but believe it should be supported as a part of tax law reform.

UNIVERSAL PAYMENT

The fifth alternative open is a universal payment to everyone in the country, without regard to income or status. This is the original definition of guaranteed income; it shall here be referred to as the "universal payment" or "universal demogrant" to distinguish it from other programs now implied by the term "guaranteed income."* The universal payment is the one comparatively radical idea mentioned here. It derives from the concept of a contract between the state and the individual, assuring that the individual will receive income and will give work. The state does not have a choice on the one hand nor does the individual on the other. As the universal payment has been discussed lately in the United States, in a not uncommon historic reversal it has become associated with the expectation that work will *not* be required.[7] For the next decade, at least, this is probably a fantasy. In any event, the universal payment, if it provided enough money for decent living, would bring about a sweeping redistribution of in-

* The term "demogrant" has been popularized in the United States by Eveline Burns, who credits William Anderson, a Canadian actuary, with inventing it.

come in the United States. It is doubtful that this objective will be reached in one step, desirable as it might be.

PARTIAL DEMOGRANT

A partial form of the universal payment is the sixth and last alternative. If we are not likely to have a universal demogrant in the very near future, it seems much more nearly practical to extend a payment to specific population groups, without income test or any qualifying test other than age. The two candidates for such a program that come readily to mind are the aged and children. We have in fact already opted for a demogrant in proposing that the aged be blanketed into social security. There will be a certain amount of academic argument over the principle involved. I venture to prophesy that scholars will decide that these old people are receiving demogrants but that they themselves will call it social security.

The one critical group that has so far been omitted in our system of income maintenance is children. A demogrant for children—that is, a children's allowance—might correct this long-standing oversight. It will be said that a children's allowance wastes money on children who are not poor that could be spent, in an income-limited program, on children who are poor. A children's allowance designed carefully in relation to the income tax system would waste little money. In any event, that money is well wasted that purchases a sense of its rightness. It will be said that children's allowances would increase the birth rate, especially among those who really should have fewer children. Since the subject requires its own paper, I simply offer a dictum (but one complete with citation): *There is no evidence that children's allowances will affect the birth rate. If any effect at all is seen, it is likely to be trivial.*[8]

Apart from the sense of rightness that may be provided by a demogrant, because it is not related to income it quite avoids interfering with incentive to work. A third point has already been made, and two estimates will underline it. A children's allowance of $50 a month would take beyond the reach of poverty three out of four children now poor. Moreover, family income is generally pooled; a child exits from poverty only when his whole family avoids poverty. If poverty were eliminated only for families with children, therefore, fewer than a third of those now counted poor would remain poor. It is perfectly plain who the citizens are who require income maintenance. How is it that we turn everywhere else?

WHAT SHOULD BE DONE?

Where have we arrived in this discussion? If we strengthen the existing income maintenance mechanisms and add a couple of new ones, we can assure a decent income to virtually everyone in the United States. In addition, many who are "near poor" would find their income improved. I have rejected fatherless-child insurance and the universal payment as means toward these ends. Each is utopian, which is to say appealing in some rational sense although we are not ready for it.

We can assure decent income, then, by seeking to improve social security, increasing minimum benefits, and reaching all the aged. We should seek to provide medical care and decent housing to all the population. We should seek to right unjust tax laws by providing at least a modest negative income tax. And we should seek a program of allowances for children.

In, the context of this ten-year objective, what of public assistance? A truly residual program of public assistance would be more practical than the mass program that has been conceived. Doubt about social services as an integral part of public assistance has been growing because, in all truth, we will not have the staff to make such a large program work. Doubt has been growing because "services" carry the implicit promise that we shall substantially reduce public assistance case loads, a promise we cannot meet with a case load of old people and mothers and children. Moreover, the means test is the community's way of keeping a vast program to manageable size.

With improvements in social insurance and the other measures that have been identified, public assistance would be a smaller program, dealing with hundreds of thousands rather than millions. Because it is difficult to know just who would need help and why, individual investigations might indeed be required.

Quite possibly these recipients would be troubled people requiring a variety of services, which should be close at hand. That model combination of assistance and services tailored to individual situations cannot operate in the current context—overwhelmed by the prevalence of stark need—and a public assistance program that tried to replace social insurance and similar programs would be a disaster in its own right.

Financing of these programs will not be discussed here. Obviously, a great deal of money is involved but not so much as the Gross National Product increases in a single year. That is to say, the cost spread over ten years would amount to substantially less than one-tenth of our *gain* in national production.

CHOICE TO BE MADE

Apart from the programs themselves, I have been concerned with suggesting how a pluralistic approach to income maintenance may assure income for all Americans. Brushing away all these programs and substituting one great new program would surely be neater. But esthetics is not the point so much as warmth and protection; it is said that a patchwork quilt may perform those tasks very well. Over time, the patchwork we have created should of course be rationalized, especially to achieve a pluralistic system that is simpler and more complete.

Two things concern me about recent interest in substituting a general approach to income maintenance for the categorical approach that has historically been used. First, it would introduce poor law concepts into our brave new programs and even into areas where we have long-established rights; this has already been dwelt on. Second, we are a deeply divided nation—we are divided between those who have and those who have not, between slums and suburbs, between those who feel competent and those who feel exploited. The national structure of income maintenance is not a small matter. It can be structured to deepen the schism by dealing with the poor in identifiably separate programs, or it can strike across such divisions and help to heal them. In the next two or three years we must make a choice.

NOTES

1. *Technology and the American Economy,* report of the National Commission on Technology, Automation, and Economic Progress, Vol. 1 (Washington, D.C.: United States Government Printing Office, February 1966).
2. See "Assembly Backs Minimum Income, Asks New Membership Proposals," and Wanda Collins, "The 1964 Delegate Assembly: A Delegate's Firsthand Report," *NASW News* (National Association of Social Workers), X, No. 2 (February 1965).
3. Mollie Orshansky, "More About the Poor in 1964," *Social Security Bulletin,* XXIX, No. 5 (May 1966).
4. Robert M. Ball, "Policy Issues in Social Security," *Social Security Bulletin,* XXIX, No. 6 (June 1966).
5. Sir William Beveridge, *Social Insurance and Allied Services* (New York: The Macmillan Company, 1942).
6. White House Conference, "To Fulfill These Rights," *Council's Report and Recommendations to the Conference,* June 1–2, 1966 (Washington, D.C.: United States Government Printing Office, 1966).
7. Robert Theobald, *Free Men and Free Markets* (New York: Clarkson N. Potter, 1963).
8. Alvin L. Schorr, "Income and the Birth Rate," *Poor Kids: A Report on Children in Poverty,* Chapter 5 (New York: Basic Books, 1966).

Index

Abbott, Edith, 76 *n.*, 128 *n.*, 129 *n.*
Abrams, Charles, 181, 192 *n.*
action sanitaire et social, see Health and Social Action
ADC (Aid to Dependent Children), *see* AFDC (Aid to Families with Dependent Children)
Addams, Jane, 232 *n.*
Advisory Council on Public Assistance, 46, 49–50
Advisory Council on Social Security (1948), 252
AFDC (Aid to Families with Dependent Children), 4–6, 18–19, 58, 61–63, 65, 285 *n.;* and absent-parent provision, 35, 36, 44–52; and family goals, 152; legislative history of, 9–12; and maternal families, 31–40; problems in, 21–36; and scapegoat phenomenon, 22–27; and socially orphaned child, 52–55, 61–62; and work dilemma, 27–31; *see also* public assistance
aged: and geographic mobility, 103, 122; and living arrangements, 77–90, 101–103; and OAA, 112–122; and OASDI, 101–105, 154; relations with adult children, 78–81; and support, 116–118
Aid to the Blind, 26, 285 *n.*
Aid to Dependent Children, *see* AFDC
Aid to Families with Dependent Children, *see* AFDC
aide médicale, 228
aide sociale, 222, 228

Alger, Horatio, 137
alienation, and poverty, 264–265, 267
American Economic Association, 57
American Public Welfare Association, 50
APTD (Aid to the Permanently and Totally Disabled), 26, 285 *n.*
Area Redevelopment Administration, 254
Ashmore, Harry S., 192 *n.*
assistantes sociale, 225, 229, 232–238
Atlanta, urban planning in, 206
Auden, W. H., 286 *n.;* quoted, 7, 277
Australia, 63
authority, attitudes toward, 47

Back, Kurt W., 161 *n.*, 175 *n.*, 191 *n.*
Baldwin, James, 16 *n.*
Bastide, Henri, 242 *n.*, 243 *n.*, 244 *n.*, 270 *n.;* quoted, 234
Bauer, Catherine, 161 *n.*, 279
Beck, Bertram M., 217–218, 219 *n.;* quoted, 218
Beveridge, Sir William, 65, 68 *n.*, 294, 300 *n.*
Beveridge Report, 65
Bittman, Richard A., 41 *n.*
Blackwell, Gordon B., 41 *n.*, 42 *n.*
Blake, William, quoted, 264
Blue Cross, 251–252
Bond, Floyd A., 95 *n.*, 96 *n.*, 98 *n.*, 127 *n.*, 128 *n.*, 129 *n.*, 130 *n.*
Bott, Elizabeth, 87 *n.*, 97 *n.*, 98 *n.*, 99 *n.*
Boulding, Kenneth E., 178 *n.*
Brager, George, 271 *n.*

Breckenfeld, Gurney, 193 *n.*, 203 *n.*, 219 *n.*

Breckenridge, Elizabeth, 130 *n.*

Britton, Jean O., 95 *n.*, 97 *n.*, 98 *n.*, 99 *n.*

Britton, Joseph H., 95 *n.*, 98 *n.*, 99 *n.*

Burchinal, Lee, 139, 142 *n.*

bureaucracy, 13–14, 266, 283; and community, 273

Burgess, Ernest, 98 *n.*, 99 *n.;* quoted, 85–86, 89–90

Burns, Eveline, 57, 65, 67 *n.*, 128 *n.*, 129 *n.*

Butts, Joseph, 204 *n.*

Cabot, Richard, 232 *n.*

Calhoun, Arthur W., 75 *n.*, 159 *n.;* quoted, 72

Campleman, Gordon, 286 *n.*

Canada, children's allowance in, 63, 64

Carter, Edward, 193 *n.*

Carter, M. P., 175 *n.*

cash incentives, 49–51; and maternal families, 31–40; *see also* incentive to work

Cassell, John, 163 *n.*

Catrice-Lorey, Antoinette, 243 *n.*, 244 *n.*

Cavan, Ruth S., 97 *n.*, 98 *n.*, 100 *n.*

centralization, of fund-giving, 247–257

child-parent relations, *see* filial relations

children, poor, 15 *n.*, 58–59, 297; socially orphaned, 53–54; support for, 57–67; *see also* AFDC; families; poverty, culture of

children's allowance, 55, 64, 65–66, 297–298

citizen participation, 216, 269–270, 281–286

Citizens Advice Bureaus (England), 256

city planning: effect of business practices on, 198–202; effect of government policies on, 184–191, 198–202; évitez faire policies in, 207–210; laissez faire policies in, 206–207

civil rights movement, 7, 269–270

Cleveland, Harlan, quoted, 146

Code de la Famille, 236–237, 243 *n.*

Cohnstaedt, Martin L., 219 *n.;* quoted, 217

Colean, Miles, 193 *n.*, 219 *n.*

Coleman, Richard P., 163 *n.*

Commission on Intergovernmental Relations, 278

Commission on Race and Housing, 181

Committee on Economic Security, 292

community, sense of, 267, 272–286, 299

community chests, 247–248

community services, 213–218; coordination of, 238–242, 254–256; in France, 220–242; future of, 247–257; *see also* évitez faire

Conant, James Bryant, 142 *n.;* quoted, 138

consumership, 177

Cooley, Charles Horton, 270 *n.*

Cooney, Timothy J., 204 *n.;* quoted, 201

CORE, 269

Corson, John J., 97, 129 *n.*

Cottrell, Leonard S., 163 *n.*

Cowles, May L., 192 *n.*

Daley, Sir Allen, 243 *n.*

Darby, W. J., 175 *n.*

Davis, Allison, 96 *n.*, 99 *n.*, 174 *n.*

demogrant, partial, 297–298

Denmark, and negative income tax, basis of, 53, 63–64

De Schweinitz, Elizabeth, 42 *n.*

DeVane, William C., 270 *n.*

Dinkel, Robert M., 98 *n.*, 130 *n.*

District of Columbia: ADC payments in, 24; poor families in, 171; and urban planning, 205–206

divorce: rates of, 23, 53, 153; and re-
marriage, 23, 59–60
Dodson, Dan W., 287 *n.*
Dorfman, Robert, 77, 95 *n.*, 97 *n.*, 102
n., 142 *n.*
Drake, Joseph T., 93 *n.*
Duncan, Beverly, 191 *n.*, 192 *n.*, 193 *n.*
Duren, Mary, 40 *n.*
Duvall, Evelyn M., 89 *n.*

Edmonson, Munro S., 56 *n.*
education, financial aids to, 266
Edwards, Hugh, 286 *n.*
Eichmann, Adolph, 14
Eliot, Thomas H., 68 *n.*
Elizabethan Poor Law, 72–74, 291
Ellison, Ralph, 16 *n.;* quoted, 173 *n.*
Ellul, Jacques, 7, 14 *n.*
equality, 264–267, 270, 274–278
Epler, Elizabeth, 107 *n.*, 113, 129 *n.*
Epstein, Abraham, 101, 126 *n.*
Epstein, Leonore A., 56 *n.*, 97 *n.*, 126
n., 142 *n.*
Erikson, Erik, 16 *n.*, 163 *n.*
évitez faire (avoid action), 207–210,
212

families: image of, 132–137; maternal,
31–36, 59–60; nuclear, 134; and residential patterns, 177–179; and social class, 54; and socially orphaned,
52–55; stability of, 36–39; trends in,
143–144, 157–158; *see also* AFDC;
filial relations
family allowance, *see* children's allowance
family cohesion, and social support
requirements, 118–122
family planning, 8, 297
family policy: definition of, 143–144;
forces for change in, 155–159; and
social security, 152; U.S. determinants of, 144–153
family responsibility, 71, 155; *see also*
filial responsibility

fatherless child insurance, 19, 55, 64,
65, 294, 298; financing of, 66–67
fathers: and ADC, 31–36; and support
orders, 38, 59–60
Federal Housing Administration, 181,
277, 281
filial relations: attitudes toward, 78–
79; and cash assistance, 79–81, 106;
by economic class, 80, 82–83; in living together, 81–90; in separate living, 77–81; *see also* aged
filial responsibility: in California, 103,
110, 117; care and affection in, 90–
92; and current practice, 77–95;
and family cohesion, 118–123; and
family image, 132–137; and family
policy, 5, 143–159; history of, 71–74;
in Maine, 109, 110, 112, 114; in Nevada, 106; in North Carolina, 115,
117; and OAA, 105–123; and
OASDI, 101–105; in Pennsylvania,
112–115; and poverty, concept of,
137–141; and social security, 101–
126; and support requirements, 116–
118; in Tennessee, 107, 117; in
Texas, 110; in Utah, 115; in veterans' benefits, 123–125; and Vocational Rehabilitation, 125–126; in
Washington, 106
fiscal zoning, 278
Fisher, Ernest M., 204 *n.*
Fishman, Jacob R., 271 *n.*
Flanders, Ralph, quoted, 150
Flemming, Arthur S., 162 *n.*
Foley, Mary Mix, 191 *n.*
Foote, Nelson N., 163 *n.*, 191 *n.*
France, 63, 64; coordination of services in, 238–241; health and social
action in, 221–232; social security
in, 221–238; social services in, 220–
242, 265, 273; social work in, 221,
232–238; technical terms, glossary,
244–246
Frazier, E. Franklin, 5, 42 *n.*
Freeman, T. W., 193 *n.*
Fried, Marc, 161 *n.*, 219 *n.*

Friedrich, Rudolph H., 218 *n.*
future-oriented programs, 48

Gans, Herbert J., 161
Gardner, Burleigh B., 96 *n.*, 99 *n.*
Gardner, Mary R., 96 *n.*, 99 *n.*
Girard, Alain, 242 *n.*, 243 *n.*, 244 *n.*, 270 *n.;* quoted, 234
Girard, G., 242 *n.*, 243 *n.*
Glazer, Nathan, 258 *n.*
Goodman, Paul, 279
Gottman, Jean, 193 *n.*
Gould, Raymond F., 41 *n.*, 42 *n.*
grandparents, 92; *see also* filial relations
Grattan, C. Hartley, 161 *n.*
Great Britain, 65, 256; cities in, 185–191; housing in, 275–276; integrated living patterns in, 89; poverty in, 265
Grebler, Leo, 160 *n.*, 161 *n.*
Greenfield, Margaret, 40 *n.*, 128 *n.*, 129 *n.*, 130 *n.*
Grier, Eunice, 192 *n.*
Grier, George, 192 *n.*
Grigsby, William G., 191 *n.*, 192 *n.*
Grimm, Peter, 202

Hamlin, Robert H., 219 *n.*
Handel, Gerald, 163 *n.*
Handlin, Oscar, 97 *n.*, 163 *n.;* quoted, 157–158
Hauser, Philip M., 191 *n.*, 192 *n.*, 193 *n.*
Havighurst, Robert J., 89, 96 *n.*, 99 *n.;* quoted, 90
health and social action (France), 221–232
Herbrich, Jacqueline, 243 *n.*
Herley, Mark K., 202 *n.*
Herron, Jane, 219 *n.*
Hervert, M., 243 *n.;* quoted, 244 *n.*
Hill, Reuben, 162 *n.*
Hitrovo, Michael V., 76 *n.*, 128 *n.*, 129 *n.*
Holland, social counselors of, 256

Hollingshead, August B., 56 *n.*, 96 *n.*
Hollis, Ernest V., 96 *n.*
homemaker service: in France, 225; in U.S., 94, 251–252
Hoover, Edgar M., 191 *n.*, 192 *n.*
housing: and family patterns, 170–172, 177–178; and national community, 272–286; and poverty, 170–171, 272–286; and residential patterns, 278–281
Housing Act of 1937, 276
Housing Act of 1949, 151, 276
Housing Act of 1961, 195
housing codes, 188; and financial incentives, 194–202; in New York City, 197
housing policies: business and taxation in, 194–202; code enforcement in, 188, 195–202; and family policies, 148–151; in Great Britain vs. U.S., 184–191; and laissez faire policies, 206–207; for the poor, 195–202; and rehabilitation, 195–202, 275–276; in U.S., 177–184; and urban planning, 205–210
Huber, Gizella, 40 *n.*
Hughes, Everett C., 175 *n.*

illegitimacy, 23, 24
in-kind programs, 282
incentive: to support, 116–118; to work, 8, 27–31, 291; *see also* cash incentives
income, taxable, related to family allowance, 55
income exemption, 8–9, 29, 48–50, 116
income levels, and privileges, 266–267
income maintenance: and children's allowance, 64, 65–66, 297–298; fatherless child insurance in, 64–67, 294, 298; and negative income tax, 294–296, 298; and social security, 292–294; systems of, 288–300; universal payment in, 296–297
income tax: children's allowance tied to, 63–64; exemptions from, 64; and

housing maintenance, 199; negative, 64–65, 66, 294–295, 298
indigenous leadership, 281–286; *see also* citizen participation
individualism, 145–146
in-kind programs, 292
in-law conflict, 88, 89

Jeffers, Camille, 68 *n.*
Jenkins, David, 163 *n.*
Jews, 13
Job Corps, 61, 156 *n.*
Johnson, Lyndon B., 66, 276
Johnson, Thomas F., 204 *n.*
juvenile delinquency, 250

Kaplan, Saul, 40 *n.*, 42 *n.*, 43 *n.*, 95 *n.*, 129 *n.*
Karter, Thomas, 258 *n.*
Keith-Lucas, Alan, 40 *n.*
Kent, James, 75 *n.*
Key, William, 205 *n.*
Keys, A., 174 *n.*
Kluckhohn, Florence, 56 *n.*
knowledge, politicality of, 8–12
Komarovsky, Mirra, 68 *n.;* quoted, 60
Kraus, Hertha, 98 *n.*
Kuhlen, Raymond G., 99 *n.*
Kutner, Bernard, 96 *n.*, 97 *n.*, 98 *n.*, 99 *n.*, 100 *n.*, 130 *n.*

laissez faire, in urban development, 206–207
Lajewski, Henry C., 98 *n.*
Lampman, Robert, 67 *n.*, 142 *n.*, 162 *n.;* quoted, 57
Laroque, Pierre, 243 *n.;* quoted, 220 *n.*
Lazarus, Esther, 43 *n.*, 126 *n.*, 130 *n.*
Lebeaux, Charles N., 98 *n.*, 128 *n.*, 160 *n.*, 163 *n.*
Lee, Alfred McClung, 192 *n.*
Leichter, Hope J., 97 *n.*, 99 *n.*, 160 *n.*, 162 *n.*
Leighton, Alexander, 153, 162 *n.*

Lenzer, Anthony, 99 *n.*, 129 *n.*
Leslie, Gerald R., 160 *n.*, 192 *n.*
Lewin, Kurt, 22
Lewis, Hylan, 8, 60, 68 *n.*, 174 *n.*, 192 *n.*
Lindemann, Erich, 161 *n.*
Litwak, Eugene, 162 *n.*
Loeb, Martin B., 47, 56 *n.*
London: housing in, 189; social classes in, 185
Lynd, Robert S., 6–7, 14 *n.;* quoted, 7
Lynn, Rita L., 41 *n.*, 42 *n.*

McCann, Charles W., 100 *n.*
Maccoby, Eleanor E., 42 *n.*
McConnell, John W., 97 *n.*, 129 *n.*
Mace, David, 162 *n.*
McEntire, Davis, 192 *n.*, 193 *n.*, 286 *n.*
Mack, Edward J., Jr., 161 *n.*
McKeany, Maurice, 162 *n.*
Macmillan, Harold, 189, 194 *n.*
malnutrition, 9, 168–170
marginal men, 13, 15–16 *n.*
marriage, *see* families
"marriage dropouts," 60
Martineau, Harriet, 270 *n.;* quoted, 264
maternal families, 31–36; and cash incentives, 31–40
Maxwell, Richard C., 75 *n.*, 127 *n.*, 128 *n.*
Mead, Margaret, 156, 163 *n.*
means test, 61–62, 249–250; and incentive to work, 30; *see also* Elizabethan Poor Law; incentive; negative income tax; public assistance
Merriam, Ida C., 163 *n.*, 258 *n.*
Merton, Robert K., 161 *n.*
middle class: goals of, 177–178; in suburbs, 185
Miller, Walter B., 56 *n.*, 160 *n.*
Millspaugh, Martin, 193 *n.*, 203 *n.*, 219 *n.*
Mitchell, Celia B., 160 *n.*
Mitchell, George W., 203 *n.*

mobility, geographical, 103, 122, 143, 184 *n.*
Moore, Wilbert E., 75 *n.*, 98 *n.*
moral attitudes, and ADC, 33
mortgage insurance, 186, 274
Moser, C. A., 193 *n.*
mother-in-law conflict, 89
Mumford, Lewis, 210 *n.*
Mydral, Gunnar, 160 *n.*, 268, 271 *n.*

national community, *see* community
negative income tax, 55, 64–65, 66, 294–296, 298
Negro groups, 269
Negroes, 13, 22, 23; effect of aid programs on, 62; family relations of, 34–35, 61, 172–173; poverty of, 171, 179, 180–184; and real estate values, 279; and segregation, 180–184, 280; and sit-in movement, 172–173; *see also* families
New Towns 279–280; in England, 187, 189
New Zealand, 63
Northwood, L. K., 205 *n.*, 210 *n.*
Nuremberg trials, 14
nutrition, *see* malnutrition

OAA (Old Age Assistance), 26, 63, 105–123, 285 *n.;* in Alabama, 106, 110, 117; and family cohesion, 118–122; and perpetuation of poverty, 112–115; support requirements in, 116–118
OASDI (Old Age, Survivors, and Disability Insurance), 101–105, 154; *see also* social security
Office of Economic Opportunity, *see* war on poverty
Ogburn, William F., 97 *n.*, 160 *n.*
Orshansky, Mollie, 68 *n.*, 78 *n.*, 174 *n.*, 217 *n.*, 300 *n.*

Paris, social service coordination in, 239–240, 256

Parsons, Talcott, 90, 98 *n.*, 99 *n.*, 163 *n.*
Patrick, Ralph, 163 *n.*
Peace Corps, 156 *n.*, 262–263
Perkins, Ellen J., 174 *n.*
Perkins, Frances, 67, 68 *n.*
Philbert, André, 244 *n.;* quoted, 236
planning, *see* city planning; community services, coordination of
PMI (*Protection Maternelle et Infantile*), 225, 232, 234, 236, 246
Polemis, Zane M., 127 *n.*
Pollak, Otto, 99 *n.*, 129 *n.*, 159 *n.*, 163 *n.;* quoted, 88, 158
Pond, Adele S., 99 *n.*, 129 *n.*
Poor Law, *see* Elizabethan Poor Law
poverty, culture of: described, 9, 46–47; as "nonculture of," 167–174; as present-oriented, 46–48
poverty and alienation, 264–265; and citizenship role of poor, 281–284; concept of, 137–138; and family relations, 59–61; perpetuation of, in social security, 112–115; and policy issues, 261–270; *see also* families; war on poverty
prescriptiveness in social work, 13, 262–264
present-orientation and programs, 48, 168
private enterprise, 146; and housing, 186, 198, 202
professionalization, 13
Protection Maternelle et Infantile, *see* PMI
public assistance, 290–291, 298–299; *see also* AFDC; APTD; OAA
public housing, 186, 187, 188, 189, 256–266

Quarantelli, Enrico, 136, 142 *n.*

relative responsibility, *see* filial responsibility
research: in civil rights movement, 269–270; in social movements, 167–

174; trends in, 3–14; and value-free orientation, 6–8

residential patterns: determinants of, 176–191; and fiscal zoning, segregation in, 208–209; stratification in, 177–186, 278–281

Reynaud, Jean-Daniel, 243 *n.*, 244 *n.*

Ribicoff, Abraham, 11, 14 *n.*, 162 *n.;* quoted, 10

Richardson, Arthur H., 192 *n.*

Riesenfeld, Stefan, 75 *n.*, 127 *n.*, 128 *n.*

Riesman, David, 156, 163 *n.*

Roosevelt, Franklin D., quoted, 67

Roosevelt, Theodore, 144

Rose, Arnold M., 98 *n.*

Rosenberg, Albert G., 219 *n.*

Ross, Elizabeth, 42 *n.*

Rossi, Peter H., 161 *n.*, 191 *n.*

salaire unique, 229

Salzman, Donald M., 192 *n.*

Saunders, Lyle, 95 *n.*

Schneiderman, Leonard, 169 *n.*

Schorr, Alvin L., 15 *n.*, 98 *n.*, 162 *n.*, 174 *n.*, 257, 270 *n.*, 271 *n.*, 300 *n.*

Scott, John, 99 *n.*, 129 *n.*

Scott, Wolf, 193 *n.*

segregation, 180–184; and urban planning, 208–209

Service of Coordination, of Paris, 240, 241, 256

servicemen, benefits for parents of, 123–125

"service amendments," history of, 9–12

Shanas, Ethel, 95 *n.*, 97 *n.*, 99 *n.*, 102 *n.*, 127 *n.*, 136, 142 *n.*, 162 *n.*

Sheldon, Henry D., 97 *n.*, 98 *n.*, 99 *n.*

Sherman, Edmund, 19 *n.*

Sherman, Sanford N., 160 *n.*

Shultz, Gladys D., 99 *n.*

Sletto, Raymond F., 161 *n.*

"slum clearance," 275–276

slums: Negro life in, 180–184

Smith, Adam, 206

Smith, Dan Throop, quoted, 199 *n.*

Smith, William M., Jr., 95 *n.*, 98 *n.*, 99 *n.*

SNCC, 269

Snyder, Eleanor M., 40 *n.*

social classes: and cities, 177–186; and families, *see* families, filial relations

socially orphaned children, 18–68

social security: and dependent parents, 103–104; and family policy, 152; and filial responsibility, 101–126; in France, 221–238; omissions in, 57–68; and parental absence, 33

social services, *see* community services; social work

social work: as advocacy, 13, 237; évitez faire policy in, 207–210; in France, 221, 232–238; prescriptiveness in, 13, 262; trends in, 51–52

Solomon, Fredric, 271 *n.*

Spiegel, John P., 56 *n.*

Springer, Vance G., 128 *n.*, 129 *n.*

Steiner, Peter O, 77, 95 *n.*, 97 *n.*, 102 *n.*, 130 *n.*

Stern, Herbert J., 203 *n.*

Stevens, David H., 128 *n.*, 129 *n.*

Streib, Gordon F., 95 *n.*, 96 *n.*, 97 *n.*, 99 *n.*, 100 *n.*

support requirements, 116–118; and family cohesion, 118–122

Sussman, Marvin B., 96 *n.*, 99 *n.*, 139, 142 *n.*

Sweden, birth rate in, 64

Swesnick, Richard H.; quoted, 199 *n.*

Tawney, Richard H., 75 *n.*

tax laws, and housing, 198, 199, 202, 274, 275

television sets, in poor homes, 59

Terry, Luther, 218 *n.*

Theobald, Robert, 300 *n.*

Thompson, Wayne E., 95 *n.*

Tierney, Brian, 72 *n.*, 75 *n.*

Timms, Noel, quoted, 214 *n.*

Tisdall, F. F., 174 *n.*

Titmuss, Richard M., 271 *n.*

Tobin, James, 65, 68 *n.*

Tocqueville, Alexis de, 75 *n.*, 159 *n.*
Townsend, Peter, 96 *n.*, 98 *n.*, 99 *n.*, 126 *n.*
travailleuses familiales, 225
Tyndall, R. Winfred, 40 *n.*

unemployment insurance, 294
united fund movements, 247–248
United States: family policy in, 143–159; and French social services, 221; housing policy in, 177–184, 186–189; income levels in, 55; OAA policies in, by state, 107 *n.*–108 *n.*
universal payment, 296–297
urban planning, 205–210
urban renewal, 186, 274, 276, 283

Vadakin, James C., 162 *n.*
value-free orientation, 6–8
Varchaver, Catherine, 98
Vaughan, John G., 219 *n.*
Veblen, Thorstein, 15 *n.*
Veil, Antoine, 244 *n.*
Vernon, Raymon, 177, 191 *n.*, 192 *n.*, 193 *n.*
veterans, benefits for parents of, 123–125
vocational rehabilitation, 125–126
voluntary agencies, 247–257

Walker, Mable, 203 *n.*, 204 *n.*
Walker, Walter L., 271 *n.*

Walkley, Rosabelle, 161 *n.*
Wallin, Paul, 99 *n.*
war on poverty, 61; and equality, 265–266; and housing, 195–202, 265–266, 272–286; policy issues in, 261–270
Weimer, Arthur M., quoted, 198 *n.*–199 *n.*
Weinstein, Karol Kane, 56 *n.*
Wendt, Paul F., 160 *n.*, 161 *n.*
White House Conference on Children and Youth, 155, 262
Wickenden, Elizabeth, 130 *n.*
Wilensky, Harold L., 98 *n.*, 128 *n.*, 160 *n.*, 163 *n.*, 286 *n.*, 287 *n.*
Willmott, Peter, 193 *n.*
Wilner, Daniel M., 161 *n.*
Wilson, James Q., 287 *n.*
Winston, Ellen, 68 *n.*, quoted, 63
women, in labor market, 27–31; wages of, 59
Wood, Elizabeth, 162 *n.*
work: in AFDC, 27–31; economic need for, 289–290; and incentives, 27–31; for women, 27–31, 59
working class, 265; and cities, 185–186

Young, Michael, 98 *n.*, 99 *n.*, 130 *n.*; quoted, 121

Zeidler, Frank P., 203 *n.*, 204 *n.*
Zender, Mary M., 40 *n.*